THE RESPONSIVE MARRIAGE

*Finding
the Path
Out of
Reactivity*

DONALD W. WELCH, PH.D., M.S., LMFT

WESTBOW
PRESS®
A DIVISION OF THOMAS NELSON
& ZONDERVAN

WestBow Press books may be ordered through booksellers or by contacting:

WestBow Press
A Division of Thomas Nelson & Zondervan
1663 Liberty Drive
Bloomington, IN 47403
www.westbowpress.com
844-714-3454

ISBN: 979-8-3850-0771-4 (sc)
ISBN: 979-8-3850-0772-1 (hc)
ISBN: 979-8-3850-0773-8 (e)

Library of Congress Control Number: 2023917735

Print information available on the last page.

WestBow Press rev. date: 01/18/2024

DEDICATION

This book is dedicated to Robin Welch: my precious wife and loving companion, beloved mother, impeccable Woman of Character, my best friend, an entrepreneurial partner, respected by all who know her, the complete Proverbs 31 Woman—with all merits of this book attributed to Robin's Christlike life example. I love, admire, respect, and thank God for you daily.

Each year on her birthday and our anniversary, I sing a song I wrote for Robin and sang at our wedding, accompanied by a small orchestra, many years ago. I wanted to include it here for you, my readers. For those of you that read music, I've included sheet music in case any of you sentimental husbands want to change the title and sing it to your wife. For those of you that don't read music, you can enjoy the written lyrics.

Chorus:
 She is so beautiful, I love her so
 She is so vibrant, I want her to know
 I treasure her, and love is ours to grow
 A gift from God

Verse 1:
 I have the love I dreamed for
 It's so true and beautiful
 The one my God conceived and gave to me

Verse 2:

    I will love and cherish you, my dear
    We will laugh and share our tears
    Thro' God's precious love and treasured years

Verse 3:

    I have found you, Lord, in a person I love
    It has given me new joy
    To know He lives and guides her precious life
    His peace to know

Robin's Song

Written by Don Welch
Arr. by David McDonald

With feeling ♩ = ca. 60

She is so beau - ti - ful. I love her so.

She is so vi - brant. I want her to know I trea - sure her. And love is ours to grow A gift from God.

1. I
2. I will
3. I have

have the love I've dreamed for.
love and cher - ish you, my dear.
found you Lord in a per - son I love.

It's so true and
We will laugh and
It has giv - en

beau - ti - ful. The one my God con - ceived and gave to
share our tears. Thro' God's pre - cious love and trea - sured
me new joy To know He lives and guides her pre - cious

Robin's Song

ENDORSEMENTS

The Responsive Marriage is a thought-provoking and immensely practical guide for married, or soon-to-be married, couples to successfully navigate conflict and build intimacy. Dr. Welch masterfully outlines what I term "the crazy cycle" that many couples fall into when trying to process emotionally charged events. In this remarkable book, he provides sage advice and effective tools for exiting the crazy cycle and preserving connection. No matter the state of your current relationship, this book will help you grow as husband and wife.

Emerson Eggerichs, Ph.D.
Author of Love and Respect

If you long-for a strong, vibrant and healthy marriage, The Responsive Marriage is a must read.

While thousands of books have been written on marriage, this unique resource is biblically-based, psychologically-researched, and informed by decades of practice with insights and tools that you'll be able to immediately apply. No matter where you are in your marriage relationship you will find help, hope, and encouragement in these pages. When you finish reading this book you will not only *view* marriage differently; you will also know how to *do* marriage differently.

This is a book that you'll want to read more than once . . . and give copies to your friends. Yes, it's that good.

Gary J. Oliver, Th.M., Ph.D.
Licensed Clinical Psychologist
Marriage and Family Therapist
Senior Facilitator of Going Deeper Together
Author of over twenty books including Mad About Us
and It's All About Relationships

What an amazing work! Don Welch offers a refreshing, unique, therapeutic approach based on excellent research that will be used by therapists working with couples, as well as provide a self-help tool for couples seeking to work through issues in their marriages or enhance already healthy marriages.

Dr. Clifford and Joyce Penner
Licensed Clinical Psychologist and Clinical Nurse Specialist
Certified Sex Therapists and Authors of Numerous Books

Don Welch's book, *The Responsive Marriage*, is an outstanding resource for all couples. In addition, his new assessment and video resources are easy to use tools for leaders, marriage mentors, and any couples who are seeking to have a "high quality" marriage. Having known Don for over thirty years, you must know his integrity is sterling, his integration of spiritual insights is refreshing, and his passion to help couples thrive is exceptional. I heartily recommend his book and resources!

Ken R Canfield, Ph.D.
Founder, National Center for Fathering and
National Association for Grandparenting

Every couple I know would benefit greatly in their marriage relationship from reading this book. I felt like I was on a personal counseling journey with Dr. Welch. At our *Refreshing Your Marriage* conferences, I challenge couples to read one marriage book a year together. Make this the book this year! Each chapter is insightful and the discussion starters at the end of each chapter are created for deeper communication. People would pay thousands of dollars for this kind of marriage content in private counseling: and you get it all in this book.

Jim Burns, Ph.D.
President—Homework
Author of Doing Life with Your Adult Children; Keep Your Mouth Shut and the Welcome Mat Out; and Creating an Intimate Marriage

Don Welch has a heart for marriages. Drawing on decades of counseling experience, he has outlined a practical approach to strengthening your relationship so that it can thrive in the way God designed it.

Jim Daly
President—Focus on the Family

Dr. Don Welch is a highly respected therapist with substantial clinical experience in California and the Midwest. In this new book, he leverages both his training and his experience to help couples learn, grow, change, and adapt. Within these pages you will find useful, practical, and meaningful insights focused on growing a strong, healthy, and lasting marriage relationship. I am glad to recommend this book as a resource for couples.

Dr. David Frisbie
Executive Director—Healthy Habits for Parents & Families
Author, Speaker, University Professor

Rarely do we have a glimpse into the tools and resources that have been developed over decades of learning, sharing, and equipping marriages and relationships. Yet the resource you are holding in your hands is exactly that: a comprehensive accumulation of Dr. Don Welch's study and practice of helping marriages and relationships thrive. As a marriage counselor and coach of forty years, I have seldom seen this golden of a treasure-trove of material in one resource. Dr. Welch is to be commended for not only his service to those God has brought under his counsel, but his generosity in sharing it with others like you; desiring to help others grow! Well done, well done indeed!

Dr. Gary and Barb Rosberg
America's Family Coaches and The Rosberg Group
Marriage coaches, authors, broadcasters, and ambassadors

This book is such a reflection of the Don Welch I have worked with for many years. He is an avid learner and a creative thinker, as demonstrated by how the university faculty and students voted him Professor of the Year. He is passionate about helping couples. This is reflected in the chapters and exercises in his book and workbook and demonstrated in his clinical work and leadership of the Center for Enriching Relationships, where I worked with Don. It is considered one of San Diego's most prominent professional Christian counseling centers. If you are looking to work on your relationship, *The Responsive Marriage* book will provide you with many creative tools and new ways to process areas of your relationship. Enjoy the journey with Dr. Welch.

Jennifer Konzen, PsyD, LMFT, CST, CCDC
Author, Director of the Center for Sexuality, San Diego

At my request, in 2006 Dr. Welch became the counseling pastor at the large church in San Diego, California where I was the lead pastor. He served in that capacity for 16 years with impeccable integrity, consummate skill, and genuine compassion. His blending of biblical teaching with psychological care for the congregation was instrumental in bringing healing, restoration, and wholeness to hundreds of marriages. I am thrilled to see *The Responsive Marriage* book now bring that potential to many more couples seeking a thriving marriage. Within these pages, you will find immensely practical improvement methods conveyed in interesting, informative, and inspiring ways. *The Responsive Marriage* is a must-read for all engaged and married couples desiring a more intimate and connected relationship.

Dr. Jim Garlow
Former Lead Pastor for Skyline Church in San Diego
Author, Founder & CEO of Well Versed

Don Welch is one of the wisest counselors we know. We have always admired his ability to combine the biblical, rational, practical, and relational truths and principles to aid couples in creating a love to look forward to living. In *The Responsive Marriage,* he guides couples to find and follow the path out of reactivity to a responsive, romantic, remarkable, and rewarding marriage. *The Responsive Marriage* will bless and benefit every marriage from the "I Do" through anniversaries decades later.

Bill and Pam Farrel
Co-Directors of Love-Wise
Authors of sixty books including the bestselling
Men Are Like Waffles, Women Are Like Spaghetti

Don Welch uses his gifts and graces to lead others into a deeper understanding of themselves and those with whom they may live, work, play—in general for every relationship in life. The insights are practical and can be woven into daily interactions at all levels. Choosing to follow this pathway offers incredible benefits for life and living. Easily understood, this book is practical and effective.

Dr., Rev. J.K. Warrick
Pastor, Parkview Church of the Nazarene in Dayton Ohio
General Superintendent Emeritus, Church of the Nazarene

CONTENTS

FOREWORD

Most people, including doctors, have difficulty with relationships. Almost everyone I know needs help navigating broken relationships. In my training to become a neurosurgeon, I was taught much about the brain but little about how the brain affects relationships.

In this important work, Dr. Don Welch reveals therapeutic counseling advice that has helped hundreds of couples during his twenty-five years as a licensed therapist. Don also has forty years of experience as professor, pastor, and a promoter of biblical truth, and this book strongly advocates a biblical view of marriage. As a pastor, Don taught a successful marriage class for many years with typically more than one hundred and fifty in attendance each week. Don has developed an assessment, handbook, video series, and textbook for *The Responsive Marriage*, thereby promoting restoration, healing, and healthy relationships. Most importantly, Don cares about marriages and has spent his life developing tools to help couples thrive. *The Responsive Marriage* is a powerful tool and is up-to-date with what is known scientifically about why problems occur in relationships.

I have come across many resources for relationships. What sets this work apart is the focus on reactivity—the biological or physiological response that hijacks many marriages. A typical couple argues over two different perceptions of the same circumstances. Perceptions are closely tied to the central nervous system as well as the history of each person. Perceptions lead to a reactive response and a reactive counter-response accomplishing nothing except a rapid, downward spiral. Dr. Welch guides couples away from debating facts and toward validating feelings. If increased intimacy is the goal, we must stop the reactivity. Once identified, the reactive person can turn down the reactivity in favor of responsiveness.

The Responsive Marriage is a "How-To" manual, a textbook, and a training manual. Dr. Welch has taken the implications of reactivity in marriage seriously. He teaches us how to move from biological reactivity to more thoughtful responsiveness which results in more enjoyable relationships. Whether you are a pastor or someone in the pew, this book will help you improve your understanding of reactive versus responsive marriage dynamics and therapy. There is much to learn about yourself, your partner, and your relationship from Dr. Welch.

David I. Levy, M.D.
Neurosurgeon; San Diego, California
Author of Gray Matter: a neurosurgeon discovers
the power of prayer...one patient at a time

ACKNOWLEDGMENTS

To my precious wife, Robin, without you this book would be a clinical manuscript lacking practical and lived-out application. To our children, Savannah and Daniel, I am constantly reminded how marriage is the cornerstone of healthy children. Mom and I are equally proud of you.

Many other people have informed my understanding of marriage, especially my parents, Dr. Lee and Pauline Welch, who exemplified the art of loving one person for sixty-eight years "until death do us part." As father of my two siblings and me, and successful author of five university mathematics textbooks, Lee (dad) exemplified his love for my mom in numerous ways. Specifically, more than once he turned to me and said, "Your mom is the smartest person I know." To mom, thank you for sharing with me your continued admiration of my dad saying to me often, "No one works harder at everything he does than your dad." It was delightful for me to regularly see my parents hold hands, hug each other, joyfully laugh, admire each other, and pray together while creating a wonderful Christian couple legacy for my sister Pam Eggleston, brother, Ron Welch, and me. We miss Mom and Dad and look forward to being with them in heaven!

To the San Diego Skyline Church 2B1 (2 Become 1) class of 600+ participants: for courageously participating in the fifteen-year weekly class; for learning the Welch Responsive Temperament Assessment (WRTA) techniques, skills, and application of its theories through the handbook while enduring my corny attempted humor. You are my and Robin's friends.

To Lance Rushing, friend, colleague, the mathematical mastermind behind the *Welch Responsive Temperament Assessment* (WRTA) ground-breaking tool that stands as the centerpiece of this book: I thank you for helping me to daily encourage and strengthen marriages across America.

To Karl Christensen and his courageous WRTA and Welch Family Therapy Institute impeccable leadership: you brought it all together. Your friendship, collegial brainstorming, and editorial gifting put your fingerprints all over these materials: you are potentially setting into motion the enriching transformation of the local church marriage ministry.

A special thanks to Anita Palmer, my long-time editor and professional writing coach, for her excellent and thorough editing skills on this book.

To Westbow Press and its effective editorial team in completing this manuscript.

To all those having invested in my marriage and contributions to this book: I am forever grateful.

INTRODUCTION

For many marriages, trouble lurks just around the corner. An insidious pattern is creeping into the couple's interactions and neither one is consciously aware of it. This is the worst kind of enemy—the kind that prowls in the shadows and operates completely under the radar. If you know who or what the culprit is, you can take steps to protect yourself and drive the adversary out. But when the enemy goes completely unnoticed and unacknowledged, that's when danger escalates.

The enemy I am speaking of, which you will learn about in this book, is *involuntary reactivity*. I use this term to encompass the behaviors and verbal replies that originate from the "feeling" part of the brain *before* we are consciously aware of them. We roll our eyes, sigh in exasperation, fold our arms, turn away, narrow our eyes, and tighten our lips. We reply with "you always," "you never," or "whatever" type statements and exhibit hundreds of other reactions. These actions are not consciously chosen. Instead, they emanate from the central part of our brain devoted to self-protection. In my thirty-plus years of counseling, I have come to believe that reactivity is enemy number one for a marriage. This is because each occurrence tends to mortar one more brick on the wall that separates a couple.

A Real-Life Example

My first defining moment for understanding the pernicious nature of reactivity came during couples therapy work. Michael and Jessica (not their real names), a couple you will read more about later, represent hundreds of couples I've worked with over decades. Michael and Jessica reacted toward each other without any conscious awareness: a word spoken, a look expressed, a turning toward or away from the other, rolling the eyes in exasperation, or sighing in disgust. Each gesture signals involuntary reactivity—negative behavior happening below the surface of cognizance.

In my counseling practice, I have observed these behaviors in many couples who seem to have no clue as to why it happens. One client said, "I just react and don't know why." They will often say, "Our responses feel like we're enemies when we started out as friends." These couples are caught in a cycle of incessant reactivity and are completely perplexed about why it keeps occurring with frustrating regularity. (Throughout this book, I incorporate many real-life stories of my clients to help illustrate the concepts presented. The names and certain facts have been changed to protect the confidentiality and anonymity of those individuals.)

In an attempt to help my clients increase their self-awareness, I hunted for a tool that would simultaneously measure out-of-awareness reactivity (involuntary behaviors) and temperament, the psychological encoding that drives behavior preference when interacting with others. Although there were plenty of assessments on the market measuring one of these elements, my quest for a tool to measure both resulted in no viable options. This led me to create the Welch Responsive Temperament Assessment (WRTA).

Welch Responsive Temperament Assessment

Reducing reactivity and increasing responsiveness are at the heart of the WRTA. I believe that when one understands and embraces their natural temperament and learns to minimize negative reactivity in the expression of their temperament, their important relationships will flourish and grow. The WRTA, the accompanying handbook, and this book you are reading can help you understand how unknown and unmanaged reactivity erodes marital intimacy. By applying practical principles and tools, which you will learn about in this book, you can safeguard your marriage from erosion and detriment.

The WRTA measures and reveals hidden reactivity. Awareness of these surprising reactions provides opportunities to respond to others with choice. The freedom to choose to *respond* rather than *react* is a gift of being human. Other mammals, for example your dog or cat, simply react. Their reactions to their environment are instinctual rather than reasoned. Their brain is incapable of analyzing response options to the degree we humans do. We may observe our favorite pet sit or lie down upon command, but they lack what we, as humans, possess—an advanced prefrontal cortex area of the brain capable of assessing response options and choosing the best course of action.

As a thirty year veteran professor, licensed marriage and family therapist, certified sex therapist, and counseling pastor for a large church for sixteen years, I have administered the WRTA to over five hundred couples and individuals. This experience has led me to conclude that unmanaged, involuntary reactivity is the most destructive force present in today's marriages. Reactions occurring without cognizance continually erode emotional connections between a husband and wife. This sends them careening towards divorce or pervasive unhappiness. In short, their hearts are closed or closing.

Check Your Heart

The human heart is a complex, mysterious, and sometimes unruly member of our essence. Not the physical heart that occupies your chest cavity, although that organ is complex as well. I refer instead to the intangible heart that occupies your soul. Through the ages, poets, philosophers, writers, psychologists, relationship experts, clergy, and researchers have tried to make sense of this implement that determines the success or failure of our relationships with God and other human beings.

Scripture tells us to guard it (Proverbs 4:23), examine it (1 Corinthians 11:28), soften it (Hebrews 3:15), encourage it (2 Thessalonians 2:17), judge it (Hebrews 4:12), purify it (Psalms 51:10 NIV), and strengthen it (1 Thessalonians 3:13 NIV). Proverbs 4:23 cautions us that it is "the wellspring of life." Consequently, this same verse instructs us to diligently guard it. When a wellspring is in good working order, it has abundant supply to prevent thirst. When a wellspring dries up, it becomes useless for its intended purpose, and the dirt around it becomes hardened. This might be the condition of your heart at this very moment in your marriage.

Before you begin reading the chapters of this book, it would be helpful for you to examine the condition of your heart as it relates to your marriage, or, if you are dating or engaged, your pending marriage. No judgment, no condemnation, no pressure. Just a way to honestly determine your starting point so you can better use the tools and resources you are about to encounter.

Where would you place yourself right now on the following continuum when you think about the current state of your heart towards your spouse, fiancé/fiancée, or boyfriend/girlfriend?

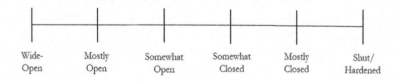

| Wide-
Open | Mostly
Open | Somewhat
Open | Somewhat
Closed | Mostly
Closed | Shut/
Hardened |

I group readers of this book into three categories based on their primary purpose for reading this book: those needing *prevention*, those needing *subvention*, and those needing *intervention*.

Those in the *prevention* group have not yet developed unhealthy habits of reacting to each other. Perhaps you are just dating, engaged, or early in your marriage. You want practical ways to avoid pitfalls and reinforce your marriage for the long haul. This book is for you.

Those in the *subvention* group need a bit more work. Subvention means furnishing aid or relief. Perhaps there is some evidence that reactivity is present in your relationship. You experience some success with managing emotion-laden interactions with each other and resolving conflict. But at other times, things tend to spin out of control and you walk away with hurt feelings and lack of resolve. This book is for you.

Those in the *intervention* group need focused, sustained work using most, if not all, of the concepts, tools, and methods covered in this book. Some may also benefit from professional counseling to guide them through these concepts and bring lasting change. You routinely experience frustrating interactions with each other and seem unable to resolve conflict in healthy ways. You may walk away from your interactions quite bewildered at how you both went off-topic and said things you wish you had not—*again*! This book is for you.

Your primary purpose for reading this book is likely linked to the current condition of your heart towards your companion. I will use the term "companion" throughout this book to refer to the person with whom you are in an intimate relationship. This is because I recognize that not all who will read this book are married. For married couples, *companion* means your spouse. For others, it will be your fiancé, fiancée, boyfriend, or girlfriend.

So, how does your current heart condition towards your companion relate to your primary purpose for reading this book? The following table will explain:

Current Heart Condition	Primary Purpose of Book
Wide-Open	PREVENTION
Mostly Open	
Somewhat Open	SUBVENTION
Somewhat Closed	
Mostly Closed	INTERVENTION
Shut/Hardened	

Now that you have an idea of your current location, often shown on maps as YOU ARE HERE, let us journey together to find a new path. Welcome to this quest to find the path out of reactivity to a *Responsive Marriage.*

PURSUING INTIMACY

Ben and Ashley are madly in love but have a lingering fear of ending up like their parents—divorced. Ashley, a serious and curious student looking for closeness, choice, curiosity, and cleaving in her relationship with Ben, attends a university marriage and family class at the local university. Ashley and Ben are functioning in their relationship at around age twelve and thirteen respectively.

As a student, Ashley regularly asks intuitive questions during her university class discussions. In counseling, she remembers her parents fighting in front of her and her little brother. "Mom and Dad's fights are repetitive, like watching reruns of *Everybody Loves Raymond*, with one telling the other what they don't like." Accusations like, "You're too demanding" and "You don't take enough responsibility" are regularly heard. Ashley's transference of this to her relationship with Ben elevates Ashley's voice as she turns toward Ben saying, "Our relationship is too dependent."

Ashley and Ben met three years earlier as freshmen in college. Now they are talking about marriage. Ben sees no correlation between his parent's divorce and dependence on Ashley. Ashley, on the other hand, is like the person discovering the final four pieces among 500 to complete a puzzle. Ashley turns from Ben and looking at me blurts out, "I depend on Ben too much." Ben retorts, "I don't agree. You are too *independent*." Ashley interrupts. "This sounds similar to my parents. We need to retain our two distinct personalities and reactions."

Our discussion deepens. Ben and Ashley's curiosity leads them to understand the difference between *closeness* (healthy connection) and *enmeshment* (too close). Awareness is the first step to retaining individuality. Validation of the other's perception and emotions is the second step. Ashley and Ben embrace this disagreement and stay curious while respecting each other's emotional choices. All of this opens the way to eventual *cleaving* (deepened connection) when they marry months later.

CHAPTER 1

ANCIENT PATHS

This is what the Lord says: Stand by the roadways and look. Ask about the ancient paths: Which is the way to what is good? Then take it and find rest for yourselves.

—Jeremiah 6:16

Getting lost in the forest is one of the most disorienting and upending experiences a person can have. Surrounded by towering trees and treacherous terrain, with no map and no compass, one can wander for days and make no forward progress. Those who have experienced this describe an overwhelming, sinking feeling when they come across human footprints—only to discover those footprints are their own. "We've been walking in circles."

When the lost and weary sojourner emerges from under the tree-top canopy into a clearing, hope sparks. But when the clearing contains a path, elation ignites. Discovering a path amid rugged terrain can be exhilarating, especially if the wandering is protracted. And when the path has clear signage giving direction to desired destinations, the discovery is particularly pleasing.

This is the outcome God intended when He inspired the writing of this verse in Jeremiah: "Ask about the ancient paths. Which is the way to good? Then take it and find rest for yourselves." It is as if He is saying, "Go back to your roots—remember and follow the 'tried and true' way."

After escaping from slavery in Egypt, the tribe of Israel physically wandered in the wilderness for forty years before settling in the land God promised to them. But over time, Israel continued to wander spiritually even though their physical wandering ceased. In the sixth chapter of Jeremiah, God takes an extremely harsh approach, introducing the specter of more treacherous terrain for Israel to navigate. He pronounces judgment in the form of war and laments how they have not listened to Him. "Listen, earth! I am about to bring disaster on these people, the fruit of their own plotting, for they have paid no attention to My word. They have rejected My instruction" (Jeremiah 6:19).

Yet the hope of finding the ancient path, the way that is good, remained for Israel during this time and still remains today. This is the hope I intend to provide you in this book—the path to a responsive marriage. There is a way that results in a great marriage. You and your companion may not be in a good place right now. Perhaps you are wandering as well having trouble finding the path. You have set off in various directions, attempting to find fulfillment in your relationship, but enduring satisfaction remains elusive. Counseling, marriage retreats, prayer, Bible study, pastoral advice—all noble efforts. Yet frustrating conflict still troubles your marriage. Your hope may be dissipating.

The Quest for Intimacy

As a marriage and family therapist, I am financially compensated to regularly "eavesdrop" on the details of people's most intimate moments. Talk about being in the front row of reality television! The counseling office is an ongoing parade of despair: broken marriages, teenagers' rebellion, and numerous emotional disorders, each tearing the family, and the person, apart. Maybe that's the reason I have no interest in TV "reality" programs. I am already saturated with it due to my chosen profession. Simply put, a counselor's job is helping people sort through relationships in which they have completely lost intimacy.

We frequently observe people risking "everything" frantically trying to get their arms around some emotional sense of connection. It is truly mind-boggling witnessing people literally risk reputation and family, the two most precious and prized parts of a person's life, in hopes of finding some form of intimate connection with another. From leaving one's spouse to starting affairs, pursuing pornography, and running away from home, people try almost anything hoping to experience intimacy.

From the early 1960s *Leave it to Beaver* television show to *The Osbournes*, a 2002 reality show featuring Black Sabbath rocker Ozzy Osbourne, the metamorphosis of TV continues to dazzle and bewilder our world. Hollywood lulls us into a mesmerizing belief that we want it as real and uninhibited as possible—and we want it now! No holding back when it comes to providing a peek into personal and up-close images of purported intimacy.

Reality TV regularly dishes up an enticing diet of what many call true intimacy—more fondly spoken of as the "real thing." The underlying message is crystal clear: the more tantalizing the better.

Why is it that much of our society thrives on catching a glimpse of up-close and personal encounters? Where does the great need for viewing others' most intimate moments come from? Frankly, why is it that pornography, one of the more lucrative and fast-growing industries on the worldwide web, ensnares millions of men and women? What drives us with an insatiable appetite for real survivors on an island or eavesdropping on the painful struggles of those wanting to be the next iteration of the TV show *The Apprentice*? The answer: people want to be right smack-dab in the middle of emotionally riddled encounters. At our core, we are made for intimacy.

IT IS TRULY MIND-BOGGLING WITNESSING
PEOPLE LITERALLY RISK REPUTATION
AND FAMILY, THE TWO MOST PRECIOUS
AND PRIZED PARTS OF A PERSON'S LIFE,
IN HOPES OF FINDING SOME FORM OF
INTIMATE CONNECTION WITH ANOTHER.

Not that Hollywood and the Bible have much in common, but both narrate a similar story line: humans in pursuit of intimacy. Hollywood continually indoctrinates us with messages like, "If only I could find my 'true love,' life will be good!" Jesus says, "You are my love, so submit and rest in me." Hollywood preaches, "Grab onto your love." Jesus proclaims, "Give away your love." Hollywood says, "Fall in love." Jesus teaches, "Receive my love—it's yours for the taking."

The question remains, though, "Am I seeking intimacy Hollywood's way or God's way?" Perhaps you and your companion believe "God first, family second, and career after those." God's economy says this is how intimacy works. It is sequential. Reality TV unabashedly entices us to design intimacy, create it, and manipulate it for our advantage—in direct contrast to God's relationship manual found in the pages of Scripture. The media teaches us to take charge of our destiny: "Conquer the other person," "Be in control of your relationship," or "Have it your way."

On the other hand, God's economy invites us to "submit to one another," to "first look out for the interests of your companion," and to "do nothing out of selfish ambition." Simple enough, right? Not! I think you would agree with me that God's way is extremely difficult. Although we have heard it taught by our Sunday school teachers and preached by our pastors for years, and we may believe it intellectually, it is difficult for the heart to comprehend.

Once viewed as a taboo subject for public consumption, our society now touts sexually intimate interplay as an acceptable form of entertainment—indeed one of the most prolific media draws. Many relish it, crave it, expect it, and make time for it—often at the exclusion of more worthy endeavors. The movie industry accumulates billions of dollars thrilling us with these real and intimate human encounters. What is the obvious psychological, emotional, and perhaps spiritual, drive behind all this? Could it be *intimacy*? Or does this unquenchable desire reflect God's highest calling—that of being emotionally close with Him and others?

It is no wonder that He declares this is our highest purpose: "And be found in him, not having a righteousness of my own that comes from the law, but one that is through faith in Christ—the righteousness that comes from God based on faith" (Philippians 3:9). And, I might add, there is an insatiable desire within each of us to feel passionate (a synonym for intimacy) about something. These secure feelings of connection let us know we are alive.

In the Mel Gibson movie *The Passion of the Christ*, one of the first scenes frames Jesus's face writhing with anguish and pain depicting His excruciating torment experienced on our behalf. Jesus passionately loved us in such a way that His death made it possible for us to have direct access to God the Father. Without a doubt, our greatest need is to experience intimacy and passion—beginning with our heavenly Father!

Intimacy: God's Design

As I have noted, God desires intimacy and closeness. His very nature exudes a desire for it. We first see intimacy depicted in the relationship of the Trinity—Father, Son, and Holy Spirit in constant communion and close relationship with one another. Jesus, while He walked this earth, often retreated to a quiet place alone to spend time with His Father. He needed the connection, the closeness, and the intimacy. Everything He did flowed from His relationship with His Father. "If you really know Me, you will know My Father as well. From now on, you do know Him and have seen Him" (John 14:7). Now that is a close, intimate relationship.

Apparently, the Father and Holy Spirit also delighted in intimacy with the Son as well. In Matthew we read the account of Jesus's baptism in the Jordan River at the start of His ministry. Contained in this story is a beautiful depiction of the intimate relationship of the Trinity. "After Jesus was baptized, He went up immediately from the water. The heavens suddenly opened for Him, and He saw the *Spirit of God descending like a dove and coming down on Him*. And there came a voice from heaven: *This is my beloved Son. I take delight in Him.*" (Matthew 3:16–17; emphasis added). The gentle caress of the Holy Spirit and the verbal affirmation of the Father. What a beautiful picture of intimacy and closeness within the Trinity.

At some point in time, God created angelic beings to occupy heaven with Him. There is no account in the Bible of how or when this occurred, but apparently God desired company—to experience interaction with His created beings. Although the angels are often portrayed in Scripture as accomplishing tasks and fulfilling work assignments, there must also be some relational component to their existence.

Lucifer, now known as Satan, was one of the premier angels. His insurrection against God and fall from heaven is vividly described in Isaiah 14:12–17. Since Lucifer was present in the garden when Adam and Eve were created, we know angels existed before human beings were created. God's desire to create another type of being, human beings, may be an indicator that something was missing or absent from His relationship with the angels. Could it have been "love," the exhilarating attraction that only emerges where choice exists?

The creation story seems to emphasize this ingredient of choice. Hundreds, if not thousands, of trees from which the couple could eat except *one,* lone tree. The consequences were made clear, "For when you eat from it you shall surely die" (Genesis 2:17). Nevertheless, you can eat from every other tree. There is no confusion here. God took a chance to experience love, the kind of true love requiring the other to "choose me" among assorted options. This is God's desire for intimacy and closeness on public display.

His creation of both *male* and *female* lends further credence to His desire for intimacy in His created order. Although we know that God is omniscient (all knowing) and, therefore, cannot be surprised by any event or development, the turn the creation story takes after the creation of Adam is quite intriguing. God apparently faces a dilemma. Having "finished," He "realizes" that Adam has no companion suitable for him. God created every animal and brought

THE CREATION STORY SEEMS TO
EMPHASIZE THIS INGREDIENT OF CHOICE.
HUNDREDS, IF NOT THOUSANDS, OF
TREES FROM WHICH THE COUPLE
COULD EAT EXCEPT ONE, *LONE* TREE.

each one to Adam so he could name them (Genesis 2:19). But among those animals "no helper was found as his (Adam's) complement" (Genesis 2:20b).

So God creates woman, Eve, for relationship and for intimacy. He separates the *male* elements from the *female* elements and locates them in two separate beings. Yet, in the experience of sexual intimacy there will continually be a yearning and longing to recombine those elements and "complete" the image of God. In Genesis 1:27, God defines His image created in "him," the man Adam, as "male and female." To give Adam a helper and prevent loneliness ("It is not good for the man to be alone..." Genesis 2:18), He extracts the female elements from Adam and makes a separate being: Eve. Then in Genesis 2:23–24, God describes the strong attraction that remains to merge the *male* and *female* back into one. "This one will be called 'woman,' _for she was taken from man. This is why_ a man leaves his father and mother and bonds with his wife, _and they become one flesh_" (emphasis added). This is the biblical description of intimacy between a husband and wife.

Intimacy: The Ideal

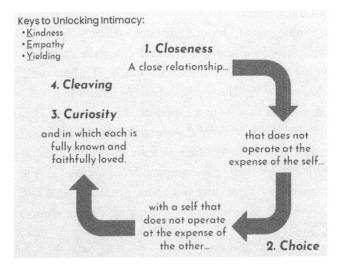

Keys to Unlocking Intimacy:
- Kindness
- Empathy
- Yielding

1. Closeness

A close relationship...

4. Cleaving

3. Curiosity

and in which each is fully known and faithfully loved.

that does not operate at the expense of the self...

with a self that does not operate at the expense of the other...

2. Choice

As depicted in this graphic, based on biblical references and scientific understanding, I define intimacy as *a close relationship that does not operate at the expense of the self, with a self that does not operate at the expense of the other, and in which each person is fully known and faithfully loved.* In other words, each maintains their individual identity while at the same time bonding together.

One of the more beautiful portrayals of this type of intimacy is illustrated in the Gospel of John where Jesus makes it plain and simple, "May they all be one, as You, Father, are in Me and I am in You" (John 17:21). If we understood what Jesus meant by "being one," would we have the key? Do you suppose He was inviting us into intimacy as an adopted blood member of his family? It seems that Jesus is suggesting more than just joining him for a warm cappuccino and a cordial chat at Starbucks. God made it perfectly clear that He has a supreme desire for an intimate relationship with His children. He does not just want to spend time with us during Spring break or Summer vacations. No, His one desire is to be in permanent relationship with us—deeply and intimately connected. He wants all of us. His desire pulsates intimacy. What could be more euphoric than becoming one with Jesus and relishing the most connected and fulfilling experience afforded a human—becoming one with our Creator?

In simple terms, Jesus sums up intimacy (submission) as the act of *kenosis*, a pouring out and emptying, a life enriching relationship with God through Jesus Christ (Philippians 2:5–8, 1 Corinthians 1:4–9). This makes absolute sense when we consider God's command that we first experience intimacy with Him before we can successfully accomplish it with another person (see Genesis 1:27 and Exodus 20:3–4). Once we fully submit to God and receive His Spirit, we are then fully equipped to be catapulted into loving our companions "as we love ourselves." That's it! That's intimacy. To begin to love, genuinely love, our companions is comparable to loving God.

Perhaps another way to get our arms around this is to look at a biblical view of intimacy in the idea of "leaving" parents and "cleaving" to one's companion. The basic core idea here is that one must leave something to join something else. Simple enough, right? If it were that simple, why are so many couples caught in an emotionally dry desert with no evidence of water?

Although "leaving" and "cleaving" are like spiritually leaving the old life and relishing the new life in Christ (2 Corinthians 5:17), many good Christian couples struggle to implement this in their marriage. They just cannot seem to keep past emotional issues from impacting their current emotions. You know, the ole' game of "Remember when you said that to me? Well, that still hurts." What may seem to be a discussion about a current topic is not. There is always some emotional memory from the past that continues to cloud and obscure a current discussion. A fog envelops you when during an argument with your companion you finally realize that what is being discussed is not at all what provoked the initial disagreement.

In a bewildered state, a couple may question, "How did we get here?" The original topic of discussion reverted to a previous disagreement, sometimes from years earlier, fueling further anger and resentment. In other words, failure to leave the past behind can cause it to replay at inopportune times. Hopefully, the couples' bewilderment can ignite change, encouraging them to deal emotionally with the past ("leaving") to resolve current issues ("cleaving").

Intimacy Interrupted

It may be that continual emotional interruptions arise from wounds inflicted before the marriage. Unfortunately, couples can easily confuse current troubles with past wounds. This dynamic threatens the health of any relationship. Many times, without any awareness, one or both within the marriage may unwittingly sabotage the relationship by rejecting their companion's loving affections. What a glorious day when the person can receive God's abundant *grace*, be freed from the past, and completely enjoy their companion.

Freedom is precious, especially for the person who has been without it for years. Susan is a notable example of this. She could not figure out why she was pushing her husband and two children away. Following one of Susan's singing concerts, a friend complimented Susan on the quality of her vocal solo. Susan began to realize she had a tough time receiving compliments. This friend reminded Susan that she tended to reject any words of praise or appreciation. It was then that Susan realized she was suffering from something that continually disabled her from receiving any type of gracious gesture. At the same time, she deeply questioned why she and her husband could not enjoy a closeness she observed in other couples.

Susan decided to enter therapy. For eight months we utilized several therapeutic methods. We continued to peel back the layers of pain until it became obvious her father had deeply wounded her spirit. At the time of our counseling sessions together, her father had been deceased for over twenty years. Despite the time distance, Susan still felt the sting of his cutting words and disfavor every day.

She had become another wounded victim behaving in ways her father predicted she would. "You will never amount to anything. You're fat, no good, and trouble." She had endured these harsh pronouncements for years. Somewhere down deep within her soul, Susan believed she was not deserving of her husband and children. So, she subconsciously fulfilled her daddy's predictions by continuing to sabotage her most important relationships.

With work, Susan came to a place where she found freedom from her father's emotional stranglehold. It was a beautiful sight for me to see her emotionally disentangle her heart from her father's dysfunction. At the conclusion of one of our sessions together, this godly woman turned to me and said, "I feel like I just got saved all over again!" How glorious it was to witness Susan experiencing release from her past emotional wounding, enriched with new and vigorous ways to unite with her husband. Her new-found grace awakening provided dynamism never enjoyed between Susan and her husband before that day.

There is no greater thrill or encouragement than the experience of a sinner shedding the "old life" and embracing the "new life" in Christ. Many new Christians have described this brand-new intimate relationship with God as one of "completeness," "joy-filled," having fully left the "old" to fully gain the "new." In many ways, emotional cleaving with another human being parallels spiritual cleaving with God. Leaving the old encourages the heart to begin again.

Many couples struggle at this very point. They just cannot shake their past. Feelings from the past are like the latest intrusive virus attacking the hard drive of their computer. With just one keystroke, one simple question put to their companion, everything becomes garbled and confused. The emotional screen fills with unfamiliar characters, incoherently assembled, making it nearly impossible for even the most astute interpreter to decipher. It would be impossible to make sense of this convoluted mess. Fortunately, there is hope for couples like this. Intimacy can be restored or experienced for the first time regardless of how scrambled the hard drive may be.

Essential Components of Intimacy

As we discover the ancient paths together, let's further unpack our definition of intimacy by examining its four essential components—closeness, choice, curiosity, and cleaving.

Closeness is the first essential component. It creates a sense of serenity and comfort for the participants. The connection is strong and stable. Closeness implies vulnerability where each can be themselves with each other without fear of judgment. Two hearts woven together in unity and oneness. When merged in this way, division results in tearing and ripping of emotional tissue. Hence the strong command from God to not try and separate what God has put together.[1]

One reason some people may not experience a sense of closeness with their companion is that the second essential component, *choice*, is missing. Intimacy is only possible when each participant has voice and choice. Choice is freedom of decision while voice is freedom of opinion. Both are essential elements for an intimate relationship. God knows this. It is why the creation story contains elements involving choice. Love only exists where choice is present. When choice is eliminated, so is intimacy. When one or both start operating in more dominant ways, reducing voice and choice for the other, intimacy is compromised. My wife, Robin, and I practice offering choice daily. "Do you have a moment to talk?" is a usual starting point in a telephone conversation. "Would you be willing to hear what I have to say?" is another expression that increases *choice* in your relationship. Questions offer choice; declarations or commands suffocate choice.

Another essential component for intimacy is *curiosity*. Curiosity motivates us to know the other person in deeper ways, to seek to fully know them—their desires, their fears, their opinions, their perspectives. Curiosity involves questioning—asking open-ended questions with empathy and without judgment.

The final essential component of intimacy is *cleaving*, the act of faithfully loving. The sense of being attached to the other in such a way that any move to separate creates a tearing or injury. This is the risk of loving—of intimacy. We risk being hurt when we love. But any of us experiencing the intimacy I am describing know that the reward of cleaving and closeness far outweighs the risk of injury.

INTIMACY IS ONLY POSSIBLE WHEN EACH
PARTICIPANT HAS VOICE AND CHOICE.

The Key to Intimacy

Creating and sustaining intimacy in marriage requires deliberate action. Intimacy grows in an atmosphere permeated with tenderness and sensitivity. I believe there are three keys to unlocking intimacy. To create the proper environment for intimacy to flourish and grow, each participant in the relationship needs to be committed to extensively using these keys: *kindness*, *empathy*, and *yielding*. With even one key missing, intimacy will diminish.

Kindness means purposely offering gestures and words that build up rather than tear down. This includes common courtesies such as saying "please" and "thank you." It requires regarding the interests of our companion as more important than ours, as we are admonished to do in Philippians 2:3–4.

The second key, *empathy*, means trying to enter and understand the other person's experience in a curious, non-intrusive manner. It involves nonjudgmental questioning to gain a deeper understanding of the other person's perspective. It goes as far as to attempt to "feel" what the other person feels. This requires more than intellectual assent. Empathy requires engaging the heart. As a family, we experienced empathy on the big screen when *Sadness* consoles *Bing Bong*, the main character's imaginary friend, in the Disney Pixar movie *Inside Out*. Although Bing Bong felt all alone when he lost his most treasured belonging, Sadness walks up to Bing Bong, sits down next to him, and displays empathy by simply listening and trying to understand Bing Bong's pain.

The third and final key, *yielding*, means "letting the other person go first." The idea here is like the rules of the road when driving—yielding the right of way to the other driver. Yielding involves a mindset of deferring to the other person, letting them "go ahead of you."

My aim is to help couples find and follow the path out of reactivity to a responsive marriage. We will employ both the wisdom of the Bible and scientifically verified practices in our quest to find that path. However, after reading this book you will not have arrived at a *Responsive Marriage*. *The Responsive Marriage* is a journey, not a destination. This is why I purposely used the term "path" in the subtitle rather than "key" or "formula." The latter terms appeal to our desire for a "quick fix" and imply finality or instant success. Developing a *Responsive Marriage* takes time and effort. It requires deliberate and focused attention. It is a journey, a quest to uncover and find the "ancient paths" that lead to a thriving relationship. Please join me on the journey as we embark.

Discussion Starter Questions

- *For Couples or Groups*
  - How have you defined intimacy before reading the definition presented in this chapter? In your definition, what does intimacy include and what does it not include?
    NOTES:_____

    _____

    _____

  - Do you think your current definition of intimacy is more Hollywood-like or more Bible-like? How did you learn your definition of intimacy?
    NOTES:_____

    _____

    _____

  - What are the implications of the Trinity—Father, Son, and Holy Spirit—to having an intimate relationship? Which member of the Trinity is it easiest for you to relate with and why? Which member of the Trinity is it most difficult for you to relate with and why?

NOTES:_____

_____

_____

○ Has there been a time when you and your companion were in a dispute about something and one or both of you lost track of what the original topic was? Describe what happened and what that experience was like for you.
NOTES:_____

_____

_____

• *For Couples Only*
  ○ What part of the definition of intimacy do you think you have in your relationship now? What part of the definition do you think is currently missing or deficient in your relationship? What will you do to ensure all parts of the definition are operating in your relationship with your companion?
  NOTES:_____

  _____

  _____

  ○ Which of the three keys to unlocking intimacy—kindness, empathy, and yielding—does your companion consistently exhibit? Which of the three keys do you think is missing or deficient in your relationship? What will you do to ensure you consistently apply all three of these keys?
  NOTES:_____

  _____

  _____

INTIMACY ERODING

On a snowy, Kansas City, Kansas morning, I'm scheduled to meet a couple married for over forty years. As their new pastor in the inner city, I noticed David and Mary several times in the church lobby. They seemed emotionally distant from each other and appeared physically separated. They routinely turn away from, rather than toward, the other. When they glance at each other, a glazed, despondent look encircles their faces. Their marriage may have, at one time, been like a lustrous, right-off-the-show-room-floor car full of vibrant colors. But now, it was washed out and faded. Something had eroded their relationship.

As they enter my office, the cold, dreary morning seems to follow them like the Charles M. Schulz *Peanuts* comic strip character *Pig-Pen* wrapped in a cloud of dust. Neither seemed much invested in the other. I asked them, "How do you keep things in your home from eroding?" They seemed stunned by my question. They remember my introduction to the church as a native Californian and must have thought I was an alien to the Midwest way of doing things.

David blurted out, "We care for our things here in Kansas."

"Help me understand how you do this, especially your car with all of the salted Kansas City roads in this winter season," I quipped.

"We wash the undercarriage often."

"How does maintaining your car and washing the undercarriage parallel how you maintained your marriage relationship over these years?" Mary half-smiled as if to say, "Now he's got my husband under a microscope." I continue. "One of the better ways to maintain a healthy marriage is to learn when to promote your expectations, alter them, or perhaps even drop them when they hurt your relationship. There are proven ways to maintain a relationship which are similar to maintaining your vehicle."

"That makes sense," David replies.

"Good," I said. "Let's start by understanding each of your expectations for the marriage and each other." After some time and work, the gleam and glow of their relationship returns.

CHAPTER 2

EROSION

In August of 2022, residents near Detroit, Michigan heard this Fox News report:

> *Severe erosion along I-94 in Roseville has prompted Macomb County to order an emergency stabilization of the banks along the freeway.*
>
> *"This is an emergency," Miller said. "Even though we've had drought conditions, we've seen these banks erode approximately six feet in some spots just in the past few months. We're concerned that very heavy rains could accelerate that erosion."*
>
> *While the summer has been drier than normal, severe weather over the past month has dumped several inches of rain on Southeast Michigan.*
>
> *The Macomb County Public Works commissioner said they were concerned that loss of the land bank near the highway could cause the road to collapse. According to Commissioner Candice Miller, the erosion at the*

Rohrbeck Extension Drain near 13 Mile and Little Mack is "the worst they have ever seen."[2]

This type of news report is common. Streets, highways, and bridges sometimes collapse when heavy rains or sustained stormwater flow erodes the land underneath them. These roadway failures often cause a heavy and substantial cost. Not only can there be extensive property damage requiring expensive repairs, the pedestrians and drivers using these roadways to arrive at their intended destinations can suffer injuries, or even death, when the cumulative impact of sustained and steady erosion goes unnoticed: until it is too late. In other words, erosion can have catastrophic consequences.

The Erosion of Marriage

To find the path to a responsive marriage, we must first understand and embrace the sacredness and sanctity of marriage—created by God so we can experience intimacy—as God does within the Trinity and with us. God sternly warns against having a casual, cavalier attitude towards marriage in Matthew 19:6. "What God has joined together, man must not separate." He then escalates the gravity of "separation by man" when He announces that Moses instituted the "escape clause" of divorce only because of the "hardness of your hearts" (Matthew 19:8). Ouch! A stern rebuke. These verses instruct us to protect marriage, guard it, and preserve it.

Yet, over many years, we have experienced a steady erosion of marriage across the globe. This assertion will no doubt elicit controversy among some readers of this book. Before drawing premature conclusions or taking a defensive position, I ask you to allow me to explain my rationale for such an indictment. Then, you can be the judge. My analysis of erosion in marriage will move from the broad institution or construct of marriage itself, to statistics that speak to the quality of marriages within large populations, and finally to the condition of individual marriages, including yours.

Examining Our Presuppositions

The term "erosion" implies a reduction in quality based on some set of standards. For roadways, the standards are based on engineering formulas and calculations of load-bearing. For marriage, the looming and necessary question is "what are the set of standards to use when measuring the quality of marriage?" These "standards" are knowingly or unknowingly contained in *presuppositions*, those assumptions, or cognitive filters, each of us has developed and refined throughout a lifetime of experiences. Presuppositions inform the development of the conclusions we draw when our senses—what we see, hear, taste, touch, and smell—are presented with evidence.

It is presuppositions that cause two people analyzing and pondering the same evidence to draw different conclusions. Let us take an example. Evolutionists and creationists analyze and ponder the same evidence and draw different conclusions for the origin of life. Direct, verifiable, evidence used in court trials falls into four categories[3]:

1. *Real Evidence:* tangible artifacts such as weapons, DNA, blood samples, fingerprints, and other material items.
2. *Testimonial Evidence:* eyewitness accounts, either verbal or written, of pertinent events associated with the case.
3. *Demonstrative Evidence:* visual depictions or representations of pertinent elements, in the form of charts or graphics, reasonably and correctly linked to Real or Testimonial Evidence.
4. *Documentary Evidence:* various types of writings containing alphabetic letters and/or numerical figures reasonably and correctly linked to other evidence categories.

These can be primary (original) or secondary (authenticated copy of the original), with a primary source receiving more credibility weight in court than a secondary source.

The dynamic of different reasonable and intelligent persons drawing different conclusions from the same evidence increases dramatically when the above types of evidence are absent or sketchy. When Real, Testimonial, Demonstrative, and Primary Documentary Evidence is not available, as in the case of determining the origin of life, analysis of indirect, present-day "evidence" may lead one to reach different conclusions based on the interpreter's presuppositions.

When one has a presupposition that God either does not exist or does not play an active role in our lives, their analysis of evidence will be skewed towards assumptions of random, indiscriminate happenings rather than purposeful design. Hence, the development of the *theory* of evolution. Not a *law* or a *fact* since there is insufficient, direct, verifiable evidence to prove its tenets. Similarly, creationists cannot prove their tenets regarding the origins of life "beyond a reasonable doubt" or with "the preponderance of evidence"—the standards of evidence used in court trials. It is also, therefore, appropriately named, the *theory* of creation. The defining of these points of view as theories is the reason for creation vs evolution debates that continue to this day.

Considering the Origin of Marriage

This same application of presuppositions to the evidence will also be present in my analysis of whether marriage has eroded over many years, as I assert. This is because part of my assertion is based on the origin of marriage. It fascinates me to ponder the fact that governments across the globe currently grapple with the crafting of legislation to codify a definition of marriage into law. An obvious presupposition to this action is that marriage is an institution or construct of changing societies or cultures, rather than a purposely designed element stemming from God's creation. It is, therefore, malleable and mutable in the eyes of secular thought leaders and governmental agents.

My firmly held presupposition on the origin of marriage is that God created it and not humans. It is, therefore, unmalleable and immutable. In my view, God is the original designer and craftsman of the two genders and the process by which they would bond and procreate. As such, He is the owner of the design, just as Microsoft is the owner of the *Windows* operating system. The book of Genesis clearly and unequivocally depicts this in the creation account, which like all Scripture, God influenced and inspired. To legislate a definition of marriage that deviates in any way from this divinely inspired description requires either a denial of God as the Designer/Owner, or a deliberate decision to tell the Designer/Owner that your new, altered design is superior. Both are equally arrogant positions to take against God, the Designer/Owner of marriage. This would be akin to demanding that Microsoft and Apple, original designers and owners of the *Windows* and *Mac* operating systems, change their designs to make one, all-inclusive operating system based on governmental edict.

The dilution of marriage caused by redefinition erodes its quality. When the definition is broadened, we erode its value in the process. This same premise is observable in economics. If the precious diamond were somehow broadened in its supply and availability to the marketplace, made more accessible to more people regardless of economic status, made less exclusive and more inclusive, the price paid for it would eventually drop dramatically. Its intrinsic value would be cheapened. This is a basic law of economics, and it holds true for anything to which we assign value. Broaden its scope and you risk cheapening its value and the perception of quality assigned to it by potential "buyers." The marriage covenant is sacred and holy, to be esteemed and revered. Jesus's treatment of marriage in Matthew 19 makes this clear. It is to be untarnished and held in high regard. Altering its definition and expanding its scope reduces its quality and value.

THE DILUTION OF MARRIAGE CAUSED
BY REDEFINITION ERODES ITS QUALITY.
WHEN THE DEFINITION IS BROADENED,
WE ERODE ITS VALUE IN THE PROCESS.

Types of Romantic Relationships

All romantic relationships can be placed in one of three categories: *casual, contractual,* or *covenantal.* The category placement is based on the degree of commitment each brings to the relationship. In a *casual* arrangement, commitment is minimal or non-existent. Most romantic relationships start out at this level. Each participant is "testing the waters," trying to determine if they want the relationship to continue. Some are satisfied to remain at this level for a while, or even permanently. However, despite how excitement-filled this type of relationship may be, it is permeated by insecurity. There is a constant uncertainty present, either consciously or unconsciously, and each participant knowingly or unknowingly withholds parts of themselves for protection against rejection.

A *contractual* romantic relationship is one built on terms and conditions. In a *contractual* arrangement, there is an exchange of things of value conditioned upon each party fulfilling all the terms of the agreement. Most contracts have a termination clause which allows each party the option to end the contract "for cause" or "without cause." A "for cause" termination will commence if one or both parties breach any term of the contract. A "without cause" termination is sometimes called a "termination for convenience" which allows each of the participants to get out of the contract for any reason, stated or unstated.

While this type of arrangement certainly involves more commitment than a *casual* relationship, it still produces significant insecurity since there is a known escape clause. It is part of the agreement. If you mess up and breach the contract, it will likely be terminated and you will lose the benefits you are entitled to under the contract. Because it is unknown whether the other will fulfill all their duties and obligations under the contract, the participants are only "partially in" and may still withhold parts of themselves for protection.

A *covenantal* relationship represents the highest form of commitment. In this type of arrangement, the parties pledge lifelong allegiance to each other. There is no "out." For mutual benefit, the parties essentially lay down their rights and privileges for the other. In ancient biblical times, covenants were a common undertaking between leaders of nations.

There were two major types of covenants: obligatory and promissory. Obligatory types dealt with the relationship of two individuals of equal standing (for example leaders of nations) while promissory types were initiated between a suzerain (master) and a vassal (slave).[4] In the latter type, the suzerain was able to offer more in the exchange than the vassal. The suzerain would primarily offer protection while the vassal would simply offer loyalty. In both types, though, the primary focus was not on fulfilling terms, although there may have been some conditions. Rather, the focus was on mutual pledges and lifetime allegiance to each other. This is the type of marriage originally designed by God. It is the most valuable and prized of all types since the level of commitment is the highest. Higher commitment means higher value. This is how God intended marriage to be treated when He created and designed it. Unfortunately, many have strayed from this original design in their marriages and settled for a *casual* or *contractual* arrangement.

Diminishing Value of Marriage

Perhaps, partially at least, stemming from the redefinition of marriage and non-covenantal types of relationships, statistics regarding the value assigned to marriage by Americans paint a rather bleak picture. Fewer adults are getting married and staying married. According to the Census Bureau, in 2022, there were 37.9 million one-person households in the United States. This represents 29% of all households in the U.S. In 1960, one-person households

A *COVENANTAL* RELATIONSHIP
REPRESENTS THE HIGHEST FORM
OF COMMITMENT. IN THIS TYPE
OF ARRANGEMENT, THE PARTIES
PLEDGE LIFELONG ALLEGIANCE TO
EACH OTHER. THERE IS NO "OUT."
FOR MUTUAL BENEFIT, THE PARTIES
ESSENTIALLY LAY DOWN THEIR RIGHTS
AND PRIVILEGES FOR THE OTHER.

represented only 13% of U.S. households. Also in 2022, 34% of people ages fifteen and over had never been married, compared to 23% in 1950.[5] In 1980, the marriage rate, expressed as the number per 1,000 of population, was 10.6. There has been a steady decline in this rate since then with the rate in 2022 standing at 4.9 per 1,000 of population, more than halving the rate in a little over forty years.[6] During the same time frame of 1980 to 2022, the percentage of households headed by a married couple declined from nearly 61% to just under 47%, a 23% decline.[7]

Clearly, the value assigned by individuals to marriage in the United States has fallen dramatically. More are choosing to cohabitate rather than make their union permanent, and many just choose to remain single.

Of course, the related statistic of divorce also speaks to the value assigned by individuals to marriage. Most of us know that only about 50% of marriages survive in the United States. The actual statistic fluctuates between 50% and 60%, the third to sixth lowest among nations in the world, depending on the data source.

Some "glass half full" folks will point to the fact that a 40% to 50% divorce rate can be cause for encouragement, that as long as the rate is below 50% it portends a better chance of staying married than getting divorced. Interesting conclusion. Except, what about the perception of value? If you purchased a car for $50,000, something of high value, and the salesperson told you there is about a 50/50 chance this car will work after you drive it off the lot, you would think twice about investing your hard-earned money in such a sketchy product. Similarly, if a commercial airline contemplated the purchase of a new passenger aircraft from a manufacturer and the manufacturer's sales rep told the purchaser that the satisfaction and safety rating for this jet is about 50%, I doubt the commercial airline would proceed with the purchase. They would perceive its value as too low and go elsewhere to satisfy their need.

The irony of these divorce statistics is that the human craving for intimacy has not changed or diminished. It is the cry of every human heart—to be fully known and faithfully loved by another. Although this desire can be suppressed, muted, and even ignored, its pull is always there, even if it has been relegated by us to subterranean depths. God created us for relationship intimacy. It is wired into our DNA. It permeates the synapses of our brain and reverberates in the chambers of our heart.

When we do not experience it in authentic ways, we search, and often settle, for counterfeits. Pornography, romance novels, affairs, sexting, cohabitation—all attempts to satisfy our cravings for intimacy. Yet we fail to understand that intimacy only exists in an environment filled with trust and loyalty. To risk being vulnerable and completely open with another person, we must trust they will be there for us, despite the circumstances, and know they are permanently and loyally committed to us.

These essential elements are noticeably absent in temporary and discretionary living arrangements, despite efforts to convince ourselves otherwise. Only the *covenantal* marriage arrangement designed by God offers the opportunity for trust and loyalty to exist in abundant supply, thereby allowing true intimacy to grow and prosper. Furthermore, trust and loyalty are sustained in responsive relationships, not those characterized by reactivity. Reactivity erodes trust and diminishes the perception of loyal attachment. Therefore, we must work to reduce and eliminate it in our intimate relationships, the most prominent being our marriage.

Zooming in Further

Now let's talk about individual marriages. Up to this point, I am sure you have realized that creating and sustaining an intimate relationship is not easy. It takes intentionality and concerted effort over a lifetime. When a couple is dating, it seems so easy—like walking. No conscious thought is needed because every interaction with one's date is exhilarating. We listen to each other intently, hang on every word, ask a lot of nonjudgmental questions, are quick to apologize, and treat the other with kindness and respect because we know, if we do not, we may not get a subsequent date with this one who is escalating our hormones and triggering an abundance of feel-good neurotransmitters throughout our brain.

Then we marry and the ease of relating gets dampened by laundry, vacuuming, paying the bills, working, raising children, carpooling, doing yard work, and the thousands of other responsibilities that come with being married, raising a family, and maintaining a household. We lose intentionality and energy for relationship maintenance, defaulting to getting things done rather than getting closer. Successful marriages are the byproduct of intentional actions, not feelings. Feelings come and go, ebb and flow, but sustaining love involves purposeful action.

Has your marriage eroded? Erosion of roadways compromises structural integrity and reduces loadbearing capacities. The same holds true for relationships. When the foundation erodes, the relationship's capacity to withstand shifting pressures is reduced and trouble sets in.

The first step to improving any condition is to assess the current situation. In business leadership development programs we learn we cannot improve what we do not measure. Businesses routinely conduct surveys of their customers to assess satisfaction levels. I suggest you conduct a survey of your relationship. Numerous public surveys of marriages have concluded that the top three relationship stressors are dissatisfaction with communication, finances, and sex. Take some time individually to answer the following ten question survey. Most of the questions in this survey relate to the existence or non-existence of the top three relationship stressors. The remaining questions relate to the general sense of well-being each companion is experiencing.

1. I am satisfied with the amount of time we spend connecting with each other non-sexually.

2. I am satisfied with the quality of our communication.

3. I am satisfied with the speed with which we repair when we are in conflict and/or one or the other is offended or hurt.

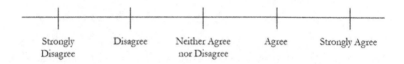

4. I am satisfied with the process we use to repair when we are in conflict and/or one or the other is offended or hurt.

5. I am satisfied with the way we manage and discuss our finances.

6. I am satisfied with the frequency of our sexual encounters.

7. I am satisfied with the quality of our sex life.

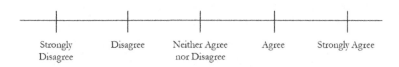

8. Overall, I feel loved by my companion.

9. Overall, I feel respected by my companion.

10. Overall, I am satisfied with the current condition of my marriage.

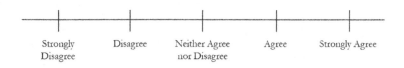

Assign a point value to each answer as follows:

- Strongly Disagree = 0
- Disagree = 1

- Neither Agree nor Disagree = 2
- Agree = 3
- Strongly Agree = 4

Add up your scores and use the following scale to determine the level of erosion to which your marriage may be subjected:

Level of Erosion	From	Through
Substantial	0	13
Moderate	14	29
Minimal or Non-Existent	30	40

Then come together to discuss your answers. This will give you, as a couple, a launching point to further discuss improvement methods. Ask open-ended questions of each other (those requiring more than just a *yes* or *no* response) to understand how your companion sees your marriage. Then discuss ways you and your companion can improve your survey responses.

Examining Expectations

It is imperative that you, as individuals and then as a couple, as part of this assessment process, define and examine your expectations for each of the areas contemplated in the erosion survey questions. Unmet expectations are relationship killers. Often, the conflict experienced in marriage is the result of these unmet expectations. Everyone enters marriage with a predetermined set of expectations whether we are consciously aware of them or not: expectations about communication, money, sex, distribution of household responsibilities,

UNMET EXPECTATIONS ARE RELATIONSHIP KILLERS. OFTEN, THE CONFLICT EXPERIENCED IN MARRIAGE IS THE RESULT OF THESE UNMET EXPECTATIONS.

procreation, parenting, involvement and interaction with in-laws, and ways we will treat each other, just to name a few.

Of course, expectations can and do alter over time, but they always exist. Often our expectations are unspoken, yet we assume our companion will "read our mind" and "just know" we possess the expectation. This is unfair and unproductive.

The first step to dealing with an unmet expectation then is to clearly communicate it. Then, as long as the expectation does not involve a "black and white," universally accepted one, such as, "I expect to not be physically or emotionally abused," give your companion the choice to meet it or not. If, after clearly communicating it, the expectation remains unmet, there are three options: 1) *promote it* (continue to seek satisfaction of it), 2) *alter it* (revise it to fit the relationship), or 3) *drop it* (let it go).

It bears repeating that Scripture tells us to consider the other as more important than ourself and promote the interests of the other just as much, if not more, than our own (Philippians 2:3–4, paraphrase mine). Therefore, there may be times when a companion needs to relinquish their expectation for the good of their marriage. This does not mean becoming a doormat. It does mean, however, considering the "we" more than the "me," something Jesus did for us on the cross, and continues to do for us daily.

Discussion Starter Questions

- *For Couples or Groups*
  - What are some of your presuppositions about the institution of marriage?
  NOTES:_____
  _____
  _____

○ Do you agree or disagree that the value assigned to marriage has eroded over time? Explain your rationale.
NOTES:_____

_____

_____

○ Read Matthew 19:1–12 and discuss the implications together.
NOTES:_____

_____

_____

○ What counterfeit or unproductive ways have you pursued intimacy in the past?
NOTES:_____

_____

_____

○ How have your expectations in marriage created conflict?
NOTES:_____

_____

_____

• *For Couples Only*
○ Would you describe your marriage as *casual*, *contractual*, or *covenantal*? What can you as a couple do to keep it in the *covenantal* category?
NOTES:_____

_____

_____

○ Take the Erosion Survey separately then come together to discuss your answers. What can you do to eliminate erosion in your marriage?
NOTES:_____
_____
_____

○ What expectations do you have for your marriage that are currently unmet? In what ways can your companion meet those expectations? In what ways do you need to alter your expectations? What expectations do you think you need to discard?
NOTES:_____
_____
_____

GETTING A REACTION

University professors can be dry, abstract, and maybe even a bit (no, maybe a lot!) out-of-touch and dull. Not my colleagues and me. We liked playing tricks on our students to get a reaction.

Take, for instance, one of our favorite pranks. I would handout an impossible exam to the students and let them struggle with it for a few minutes. Then, another professor would enter the classroom and pronounce, "Hey, Dr. Welch, I think you're giving your class the wrong test." We performed this dastardly deed more than once. As the students began attempting to answer the questions, they immediately became uncomfortable trying to make sense of the bewildering questions. Soon, involuntary reactivity began to occur like groaning and deep sighing, all of which tend to be neurologically prompted behaviors outside of conscious awareness.

Both of us pranksters stood there as if in amazement as the mayhem and reactivity in the room unfolded. We noticed the collision of the extroverts and. introverts. One of our introverted-contemplators shut down, bowed his head, dropped the exam on the floor, and placed his head on the desk in front of him. The introverted-stabilizer looked around the room, folded the defunct exam, quietly laid it on her desk, and began consoling and encouraging her classmates. The extroverted-influencer blurted out, "You've got to be kidding me. I'm going to get both of you back. You better watch your backs." He then wadded up the exam, bit off a piece of it in his teeth, and spit it out toward both of us. An extroverted-director, who happened to be the student body president, stood on top of a desk and issued a condemnation statement. "This isn't funny at all and you will be reprimanded for such behavior." The room grew silent. All eyes were on the student body president who then threw the exam in the air and started laughing about the entire ordeal. Other students got on top of their desks chanting, "We'll get you, professors. Don't think you're going to get away with this!" It was one of my finer moments. I think it helped my students view me as more relatable. I come across quite nerdy, just ask my children. One student later reminded me of this when she voted for me as *teacher of the year*.

CHAPTER 3

COLLISION

In the United States, traffic collisions are one of the leading causes of death. More than 46,000 people die each year in traffic accidents and another 4.4 million are injured seriously enough to require medical attention.[8] The collision of two or more motor vehicles moving in different or opposing directions can be injurious to human health, even fatal.

In like manner, the collision of two individuals in a close relationship can be equally detrimental. In marriage, our personalities, our respective genders, our family of origin (family we grew up in) experiences, and our preferred ways of interacting with our worlds often generate opposing forces that collide with frequent regularity. In this chapter, we want to understand the differences that lead to relationship collisions and learn to embrace these differences rather than be frustrated by them.

Variety: The Spice of Life

In case you haven't noticed, we human beings love variety. We like experiencing new things. Our brains are enticed by the allure of novelty. We see this played out every day at restaurants, eateries, and coffee shops. These establishments would not survive without the human desire for variety, both among them and within them. At times we want a good hamburger; at other times we desire Chinese, or Italian, or sushi. At Starbucks, there are hundreds, if not thousands, of different ways to order and design your coffee by manipulating size, number of shots, toppings, foam quality, liquid additives, and temperature, just to name a few. The more items on the menu and the more mix-and-match options the better. A restaurant with only one item on the menu in one form will quickly go out of business.

Yet, when it comes to marriage we shun variety. At first, when dating, we are attracted to the other person precisely because of variety. They are different than us and we love it. Then, after marriage, we attempt to make the other person more like us. We get irritated when they do not think like us and wish they would just "see things my way." In short, after marriage, we often lose the attraction to the variety our companion brings to the relationship. This is one of the most interesting dynamics I have observed in the thousands of couples I have counseled over the years. It shows up repeatedly and can be summarized in this poignant axiom—"opposites attract, then they attack."

Temperament Differences

God designed each of us with unique characteristics. No two of us are exactly alike in either physical form or cognitive and emotional attributes. In Psalms we learn that God "knit me together in my mother's womb" (Psalms 139:13). This implies crafting and assembly with purpose and forethought. One manifestation of our uniqueness displays in our temperament, the personality components through which we filter and process our world. Two people can view and experience the same event but have different interpretations, perspectives, and opinions. These differences in perspective are largely due to differences in temperament.

Different temperaments filter information differently. This dynamic has always intrigued me as a counselor and researcher. Much of my work with couples in the counseling office is focused on trying to encourage each participant to see things from a different perspective. It is this condition that led me to become fascinated with temperament assessments.

Many of us know that temperaments, or personalities, are most often categorized into four distinct types. First promulgated by Hippocrates in ancient Greece, the most common temperament categorization still used today is Choleric, Sanguine, Phlegmatic, and Melancholic. Hippocrates derived these words from four body fluids, since he believed that personality, as well as many diseases and ailments, was determined by the dominant presence of yellow bile in the Choleric, blood in the Sanguine, phlegm in the Phlegmatic, and black bile in the Melancholic. Although the body fluid connection was later abandoned as scientific understanding progressed through the ages, the resulting personality types endured and still form the basis of our analysis of temperaments today.

There are hundreds of assessments existing today that measure temperament. In my counseling work, I have used quite a few with varying degrees of success. However, I was never able to find an assessment that went deeper into how an individual expresses their temperament. I was noticing a common characteristic in couples I was counseling who were struggling with communication in their marriage—one or both were reacting to the other involuntarily and without initial conscious thought. Rolling the eyes, sighing in exasperation, quickly escalating—all signs of reactivity. Only after the reaction occurred was the individual aware of it.

This made me think, "What if we could measure the degree to which one exhibited *reactive* tendencies as opposed to *responsive* tendencies?" Hold on, we will define those terms shortly.

My reasoning led me to conclude that certain temperament types would no doubt exhibit certain types of reactive tendencies. If we could measure both temperament and temperament expression, and then provide the individual with a profile of their responsiveness vs reactivity, we could increase awareness and provide the opportunity for the individual to choose alternative responses *before* muddying the waters with their involuntary reactivity.

This line of thinking birthed the Welch Responsive Temperament Assessment, or WRTA. Since there was no assessment on the market that measures both temperament and temperament expression, I needed to invent one. I teamed up with a software developer, conducted extensive scientific research, and created the WRTA. We are now providing this tool to counselors, churches, and mental health practitioners. It has revolutionized my counseling practice. I have been fortunate to see hundreds of individuals and couples finally recognize the ways they might be unknowingly sabotaging their intimacy with reactivity and take action to increase their responsiveness to each other.

With the WRTA, we measure temperament within a range of four we refer to using the acronym DISC—"D" for Director, "I" for Influencer, "S" for Stabilizer, and "C" for Contemplator. The following table summarizes the characteristics and differences between the temperaments.

WELCH RESPONSIVE TEMPERAMENT ASSESSMENT (WRTA)				
TEMPERAMENTS [ENDURING]- Highest % = Primary, 2nd Highest % = Secondary				
Element	D	I	S	C
Known For	Directing	Influence	Steadiness	Conscientiousness
Known As	Director	Influencer	Stabilizer	Contemplator
Common Personality Test Equivalent	Choleric	Sanguine	Phlegmatic	Melancholy
Complementary Temperament	Influencer	Director	Contemplator	Stabilizer
Opposite Temperament	Stabilizer	Contemplator	Director	Influencer
Animal Metaphor	Lion	Otter	Dog	Owl
Motivating Pattern	Assertive-Directing	Engaging-Influencing	Altruistic-Nurturing	Analytical-Autonomizing
Primary Orientation	Task	People		Task
Primary Type	Active [Extroverted-Optimistic-Sociable-Responsive]		Passive [Introverted-Careful-Controlled-Reliable]	
Strengths When Responsive GOAL=Fortify/ Expand	*Ambitious *Competitive *Self-Confident *Forceful	*Spontaneous *Influential *Sociable *Adaptable	*Helpful *Caring *Peacemaking *Sensitive	*Independent *Rational *Organized *Self-Sufficient
General State for Responsive Strengths	*Steadied by Internal Calm*			
Weaknesses When Reactive GOAL=Mitigate/ Minimize	*Ruthless *Combative *Arrogant *Dictatorial	*Self-Centered *Attention-Seeking *Disorganized *Emotional	*Submissive *Gullible *Spineless *Impractical	*Critical *Suspicious *Rigid *Unfeeling
General State for Reactive Weaknesses	*Agitated by Internal Anxiety*			

WRTA Temperaments

Each temperament has a complement and an opposite. The Director and the Contemplator tend to be more task-oriented, while the Influencer and the Stabilizer tend to be more people-oriented. When we are functioning optimally within our temperament, we exhibit strengths that fortify our relationships and promote general success in life's endeavors. But when we over-function or under-function in our temperament (occurring when we are agitated by anxiety), the weaknesses of our temperament start to dominate resulting in fractured relationships and inhibited success in life. Such was the case for Michael and Jessica (not their real names), a real-life couple I mentioned earlier who I counseled.

A desperate voice filled the airwaves as Jessica called my office. "My marriage is falling apart," she said. "My husband doesn't see any hope for our marriage. He's lost all confidence in me. He really wishes I were somebody that I'm not. Do you think that there's any hope for us?"

Attempting to answer her question, I asked if she thought there was any possibility her husband would agree to come with her for counseling. Hesitantly, she said she thought Michael might be willing. I then tried to reassure her. "Although I can't promise results, there's always hope for a restored relationship if two people commit to working through their issues." Our conversation concluded with Jessica gaining some sense of reassurance.

It was not too long after that telephone call that Jessica and her husband, Michael, entered counseling. She was a registered nurse and he was an attorney. As they began telling their story, I outwardly smiled and inwardly thought to myself, "Their temperaments (their basic life approach) are the exact opposite, which is a very normal temperament combination for most couples." Jessica was the outgoing extrovert, motivated by being around lots of people, and Michael was the shy introvert who emotionally recharges by being alone.

The outgoing personality (extrovert) tends to rejuvenate by being with people and talking about whatever comes to mind. The introvert personality needs more time alone to process life's circumstances and events. Neither temperament is healthier than the other—they are simply different. These differences can cause friction and, without proper recognition and management, tend to lead to conflict and turmoil.

From the beginning of counseling, it was apparent that Michael preferred being alone. He was very analytical and lacked visible manifestations of emotion. During the first few minutes of the session, the introvert was conducting a legal proceeding with his wife hoping that "the judge" (me, as the counselor) would rule in favor of his carefully crafted defense.

Jessica, the extrovert, was extremely emotional about their relationship. Her way of working through the pain was to get the emotion out through words. Every word for her was fraught with feelings and painful outbursts. Unbeknownst to the couple, the emotional collapse of their marriage was being caused by their unmanaged experience of temperament differences. Although they were both originally attracted to the others' temperament, that original attraction had now become the Achilles heel for them individually and as a couple.

Early on in counseling, Jessica blurted out her pain as though desperately attempting to gain her husband's approval. "You never, ever, give me a compliment, it's all business with you," shouted Jessica. Michael, in his desperation to drive home his carefully thought-out points, made it clear that he did not respect his wife but instead viewed her as emotional, indecisive, and highly manipulative.

This relationship had moved from one in which each was attracted to the opposite temperament to one in which complete resentment for just how different they were from one another had taken root. Their experience of temperament differences kept the relationship stuck: both companions were unable to respect, nurture, or listen to the other. We have all heard it said, "Respect takes a lifetime to build and can be lost within seconds." Well, this couple had lost respect for one another long before coming to counseling, thereby disabling them from successfully nurturing each other. This is a formula for divorce if there ever was one. A relationship lacking nurture wipes out any trust one may have in the other person and, in turn, completely eliminates the possibility for loving feelings to exist.

Michael and Jessica's relationship was in a stranglehold. It is devastating and heart-wrenching to witness a relationship so wounded as that exhibited by Michael and Jessica. The loss of respect and nurture can squeeze the life out of any relationship. Michael and Jessica's relationship was no exception. During years of emotionless

A RELATIONSHIP LACKING NURTURE
WIPES OUT ANY TRUST ONE MAY HAVE
IN THE OTHER PERSON AND, IN TURN,
COMPLETELY ELIMINATES THE POSSIBILITY
FOR LOVING FEELINGS TO EXIST.

interactions and a growing disdain for one another, their relationship had been drained of life and vitality rendering them both angry and hostile toward each other.

Michael and Jessica lacked the ability to take what I call a step of "love + faith" toward each other. Taking this step involves one risking *again* with their companion. Although Michael and Jessica had done this during the earlier years of their marriage, their respect for the other had all but evaporated. Loving feelings had changed to frustration and disgust. They had lost all ability to negotiate and enjoy life together.

Could this be your relationship? Is it cold and lacking emotion? When you see your companion, does your heart slump to a snail's pace rather than energize with happiness? The collision of your temperaments may be the reason.

Gender Differences

In addition to temperament differences, couples routinely collide over gender differences. Men and women are different. This is not particularly earth-shattering news for anyone. We intuitively get that. Yet confusion regarding what a man is and what a woman is has grown exponentially in our culture. The lines between masculinity and femininity seem evermore blurred these days.

Our culture seems to have a challenging time accepting that men and women are different. On the contrary, many initiate significant efforts to make them more alike. It is this goal that galvanized the four waves of feminist movements we experienced over the last two centuries.[9] Although focused on creating equality for women, as compared to men, in education, property rights, political affairs, social status, and workplace pay and conditions, the later movements seemed to try to move women towards sameness with men in all material respects. Examples of this desire for gender sameness are everywhere.

Nowadays, we routinely see movies with the woman as an action hero who uses martial arts, weapons, superhuman tactics, and elevated physical strength to overcome the enemy. But prior to the late 1970s, men were the only action heroes in movies. This changed in 1977 with the release of *Star Wars: The New Hope*. Princess Leia, played by Carrie Fisher, took up a blaster and led the escape mission. She overcame her captor, Jabba the Hutt, who was several times her size, by strangling him while wearing a slinky bikini. She walked the line between sexy and powerful. This was brand new to the big screen, but it created a wave of change as more women were cast in action hero roles previously played only by men.

In 1979, Sigourney Weaver's character in *Alien*, Ripley, shed stereotypes of the woman with intense ferocity. Since then, producers have made hundreds of blockbuster movies with the woman displaying tremendous strength and intensity to overcome overwhelming odds. In the 1970s, this was groundbreaking and controversial. Today, it is not even questioned.

The quest for gender sameness has now shifted to society's current fascination with gender confusion. A recent *Healthline* posting found on the Internet describes sixty-eight different terms for types of gender, gender identity, and the like.[10] This expansion of gender from a fixed, binary system to a fluid, multi-faceted one has only blurred the lines of male and female differences further.

The concerns of women for equal treatment under the law and society encapsulated in the various feminist movements we experience are certainly legitimate. For thirty years in the university classroom, I have followed, researched, and spoke on the feminist movements. Unfortunately, the patriarchal structure of society degraded women to an inferior status. Change was needed. Inferiority was certainly not what God envisioned when He created Eve. However, God did overtly assert, through the creation story, that the roles and contributions of men and women are different. Not different in value, simply different in function and purpose. God made men and women with different bodies and different ways of processing mental and emotional input. Not inferior, simply different.

Parents would proclaim from the mountain tops that their little boy is quite different from their little girl. Take for instance my two little charmers. From an early age, my little boy, Daniel, was overwhelmingly more physical than my daughter, Savannah. He would take every opportunity to wrestle and, in his words, "take me down." Daniel could make anything into a gun or rifle and begin shooting at any moving target: a shoe, a pole, a broom, a hanger—you name it. With a little imagination, he could fabricate any object into a shooting weapon. On the other hand, our daughter, Savannah, from an early age, wanted toys that represented relationships. Barbies were her favorite dolls. Savannah and I had some of our best talks while outfitting her Barbies.

Although Savannah would indulge Daniel and willingly follow him on his hunting expeditions in our backyard, I never saw her take any of Daniel's make-believe guns and shoot at someone or something. Apparently, she enjoyed relating to Daniel during his hunting escapades as she tagged along with him but wasn't willing to join him in the fight.

I think Rick Warren, author of *The Purpose Driven Life*, describes well the differences between males and females.

> *My wife and I are the exact opposite in every single area of life except [for] our commitment to Jesus Christ. We are! Sometimes we look at each other and we want to go, 'What planet did you get off from?' And yet, I have found in counseling this many years that the couples that have the greatest potential for growth have the greatest differences.*[11]

God made us unique and we can choose to fight the differences and experience a life of great pain, or we can embrace and respect the differences and find some of the greatest joy in life.

Trying to Change Our Companion

So why do companions tend to "fight" rather than "unite?" Simply put, it is easier to understand someone who is more like me. We want to change our companion to behave and respond to life like we do. It is called *influence*, an innate need in every human being to provoke others to adapt their thinking and behavior to our way. You take any leadership book out on the market and at the top of the leadership purpose list is *influence*. It really meets an ego need within every human being to influence another to change.

In a counselor's office, it is very typical for the clients to each say, "If he (or she) would just do it my way, everything would be fine!" But this grandiose idea of getting everyone to think alike can be quite detrimental to progress and quality. Married couples are not the only ones that fail in this area. Hundreds of major corporations have succumbed to this temptation.

We tend to like people who are more like us. But it is differences, not similarities, that create success in business. Many experts call the inability to appreciate and respect differences *groupthink*. Henry Ford said it best, "if everyone is thinking alike, then someone isn't thinking." To be even more blunt, if two people are exactly alike, one of them is not needed. The most successful couples think differently and combine their differences to create synergy and growth.

Groupthink can create disasters. Some historical examples include John F. Kennedy and the Bay of Pigs invasion in 1961 and the crash of the Space Shuttle Challenger in 1986. In both instances, the leadership was unable to consider differences in opinion and perspective. They all began thinking alike rather than benefiting from their differences. The results were catastrophic.

Groupthink can lead to *entropy*, a term used to describe an organization that turns in on itself, fails to listen to its constituents, and declines in quality and financial stability. Numerous international organizations spend thousands of dollars annually developing teams with diversity comprised of people who not only look different but also think and work differently.

Basic relationships between men and women are no different than the marketplace. Relationships can exhibit the same symptoms of *groupthink* and *entropy*. No negotiation, no differences, just the same 'ole status quo: dead! It has been said that you are either green and growing or ripe and rotting.

All the research is clear. The greater a couple's differences the more likely they are to succeed in their marriage. Conversely, too much similarity in a couple creates the potential for boredom and disillusionment. It is utterly amazing how God designed relationships. We are created to be inspired by our differences not neutralized by our similarities.

Men and Emotions

One area where these differences show up is in how men and women process and deal with emotions. Women naturally "feel" and men naturally "act." Does this mean that men are emotionless, that they are clueless about relationships, that they [we] need an emotional transfusion? Absolutely not! Men have feelings. They just may need some help to know how to identify and describe them.

Recently one of my students, after watching a video titled *Men and Emotions*, described his anger problem as a young boy. He said, "My parents wanted the angry outbursts to cease so they wouldn't allow me to be angry." I was amazed at how blunt and emotionless this student was as he described his parents teaching him not to feel but rather to avoid or suppress his feelings.

Most counselors would agree that the number one challenge for men is managing anger. Why is that? Is it because they are born angry? Do they have an anger streak that runs throughout their gene pool? Do they have an overdose of testosterone? Is a male's brain structure associated with the generation of anger, the amygdala

ALL THE RESEARCH IS CLEAR. THE GREATER A COUPLE'S DIFFERENCES THE MORE LIKELY THEY ARE TO SUCCEED IN THEIR MARRIAGE. CONVERSELY, TOO MUCH SIMILARITY IN A COUPLE CREATES THE POTENTIAL FOR BOREDOM AND DISILLUSIONMENT. IT IS UTTERLY AMAZING HOW GOD DESIGNED RELATIONSHIPS.

(two small brain neural clusters associated with the emotions of fear and anger), larger? Yes to all of the above.

Children are not born devoid of emotion regardless of their gender. Their emotional expression is one of the first things we notice. Both male and female children exhibit ongoing outbursts when they are tired. Both cry when embarrassed. Well then, why do men struggle expressing most emotions but seem to have no problem expressing anger? Why is it that my brother and I would fight my sister to watch *Combat*, an army program we loved, rather than *Father Knows Best* which we thought was dorky? I think my brother, Ron, and I were attempting to find an appropriate and acceptable place to express emotion. We started early. In fact, one of the first pictures of me as a little boy in our backyard displays my Roy Rogers's regalia as I fought the bandits of the world.

Why is it that my wife will walk out of the room as I am watching the FBI bad guy chase? And before she leaves the room she says, "I can't really watch this; it's too violent!" On occasion, I have asked myself, "Do I have an anger problem? Why doesn't this violence bother me?" I do not believe I have an anger problem, but watching aggression is a way to get some release from the stress in my life. I have observed this to be true in many men. It is why men would prefer watching *Braveheart* rather than *Romantic Heart* or some other relationship focused movie.

While engaged in a violent program or video, I am in a mode of protecting and hunting down the enemy. The feeling is a secure and motivating one rather than an insecure and debilitating one. That is why wrestling, boxing, and football are the preferred sports for men. Men can get their frustrations out through a controlled environment (or I should say a *somewhat* controlled environment).

Take, for instance, my ninth-grade baseball experience. I was playing third base and we were leading by one point. It was the ninth inning, bases loaded with two outs. Bottom line, either we got the next guy up to bat out or the other team would score and win the game. The unbelievable happened. The guy on third base got a little too far away from the base and we caught him in a squeeze. He was now in between third base and home.

The pitcher threw the ball to me. Our catcher and I began tossing the ball back and forth, as we had previously practiced, attempting to squeeze this runner and hoping one of us would tag him out and end the game thereby finalizing our victory. As the runner finally took a risk and headed for third base, the catcher threw the ball to me and, luckily, I caught it. The base runner ran right over me attempting to reach third base without being tagged out.

Fortunately, I was able to keep the ball in my glove, and in doing so the ump proclaimed the runner out. Unfortunately, what I did not realize at the time was that the runner had chipped my tooth and my mouth was bleeding. Blood was running down my cheeks and onto my jersey. I became an instant hero. The coach congratulated me, my team members applauded me, and there I was standing before everyone with a damaged tooth and a bloody mess. As the other guys and the coach were slapping me on the back and giving me high fives, do you think they were at the same time asking me how I was feeling? No, they knew I was feeling elated despite my injury: I was the newest hero on the block.

I was for a few brief moments the "respected" man. What man (a boy with a squeaky voice) would not sacrifice a tooth to be a hero? Certainly, by nature men tend to think more than we feel. However, our world teaches us to be a hero devoid of feelings. Warriors don't feel; they just conquer.

Friendship Development

Most men do not have as many friends as women do. Men tend to have few friendships and most are superficial. Women develop friendships more readily than men. Therefore, men depend on their wives to fulfill the friendship role. After a divorce, men remarry at twice the speed of women.[12] Men need their wives' respect and friendship. They need a woman who respects and honors them. In contrast, a woman needs a man who will nurture her.

We've all, no doubt, witnessed the young woman "falling" for the older man. It is obvious—he needs someone who respects and admires him. She needs someone who understands her and is skilled at nurturing, much like a father would his daughter. He needs a friendship offering "respect" and she needs a relationship laden with "love."

Years ago, I decided to resign from my administration post at the university where I had been working for over a decade and take a full-time teaching position so I could devote more time to my private counseling practice. As an administrator, I was responsible for thirty faculty members and 180 students. Now, I would just be responsible for the students in my classroom.

During this transition period, it was intriguing to hear the dichotomous responses from my colleagues. Invariably, the men viewed my decision through the lens of respect by commenting that I was taking a "step down." You see, administration positions are respected more than pure faculty positions. My decision caused some of the men who wanted to gain future advancement at the university to no longer make the effort to connect with me. One of the coaches at the university piped up during an intramural basketball game saying, "Wow, Welch, you've really taken a step down."

The women at the university, on the other hand, responded through their nurturing lenses with statements like, "Wow, you'll now have the opportunity to really connect [nurture] with students," or "You'll be able to make a real contribution in the lives of your students." All statements about relationship improvement.

So, how do men and women befriend one another? She needs a friend who will listen, empathize, and exchange emotional intimacy with her. He, on the other hand, needs a playmate, someone who will support him in his interests, and respect him as a husband, father, and provider.

Husbands, find ways to increase the friendship factor by nurturing your wife's need for tender care. Ask her open-ended questions like, "Tell me about your day," "Please explain how that event made you feel," "Please explain to me how I may help you work through this situation," or, just say, "I love you—how can I help?" Assisting with the domestic chores speak volumes to her.

For the wives, find ways to offer him gifts of respect by noticing things he does, offering praise, and joining him in his interests and pursuits. Thank him for consistently going to work and helping to make your life easier. If he gets to work on time, compliment him on this consistency. If he faithfully exercises, let him know that you recognize his conscientious efforts. Find little things for which you can offer gestures of respect such as his grooming techniques, being punctual, etc.

The Creation of Gender

Now let's take a closer look at the creation account and what it tells us about gender differences. In Genesis 1:27 we read. "So God created man in His own image; He created him in the image of God; He created them male and female." Here we first learn that we bear the image of God in our gender. Our gender is an expression of God and honors Him when we are male and when we are female. In Genesis 2, we read more details about the brief summary contained in Genesis 1:27. Genesis 2:7 tells us the Lord God formed the man, whom he would name Adam, from the dust and breathed into him the breath of life. This was before Adam's companion, Eve, was created.

Since God displays both male and female attributes in His character, we can assume that making Adam in God's image meant giving him characteristics of both genders. Perhaps not physical characteristics but certainly mental and emotional attributes we see God portraying in the pages of Scripture. Most notably, strength and power (male attributes), and beauty and nurturing (female attributes).

Genesis 2:15 tells us that after creating Adam God took him and placed him in the garden of Eden to work it and watch over it. But then in Genesis 2:18, immediately following giving instruction to Adam about what plants in the Garden to eat and not eat, God "realizes" Adam has lots of work to do to take care of the garden and will, therefore, need a helper as his complement. However, none of the animals God had formed were suitable to be a helper for Adam. So, He puts the man to sleep and takes a part of him to make Eve. This is a beautiful depiction of God extracting the female attributes from Adam to form a separate and distinct complement for him. Thus, Eve took into her being the same image of God that Adam had, only with different attributes: female attributes.

We see a further declaration by God of gender differences when He pronounces the punishment each will receive for disobeying God's single instruction to not eat from the tree of the knowledge of good and evil. For Adam, his punishment relates to work and accomplishment. He will toil all the days of his life. For Eve, her punishment was in childbearing and her relationship with her husband, both representative of familial relationships. Hence, we see in each gender a different focus, men on work and accomplishment and women on relationships.

More Gender Differences

Let's review some other significant differences between men and women described in the following table. In doing so, I hope you will see how these gender differences can be honored and appreciated. Both the husband and wife bring valuable elements to the marriage resulting in "two being better than one."

Category	Aspect	Men	Women
PHYSICAL BODY	*Muscle Mass*	More	Less
	Body Fat	Less	More
	Sex Organs Location	External	Internal
	Body Image	Less Dissatisfied	More Dissatisfied
BRAIN ANATOMY	*Connectivity*	Less Hemisphere Connection	More Hemisphere Connection
	Size Relative to Body	Larger	Smaller
	Gray Matter (Processing)	Less	More
COGNITION	*General Functioning*	Compartmentalized	Integrated
	Task Processing	Single Task	Multi-Tasking
	Superior Function	Visio-Spatial, Working Memory Processing	Verbal, Reading Comprehension, Writing, Fine Motor Coordination
	Environment Navigation	Direction and Distance Calculation	Landmarks
	Primary Motivator	Accomplishment	Relationship
	Primary Fear	Failure	Abandonment
	Imbalance Tendency	Passive --> Aggressive	Enmeshment -->Ruling
RELATIONSHIPS & COMMUNICATION	*Emphasis*	Status, Independence, Competition	Interdependence, Interpersonal, Cooperation
	Comparison View	Differences	Similarities
	Preferred Communication Type	"Report Talk"	"Rapport Talk"
	Communication Focus	Data	Feelings
	Communication Objective	Solve the Problem	Deepen Intimacy
	Memory of Relationship Events	Less Detailed	More Detailed
	Core Desires in Marriage	Recreational Companionship	Relational Companionship
		Admiration	Security
		Support	Significance
		Physical Responsiveness	Emotional Responsiveness

The first set of differences relate to the physical body. Men generally have more muscle mass than women and women have more body fat than men. I recognize that the more body fat difference may be perceived as unwelcome news by the women. But this is purposeful on God's part, for her body to be more curvaceous, part of her beauty. It also makes her body more prepared for childbirth. The additional muscle mass for men is likely due to God's pronouncement to Adam that he was to work the garden and take care of it. More muscle mass is needed for physical labor.

Of course, we know that the sexual organs are located on the exterior for men and on the interior for women. Finally, we know from experience that women tend to have a more challenging time accepting their body as it is than men do.[13]

Imaging techniques that allow us to map brain structures and function have exponentially increased our understanding of brain anatomy. The way each of our brains process information is quite different. Anatomically, women do tend to have more connections between the two hemispheres of the brain. In general, the left hemisphere controls speech, comprehension, arithmetic, and writing. The right hemisphere controls creativity, spatial ability, artistry, and musical skills.[14] The additional connections between the brain hemispheres for women means they can transition more quickly between topics and activities that involve the opposite hemisphere, or both hemispheres. Although men can boast of having bigger brains than women, in proportion to body size, this certainly does not make men more intelligent. In an ironic twist, God may have given men less "gray matter," or processing neurons, as compared to women.[15] Bigger brains but fewer thinking neurons. Seems so unfair.

The last two categories of gender differences provide the most opportunity for husbands and wives to rely on the strengths of each other to gain new perspectives and see things from multiple points of view. Let's look first at cognitive processing.

Men tend to mentally process in a compartmentalized fashion. This means we attend to one set of thoughts at a time. This does not mean we cannot think about or attend to more than one thing at a time, it just means our brains tend to process input in a more linear fashion. Pull the file out of the cabinet, think about it for a while, then put the file back. Pull out a new file, think about it, put the file back, and so on. Women's brains are more integrated, meaning they pull multiple files out at a time and deal with them in a holistic fashion.

This is why men and women may get frustrated with each other as anxiety elevates. Men are attempting to deal with the single compartment, and women are attempting to link multiple compartments together for deepened clarity. Men can easily get frustrated when the multiple compartments being examined by the woman do not seem to relate. "Can't we just stick to the subject at hand?" is the typical response. The woman may get frustrated with the man when he cannot seem to keep up in the conversation.

Because of this propensity for integrated thinking, women tend to be better at multitasking while men generally focus only on a single task. As with most things in marriage, we must learn to honor our differences in the way we process mental input and find ways to allow both types of processing to occur. Neither is better than the other: they are simply different.

Although there are exceptions, men tend to be better at visuospatial and working memory processing while women are better at language dependent tasks and fine motor coordination. Hence, women verbalize more than men, and men are more adept at visually assessing the distance and spacing between objects. Robin and I have experienced this on more than one occasion. She is in the passenger seat of the car announcing that I am "following too close to the car ahead" when I think there is plenty of room. She can quickly become agitated with, in her mind, too short of a braking distance. Differences in visuospatial orientation are likely the cause of this dispute.

Men and women navigate their environments differently. Because of visuospatial orientation, men tend to mentally refer to directions and calculate distances when walking or driving. Women look for visual references when walking or driving and, therefore, tend to navigate with landmarks. This is why a woman gives driving directions to another person in a different manner than men. Men will tend to give left-right directions with estimations of miles between, while women will supplement the directions with visual markers to help guide the driver. "Turn right after you pass the Starbucks" or "Look for the white picket fence on the left" are typical driving directions given by women.

As I mentioned when we were reviewing the creation story, men tend to be more accomplishment driven while women are more relational driven. Consequently, men's biggest fear is failure while a woman's biggest fear is abandonment. A wise husband and wife will provide constant reassurance to the other in the area of their primary fear. To the husband a wife might say, "Honey, you did a great job on that fence repair" or "I sure am proud of the work you do." To the wife a husband can say, "I know we'll be together the rest of our lives" or "I'm always here for you, baby."

In concert with our primary motivator, men and women can easily gravitate to an out-of-balance condition on one end of a spectrum or the other. For men, with the motivation of accomplishment, we can either go passive with too little involvement or become too aggressive with too much involvement. For women, with the motivation of relationships, they can either become enmeshed and lose or blur their individual identity or become ruling and controlling of the other person. The key here is to recognize your tendency and intentionally move toward the center of your respective spectrum. For men, the balance is being assertive with optimal involvement—not too much, not too little. For women, the balance is being the helper to aid but not to dominate or become indistinct. In other words, honor the self and the other person.

In relationships, men tend to emphasize status, independence, and competition while women tend to emphasize interdependence, interpersonal elements, and cooperation. When comparing themselves to others, men tend to look for differences while women tend to look for similarities. When talking, men tend to use "Report Talk" that focuses on data and solving the problem. Women tend to use "Rapport Talk" that focuses on feelings and deepening intimacy. When reviewing relationship encounters, men tend to remember less details than women.

Finally, in marriage, men and women have different core desires and reasons for marrying. Men want recreational companionship while women want relational companionship. Men want admiration while women want security. Men need support and women need significance. Men desire their wife to be physically responsive to them while women desire their husband to be emotionally responsive to them.

Reactivity in Relationships

Now that we understand the differences that exist in marriages, let us turn to the possible results stemming from these differences. One of the primary ways the collision of differences manifests in marriage is through our communication patterns.

Throughout this book, we will be probing two different forms of message exchanges between companions in an intimate relationship—those that are *responsive* and those that are *reactive*. Much of my work in counseling involves helping couples to analyze their communication and interaction patterns to identify the productive, and unproductive, ways they convey messages to each other.

Human interactions are a series of "send and reply" messages similar to an exchange of emails. Unlike emails though, in face-to-face interactions one "messages" the other using a mixture of words, tone, voice volume, pace, facial expressions, and body gestures—sifted through various personal perception filters accumulated throughout their lifetime—forming a complex array of output sent to the receiver. The receiver absorbs, digests, and interprets the messages as input, forms conclusions, and then replies to the message—either verbally, non-verbally, or both—sifting their reciprocation through their own, independently constructed, personal perception filters. It is these "send and reply" messages that we will define as either *responsive* or *reactive*.

Responsive messages are thoughtful, deliberate, and controlled expressions while *reactive* messages are involuntary, mostly unconscious, and usually unregulated. These messages originate from different sections of the brain. We will explore this in more detail later in this chapter. Suffice it to say for now that *responsive* messages emerge from the thinking part of the brain while *reactive* messages emanate from the feeling part of the brain. In the relationship arena, *responsive* messages are desirable while *reactive* messages are undesirable.

Reactive messages are those occurring because of the over-functioning or under-functioning of one's temperament. A responsive marriage, then, is one in which both parties are endeavoring to increase their *responsiveness* and reduce or eliminate their *reactivity* with each other. Doing so creates and expands intimacy.

Responsiveness

What does a responsive message look like and how does it differ from a reactive one? The following table may help to provide more definition:

AREA	RESPONSIVENESS	REACTIVITY
Focus	Us	Me
Origin	Voluntary	Involuntary
Dominant Brain Region	Cerebral Cortex	Limbic System - Amygdala
Force Invoked	Magnetic	Repelling
Limitation	Regulated	Uncontrolled
Result	Closeness	Distancing/Withdrawal

Because a *responsive* message is deliberate and thoughtful, it would tend to have a focus on promoting the interests of both parties rather than just the individual. It would be regulated rather than uncontrolled and would tend to draw the other person closer. A *reactive* message would tend to create distance between the two causing the receiver to withdraw either physically, emotionally, or both. In short, *responsive* messages are magnetic while *reactive* messages are repelling.

The Bible contains many wise and relevant principles for developing and sustaining healthy relationships and marriages. In fact, many of the characteristics of thriving relationships enumerated by mental health science can be found in the pages of Scripture. In my counseling work, I routinely learn of some "new" understanding of relationship dynamics promulgated by recent scientific research that God inspired the writers of the Bible to pen thousands of years before. Researchers today regularly confirm biblical wisdom. One such "confirmation" involves our understanding of *responsiveness* and *reactivity*.

James 1:19-20 instructs us to be "quick to listen, slow to speak, and slow to anger." This is a perfect definition of *responsiveness*. When we reverse these three directives, it results in the perfect definition for *reactivity*—slow to listen, quick to speak, and quick to anger. The secular equivalent to this idea is contained in Steven Covey's seminal leadership book titled *The Seven Habits of Highly Effective People*.[16] Habit five in that book, "seek first to understand, then to be understood," is *responsiveness* in a nutshell. Reverse those—seek first to be understood, then to understand—and we risk violating the Bible's guidance on avoiding *reactivity* in relationships contained in James 1:19-20.

If you polled pastors and mental health practitioners, most would say something like, "If only couples would adhere to the guidance provided by James 1:19–20, their communication conflict would cease and my job would be done." Oh, if it were only that easy. The problem is that awareness is only part of the equation.

Awareness, of course, is essential. Without awareness, we flounder in our troubles. Hebrews 4:12 tells us God's word provokes awareness. Its sharpness and precise accuracy can "judge the ideas and thoughts of the heart." In other words, it makes us aware of tendencies and proclivities that influence the outward manifestations of our heart. However, awareness, by itself, creates little change. We must also initiate the second half of the equation—training. 2 Timothy 3:16 calls it "training in righteousness." In the counseling field, we call it "behavior modification therapy." To invoke lasting change, we need both *awareness* and *training*: the aim of this book.

Nevertheless, most commands in Scripture can rarely be consistently applied in isolation. Other commands must also be followed, thereby requiring training in more than one area. I would contend, for example, that to adhere to James 1:19–20, one would

JAMES 1:19-20 INSTRUCTS US TO BE "QUICK TO LISTEN, SLOW TO SPEAK, AND SLOW TO ANGER." THIS IS A PERFECT DEFINITION OF RESPONSIVENESS. WHEN WE REVERSE THESE THREE DIRECTIVES, IT RESULTS IN THE PERFECT DEFINITION FOR REACTIVITY—SLOW TO LISTEN, QUICK TO SPEAK, AND QUICK TO ANGER.

also need to be working on assimilating the "fruit of the Spirit" and avoiding the "works of the flesh" described in Galatians 5:19–23 and enumerated in the following table:

Generates RESPONSIVENESS	Generates REACTIVITY
Love	Hatreds
Joy	Strife
Peace	Jealousy
Patience	Outbursts of Anger
Kindness	Selfish Ambitions
Goodness	Dissensions
Faithfulness	Factions
Gentleness	Envy
Self-Control	Anything Similar

I think most would agree that we, as human beings, do not intrinsically possess the fruit of the Spirit in any discernible measure. Just think of your children or grandchildren. If left to themselves, without guidance or training, on which side of the table would their resulting behaviors likely fall? If yours are like mine, strife, outbursts of anger, and selfish ambitions would abound. Therefore, they need consistent and focused training.

Increasing Awareness of Reactivity

Let us go back to the concept of *awareness* for a moment. Many times, there are contributing factors that create or exacerbate our reactivity in relationships. Early life experiences shape and form the filters through which we sift our lives. These filters can, at times, distort our perceptions, thereby causing disagreement and conflict to erupt as we misinterpret our companion's messages and draw inaccurate conclusions.

Our family of origin often influences the way we send and reply to messages processed during our interactions. If your parents

EARLY LIFE EXPERIENCES SHAPE
AND FORM THE FILTERS THROUGH
WHICH WE SIFT OUR LIVES.

communicated in reactive ways, you are predisposed to propagate these patterns. When temperament and gender specific tendencies are added to the mixture, our marital exchanges can degrade over time. Then there are the proclivities we all have to live from "the flesh" rather than the Spirit. We want our own way and often defer to reactive and selfish means to get it. We develop poor habits rooted in our flesh when we are not actively allowing the Holy Spirit to rule our lives. The subterfuge of all these contributing factors propels reactivity.

To change this dynamic, we need *awareness* to help inform us, awareness of the factors that create and exacerbate our reactivity. It is this element that makes the Welch Responsive Temperament Assessment unique.

With the Welch Responsive Temperament Assessment (WRTA), we measure your temperament and the responsive or reactive ways you express your temperament to others within nine trait pairs we call *Dimensions of Expression*. It is the analysis of these dimensions that empowers you to consciously choose responsiveness and reject reactivity. There is a margin, a space between when we experience a circumstance or event and when we counter or retort. It is within this margin where we have choice and control. It may not seem like it since our reactions happen nearly instantaneously, often within imperceptible micro-seconds. Nevertheless, there is a space, and we can elongate that space for the purpose of generating responsiveness. But we need to bring the reactivity into conscious awareness. This is where the WRTA helps.

By answering a series of Yes-No questions, the WRTA generates a profile of the individual measuring the degree of responsiveness or reactivity the person exhibits within the nine Dimensions of Expression. When a couple takes the WRTA together, they are also provided a combined profile that overlays their self-assessment on their companion's assessment of them. With this "couple-comparison" analysis, couples gain deeper insight into their relationship and ways they may be triggering each other with reactive messages. This increased awareness provides the opportunity to choose more responsive ways of interacting consistent with the principles described in this book.

The Dangers of Unmanaged Reactivity

Unmanaged reactivity puts a couple on a collision course with each other and can lead to the demise of their marriage. Remember that reactivity is much more than just exhibiting anger or escalating during an argument. It occurs whenever one over-functions or under-functions in their natural temperament. These extremes of behavior tend to push others away and create distance. A "Director" temperament, when over-functioning, may become too competitive during game night or combative during interactions. When under-functioning, they can be passive-aggressive, controlling through silence.

In contrast, the "Stabilizer" temperament (opposite/complement of the "Director") may become overly peacemaking at the expense of self when over-functioning, or submissive by essentially saying "whatever" when under-functioning.

An over-functioning "Influencer" may become too spontaneous, shifting from one project or topic to another. When under-functioning, the "Influencer" may exhibit too much emotion, causing others to acquiesce to their over-the-top feelings.

The over-functioning "Contemplator" (opposite to the "I") may become too self-sufficient and exclude others. In contrast, when under-functioning, the "Contemplator" can be unfeeling saying internally, "I don't care that the other person is suffering." These, and many more, out-of-balance behaviors within one's natural temperament tend to undermine relationship intimacy and closeness.

My experience counseling couples has taught me that a significant correlation exists between unmanaged reactivity and predictors of divorce. Dr. John Gottman, the premier researcher on the topic of marriage and intimate relationships, identified four predictors of imminent divorce that he characterized as the "four horsemen." Those who have read Revelation, the last book of the Bible, will no doubt recognize the reference to "four horsemen of the apocalypse" as that depicted in Revelation chapter 6. In this passage, John, a disciple of Jesus, describes in vivid and disturbing detail the vision he saw on the Isle of Patmos in which four horsemen are released during the Great Tribulation to wreak havoc on the earth (Revelation 6:1–8). Here, the four horsemen represent conquest, war, hunger, and death.

Dr. Gottman first began observing real couples in a laboratory setting at the University of Illinois in the 1970s. In 1986, he and Robert Levenson, a fellow researcher, built an apartment laboratory at the University of Washington which became known as the "Love Lab." Over the years, Gottman has observed and analyzed over 3,000 couples documenting their facial expressions, heart rate, blood pressure, skin conductivity, and the words they use during interactions.

From this work, the researchers discovered that couples at "low risk" for divorce maintained what they deemed the "magic ratio" of five positive interactions to every one negative interaction during conflict.[17] Couples at "high risk" of divorce exhibited one, several, or all of the four relationship horsemen of the apocalypse.

These horsemen enter the bloodstream of the relationship like poison, infiltrating the command-and-control center of intimacy and blowing it up from the inside. The wise couple will be familiar with these four horsemen, described below, and work to remove them if they exist and avoid them at all costs:

1. *Criticism*: Dictionary.com defines criticism as "the act of passing severe judgment; censure; faultfinding." [18] Gottman's research distinguishes criticism from the more innocuous responses of offering a simple critique or voicing a complaint. A critique or complaint relays a perspective on

a specific issue whereas criticism is a global attack on the person's character. For example, "I was scared when you were running late and didn't call me. I thought we had agreed that we would do that for each other" is a complaint. "You never think about how your behavior is affecting other people. I don't believe you are that forgetful, you're just selfish. You never think of others! You never think of me!" is criticism.[19] Gottman points out that this first horseman can lead to the emergence of the other horsemen if not eradicated from the relationship posthaste.

2. **Contempt:** Dictionary.com defines contempt as "the state of being despised; dishonor; disgrace."[20] Gottman concludes that when we communicate with contempt, we are truly mean—treating the other person with disrespect, mocking them with sarcasm, ridicule, name calling, or demeaning body language such as eye rolling or scoffing. While criticism attacks a person's character, contempt assumes a position of superiority. "Contempt is fueled by long-simmering negative thoughts about the partner—which come to a head when the perpetrator attacks the accused from a position of relative superiority."[21]

3. **Defensiveness:** Dictionary.com defines defensiveness as "protective; made or carried on for the purpose of resisting attack."[22] Gottman recognizes this third horseman as a response to criticism. One of the companions feels unjustly accused and fishes for excuses, playing the victim so their companion will back off. When responsiveness is present, the companion will instead accept responsibility, admit fault, and understand their companion's perspective.[23]

4. **Stonewalling:** Dictionary.com defines stonewalling as "the act of stalling, evading, or filibustering." Gottman describes this horseman as a typical response to pervasive contempt. The listener withdraws from the interaction, shuts down, and simply stops responding to their partner. They may tune

out, turn away, act busy, or engage in obsessive or distracting behaviors. This horseman rides into the scene when the person feels physiologically flooded.[24]

Notice that the first two horsemen often birth the last two. Criticism breeds defensiveness and contempt breeds stonewalling. Therefore, to starve the last two of nourishment (defensiveness and stonewalling), the couple must kill the first two (criticism and contempt). Of course, habits of defensiveness and stonewalling can still exist even when criticism and contempt are absent. But eliminating the first two horsemen, if they exist, is a good start.

Fortunately, these four horsemen can all be removed from the marriage but only with purposeful and dedicated actions. From a biblical perspective, we are offered remedies for all of them. Couples sometimes forget that the counsel offered by God for developing and maintaining relationships in general must also be followed in marriage. Let's take a closer look.

Condition	Description	Remedy	Scriptural Support
Criticism	Attacking Character	Encouragement	Let no corrupting talk come out of your mouths, but only such as is good for building up, as fits the occasion, that it may give grace to those who hear (Ephesians 4:29 ESV).
Contempt	Disrespecting Person	Gratitude	I give thanks to my God for every remembrance of you (Philippians 1:3).
Defensiveness	Protecting Self	Vulnerability	Therefore, confess your sins to one another and pray for one another (James 5:16).
Stonewalling	Evading Engagement	Perseverance	It [love] bears all things, believes all things, hopes all things, endures all things. Love never ends (1 Corinthians 13:7–8).

We counteract criticism when we embrace a posture of encouragement. Encouragers work to instill value in others rather than devalue them with criticism. Encouragers build up rather than tear down. They see the potential in others rather than just present circumstances. What is ironic is that both encouragers and critics are attempting to motivate change in the other person. What critics fail to understand, however, is that being presented with a litany of your faults in repetitive fashion is demotivating.

School teachers know this by experience. If you want a child to change their poor behavior, continuing to point out the fault with negative reinforcement rarely produces lasting change. In fact, it often perpetuates it. Positive reinforcement is much more effective. Simply communicating the expectation, expressing genuine belief in the child's ability to change, and then rewarding them when you see any progress, does wonders to provoke more positive behaviors. The same holds true for adults.

If your criticism communicates a lack of belief in your companion's character and capabilities, you have essentially condemned them to repeat the failures. This concept of "encouraging one another" is etched in my memory while, as a team member of my high school varsity basketball team, I read John Wooden's 1972 book titled *They Call Me Coach.*[25] Over the course of twelve years, Coach Wooden led his UCLA Bruins to ten NCAA basketball championships. He demonstrated this *encourager* attitude when asked how he helps a high school superstar become a team player on the UCLA Bruins. His response, "I find them doing something right." If criticism exists in your marriage, commit to replacing it with encouragement. Over time, you will see amazing results.

Gratitude counteracts contempt. A person exhibiting contempt towards another has lost, or perhaps never had, appreciation for them. It might be helpful for the one with contempt for their companion to make a list of their mate's positive qualities or contributions, especially those that drew you to them before you were married. Spend less time focusing on what they do not do, or do poorly, and more time focusing on what they do well. Everyone has redeeming qualities. Perhaps you need a gentle reminder of the deplorable condition you were in when Jesus forgave your sins with the blood He shed for you "while you were still a sinner" (Romans 5:8). Forgiven people forgive and appreciate the unconditional forgiveness

Jesus offers so much that they can forgive the seemingly unforgivable treatment they may receive at the hands of another.

We counteract defensiveness with vulnerability. Defensiveness puts one in a victim role causing them to deny or deflect responsibility for their part in the conflict. It is interesting to me that we are told to confess our sins to God to receive forgiveness, and we are told to confess our sins to one another to receive healing.[26] I dare say that confessing our sins to another person may require more humility than confessing our sins to God. Doing so places you in an extremely vulnerable position. You open yourself up to all kinds of possible responses from those who possess the ability to annihilate your well-being. Will you receive judgment, condemnation, ridicule, and embarrassment, or will you receive acceptance, relief, encouragement, and appreciation? This is the risk of vulnerability. Yet, we are called to be vulnerable with each other, especially in marriage. It is the only way to create and sustain intimacy.

Perseverance counteracts stonewalling. A steady onslaught of contempt and scorn can render even the best of us incapable of staying present. Emotional flooding is inevitable in this environment. But, as much as contempt is disrespectful, stonewalling is equally disrespectful. It sends a strong message to the other person that they are not worth your effort. It is the proverbial "whatever" response magnified to extreme proportions.

The love described in 1 Corinthians 13 is not for the faint of heart. It requires resolve, courage, and perseverance. But this is the kind of love Jesus demonstrated for us. Our companion deserves no less. Dr. Gottman recommends that when stonewalling starts in a conflict, you take a break and spend time doing something psychologically soothing and distracting. Then come back to re-engage with your companion when the emotional floodwaters have receded.

Brain Function and Dysfunction

Earlier, I asserted that responsiveness originates from the thinking part of the brain while reactivity originates from the feeling part of the brain. Let us explore this idea further.

Our brains are a complex and fascinating organ. Until recently, the inner workings of the brain were largely a mystery to us. However, advances in brain imaging techniques over the last thirty years have allowed us to construct detailed maps of how the brain processes information, governs our daily activities, regulates body functions, and influences interactions with other human beings and the outside world.

Efficiency and flexibility are hallmarks of its functioning. Billions of neurons all interconnected and communicating across tiny spaces called synapses using a combination of chemical and electrical impulses that, when repeatedly fired, create enduring pathways. These pathways form the unique ways we each interpret and act upon events and circumstances we encounter throughout our lifetimes. This phenomenon is captured in the scientific axiom, "neurons that fire together, wire together," and in the biblical proclamation of Psalms 139 that we are "fearfully and wonderfully made."

Early in life, this "fire-wire" activity occurs passively without our intervention or conscious awareness. As we grow up and develop language and cognitive skills, our choices and purposeful actions begin to influence neuronal activity thereby allowing us to mold and shape the outcome. Yet, factors beyond our control continue to shape this process, including "nature and nurture" influences, circumstances inflicted upon us by others, and temperament tendencies coded within our DNA.

These neuronal connections, created by a combination of personal choice, perpetrated action, and personality design, form the basis for who we are today. But they are not permanent. Extensive research on the functioning of our brains reveals an amazing capacity to rewire. *Neuroplasticity* is the technical term used for this characteristic. We can alter the pathways of our brain, no matter how ingrained or embedded they may be, and thereby change our present circumstances.

The brain can be visually partitioned using a side-to-side orientation (rear-facing view) and a top to bottom orientation (aerial view). In the rear-facing view, the brain is divided into two hemispheres with the left hemisphere primarily devoted to linear, logical reasoning and the right hemisphere primarily devoted to holistic, multi-faceted reasoning.

In the aerial view, a progression of complexity is exhibited in a bottom-up approach with primitive, unconscious functions such as breathing and vital organ regulation in the brain stem, emotion processing and survival functions in the mid-section, and higher-level reasoning functions and cognitive processing in the top sections known as the cerebral cortex. The top sections are composed of gray colored matter (thinking cells) while the lower sections are composed mostly of white matter (feeling or function cells).

Our emotions are governed by the *amygdala*, an almond shaped structure in the center of the brain in an area called the limbic system. The limbic system is a set of neural structures at the border of the cerebrum and brain stem composed of several components including the amygdala, the hypothalamus, and the hippocampus. It supports a variety of functions including emotion, behavior, motivation, long-term memory, and olfaction (smell).

Our emotional life originates from here. The amygdala is responsible for the initiation of several emotions, including fear and anxiety. The hypothalamus regulates many autonomic responses, and the hippocampus plays a vital role in the formation of new memories. Together, these structures are the primary ones from which our anxiety and reactivity originates. Calming the limbic system is one of the goals of the WRTA.

While reactivity originates from the limbic system, responsiveness originates from the cerebral cortex, the intricate fabric of interconnected neural thinking cells that cover the cerebral hemispheres. It is the body's ultimate control and information processing center, much like your computer's operating system software. However, in order for it to function well, the limbic system needs to be in a relatively calm state. Otherwise, the limbic system takes over primary control and accelerates reactivity while the cerebral cortex dampens its activity thereby impeding responsiveness.

The body has two nervous systems: the sympathetic and the parasympathetic. The sympathetic nervous system is akin to the accelerator pedal of a motor vehicle, while the parasympathetic nervous system is akin to the brake pedal. When the amygdala triggers anxiety, it picks up speed flooding the body with chemicals to heighten awareness and focus attention on the perceived threat.

The parasympathetic nervous system is responsible for bringing calm back to the body. However, when anxiety is triggered more frequently, the parasympathetic nervous system can become "lazy," taking longer and longer periods to finally bring calm. When this occurs in dialogue with your companion, the delay in bringing calm makes you more susceptible to reactivity which hinders productive interaction.

Our goal is to increase awareness of our reactive tendencies and understand how they are perpetuated so we can choose responsiveness and allow intimacy to flourish and grow. In the next chapter, we will learn some practical ways to initiate this change.

Discussion Starter Questions

- *For Couples or Groups*
  - Based on the descriptions provided, or the results of your WRTA, which of the four temperaments are you? Give an example of your behavior or tendencies that fit this temperament.

NOTES:_____

_____

_____

o What strengths and what weaknesses listed in the WRTA Temperament table do you exhibit?
NOTES:_____

_____

_____

o What gender differences have caused the most frustration for you in your marriage? What gender differences have been the most beneficial for you in your marriage?
NOTES:_____

_____

_____

o What insights did you glean from the notion that men's brains function in a more compartmentalized manner and women's brains function in a more integrated manner? How have you experienced this difference in your relationship?
NOTES:_____

_____

_____

o In what ways have the differences in how you and your companion drive and navigate your vehicles created irritating or amusing outcomes?
NOTES:_____

_____

_____

o How successful are you at being quick to listen, slow to speak, and slow to anger?
   NOTES:_____

   _____

   _____

o Which fruit of the Spirit do you have the least trouble exhibiting? Which fruit of the Spirit do you have the most trouble exhibiting?
   NOTES:_____

   _____

   _____

o What percentage of the time do you think you exhibit the fruit of the Spirit and what percentage of the time do you think you exhibit the works of the flesh?
   NOTES:_____

   _____

   _____

• *For Couples Only*
   o Read the table on responsive and reactive messages together. Which of these types of messages are most prominent in your marriage?
      NOTES:_____

      _____

      _____

   o Do any of Dr. John Gottman's four horsemen of the relationship apocalypse exist in your marriage? What can each of you do to eliminate them?
      NOTES:_____

      _____

      _____

GETTING LOST

In my earlier years as a university professor, my wife and I would take students on missionary excursions we called "work and witness" trips. We usually led a group of thirty students to developing countries where full-time missionaries were established and serving.

One such trip is particularly memorable for me. Typically, we started by spending a semester in preparation for the eventual seven-to-ten-day trek across the world—meeting, planning, and organizing everything from raising money to dispensing duties to a team leader, worship organizer, van driver, food coordinator, and many others. Back then, we depended upon paper road maps and those capable of reading while announcing directions.

During this trip to Monterrey, Mexico to help a pastor prepare his sanctuary church floor for an upcoming cement application, one of our students cut his face while mishandling a pole connected to a tamping tool used for flattening the dirt floor. Immediately, the student and I got into one of our two rental vans to race to the nearest emergency room. We soon learned that the facility we entered served as both a veterinary clinic and people clinic all in one. In the waiting room, we were surprised when one of the doors opened and what appeared to be a medical doctor emerged to reunite a dog with its owner. He said, "Who's next?" To our amazement, it was my student and me.

What I didn't tell you is that we got lost while trying to find this so-called health clinic. While focusing on trying to understand the map's Spanish words, I was rotating the map to gain orientation. Apparently, I lost track of my map rotations causing me to inadvertently read the map upside down. What I thought was north was actually south. So, instead of heading to the closest health facility for humans, I was heading toward the southern portion of Monterrey called Santa Catarina, fifteen kilometers southwest of central Monterrey, one of the less developed areas of the city and one known to be unsafe.

Despite my road map challenge, the veterinarian did a superb job stitching up my student's lacerations and we were soon on our way back to the construction location. Sometimes getting lost turns out well in the end.

CHAPTER 4

ROAD MAP

Getting lost is a bummer. Those of us who have gotten lost on the way to our destination know the confusion and anxiety that develops when we realize we do not know how to get there. Prior to the advent of smartphones with Global Positioning System (GPS) technology, travelers had to rely on paper maps to plan their trip and navigate to their desired destinations.

I remember using a *Thomas Bros* map to find locations in San Diego where I live with my family. With the Internet in its infancy, to drive to a new restaurant across town I would call the restaurant to get their physical address. Then I'd pull out my most recent copy of the *Thomas Bros* hoping it was up to date. I'd look up the street in an indexed table containing page, row, and column coordinates; turn to the page where that street was pictured; then use my forefinger to trace down the page to the indicated row and across the page to the indicated column to zero in on the general area where the restaurant was located. I then had to trace back and forth, up and down, street meanderings to go back to my origination point, all the while writing down connecting streets and turns. The process was arduous but productive. It was the most "technologically advanced" method we had at the time. This process was, of course, prone to errors, so using the map did not guarantee you would not get lost on your travels, but the chances of getting lost were somewhat reduced.

This physical mapping process was used for decades with varying success rates. The degree of complication caused by city street design would sometimes frustrate all efforts to create a comprehensible route. A friend of mine got horribly lost in the city of Boston despite his best efforts to navigate using a physical map. Boston, a city of one of the original thirteen American colonies, started out as a small settlement with dirt cow paths laid out in no discernible pattern. Over time, planners paved these same roads and made them part of the overall "modernized" design. An aerial view of Boston's streets looks more like a spider web than the square grid pattern typical of most modern cities.

Consequently, vacationers and visitors to the city regularly report getting lost trying to drive around. This happened to my friend when he vacationed there with his wife many years ago, rented a car at the airport, and tried to drive to his hotel on the other side of the city. After several hours of aimless navigating and maneuvering around double and triple parked vehicles on circuitous roads, my friend gave up, returned the rental car, and opted for walking or using public transportation.

What is Responsiveness?

In this chapter, I want to give you a clear road map for how to navigate the path to a responsive marriage. I will start by describing the destination—responsiveness. What does responsiveness look like?

Most couples seeking therapy are hoping for a miracle worker or, perhaps, a cancer-removing-surgeon, one who will extract the deadly disease, stitch up the broken heart, and somehow resurrect the deceased relationship. This desire is no different in a faith-based relationship. Once basic trust is established, the other person will be trusted until they are proven to be untrustworthy. Unfortunately, lots of couples never reach this plateau. Trust is never established.

Secular research helps Christians understand this. For instance, more recent scientific literature has unmistakably proven that couples who cohabitate before marriage are more likely to divorce after marriage. Premarital sex impedes relationship development. A 2021 article in Psychology Today outlines a study by Rosenfeld & Roesler conducted in 2019 that found the odds of divorce were 1.31 times higher for women who cohabitated prior to marriage across all years examined in the study.[27]

Jesus said, "I am the way, the truth, and the life." In so doing, He amplified the essential elements for a healthy relationship—truth and trust. The basic fact that we accept Jesus into our heart tells us, and others, that we trust Him. We express trust when we take a step of faith toward God. His loving nature is what causes us to trust him and to place our faith in him. Basically, there is no faith without trust and no trust without love.

How, then, do we integrate this love and faith into a marriage relationship—especially one that is in trouble? I have heard people and theologians alike try and explain faith in practical terms with statements like, "It's a tug on one's heart with a subtle yet increasingly intense feeling of needing to be forgiven," or "It's a heavy conviction that something's not right in my life," or "It's a keen awareness that I need to submit to something greater than me."

Even though there are many varied traditions espousing many different views of faith, the Bible clearly describes it. Revelations 3:20 helps us understand how we are to take a step of faith toward God, and eventually toward our mate. "Listen! I stand at the door and knock. If anyone hears My voice and opens the door, I will come into him and have dinner with him [have fellowship], and he with Me." In other words, when God comes to us, he *invites* us to take a step of faith toward Him (submission) to experience fellowship with Him. Our faith-walk is similar to how we extend faith to our companion.

Responsive Relationships Move Toward Each Other

Taking a step of faith toward our companion (reconciliation effort), even during the most trying moments of marriage, involves submission. Both faith and submission are vital for a healthy marriage. Unfortunately, the love tank of many good and well-meaning Christians is depleted. Ephesians 2:8–9 says it so well. "For it is by grace you have been saved, through faith…." Faith plays a vital role in our ability to experience successful relationships, not only with God, but with our companion as well. As we take a step of faith toward God, we learn what it means to also take a step of faith toward our companion. Intentional submission opens the opportunity for reconciliation.

Think with me, if you would, about Jesus's love for you and His faith in you. It is truly an *amazing love*! It is amazing because there is no earthly reason for God to love us. We are unlovely but we become emotionally attractive when Jesus enters our heart. We become desirable due to *His* attractiveness.

When I first met my wife, Robin, I was absolutely attracted to her. I mean *really* attracted to her! I had never experienced this feeling with any other woman. What I experienced was a soothing peace that came over me. Simply put, I felt serene and calm in her presence. My soul was ultimately attracted to her soul. Now, I would not go as far as to use a phrase penned by a church father to describe this feeling, "My soul is not at rest until it finds its rest in thee Oh Lord."[28] But I would say that all fear dissipated, and I felt "at home" with Robin. Yes, I was attracted to her physically, emotionally, and psychologically—but I was most attracted to her soul. There was something about Robin that distinctly reminded me of God. To have a soulmate means you are attracted to the other person's soul. It is what draws a couple into the deepest of *soulmate* relationships. If this important and foundational component of your relationship is damaged or missing, please continue reading. The focus of this book is discovering or restoring this type of relationship.

To consider how Jesus took a step of faith toward us while He was on the cross continually astounds me. It was an obvious choice on the part of Jesus. He intentionally laid down His life so He could reconcile us to God. Jesus's step of faith, in love, is the supreme example of how we are to intentionally take a step of faith, in love, toward our companion. The Bible clearly states, "But God demonstrates his own love for us in this: while we were still sinners, Christ died for us…." (Romans 5:8 NIV).

He comes to us intentionally, without wavering or hesitating. It is important to continually remember that He (Jesus), who was without sin, became sin on our behalf. He did something we could not do for ourselves, and He did this willingly and with intense resolve. This same degree of willingness and resolve to move towards each other generates responsiveness in marriage.

Jesus is Always Responsive to Us

Remember Jesus on the cross and how he quoted the famous Psalm of David (Psalms 22:1), "My God, my God, why have you forsaken me?" These words were spoken during Jesus's last moments on this earth. They illustrate how He not only took on our pain, but He also entered our pain. Our pain became His. It had to have been the most heart-wrenching moment in human history watching Jesus, all alone, tortured by every sinful human act, and feeling abandoned by God the Father himself. Nevertheless, Jesus never wavered from His mission. Rather, He headed straight for the cross with intense resolve.

His commitment to us drove His passionate faith during those final moments on the cross. A remarkable thing happened as Jesus took a step of faith toward us. He chose life (ours) over death (His). Jesus could have called on "twelve legions of angels"[29] and spared himself from excruciating pain. Yet, He chose reconciliation over relief, and He did it for you and me. He embraced pain rather than running from it. He chose relationship over soothing His own pain. Jesus chose to do what he knew was right: He died for your sins and mine because, without His sacrifice, we would be lost to sin's dooming consequences forever.

He orchestrated His own crucifixion so He could liberate us from the ongoing effects of sin. Our well-being was more important to Jesus, even during the most horribly painful moments of the crucifixion, than momentary relief. For He had based His relationship with us on a faith-based relationship with God (commitment). "My Father, if it is possible, may this cup be taken from me. Yet not as I will, but as you will" (Matthew 26:39 NIV).

If troubled marriages could only partially capture Jesus's illustration of true commitment through faith, divorce would be out of the question. There is no doubt in my mind. I have sat with hundreds of couples who could change some behaviors and begin to be kind toward one another yet could not take that step of faith. If only they could put on another pair of glasses and take a fresh faith-look at their companion before giving up.

I often reflect on my own father, Dr. Lee Welch, who received national attention for the five university math textbooks he authored. He would periodically turn to me and say of my mother who did not finish college, "Your mom is the smartest person I know." He got it. Dad regularly and continually had a fresh faith-look at my mom. Thank you, dad, for such a powerful example of viewing my mom with complete trust. But to many couples, this seems impossible. *They simply cannot seem to trust!* I deeply hope it is a possibility for you and your companion. If this were possible, there would be far less broken marriages. It is incredible to think that the God of this universe thought enough of you and me to stay the course and become our sin in order that we could be free to live a "full life "(John 10:10 NIV).

Please hear me. Most people divorcing their companions do so because they just cannot take the pain anymore. Their stubborn stance is typically an inability to take a step of faith and nurture one another. Although there are situations where serious abuse is occurring, many divorcing couples decide to quit simply because their relationship is too emotionally painful. They believe they need release from it. As a counselor I hear way too often, "Doc, it's just too painful," "I can't take this one more day!" "I'll die if I stay in this relationship!" "The pain got to me so I got out!" If we step behind these statements, we will find that most are saying, "I can't endure the pain of this relationship any longer—I don't feel loved or listened to!"

Does this sound familiar? Yes, Jesus also described His pain as too much for one person to bear. Did He give in? No. Did He want to? It sure sounds that way to me.

I have often wanted to say to the person desiring to get out of a marriage, "In other words, your perceived pain is greater than your desire to stay in the relationship." That may sound harsh considering their intense suffering. But I think that's why God hates divorce: giving up on a relationship diminishes the reality that Jesus embraced our pain on the cross and did not give up on us. Giving up on a human relationship suggests that Jesus's act of faith and dedication to a purpose on the cross is confined and limited. It fails to recognize that God sent His absolute best (God Himself) to provide reconciliation.

Perhaps it says, "Jesus, I really don't care what kind of pain you endured on the cross. I can't do my pain any longer!" Fortunately, Jesus did not take the easy way out. He faced His pain with unflinching resolve. While He was enduring the excruciating pain of the cross, aren't you glad Jesus did not feel toward us like many of us do toward our companion? Well, if Jesus had not been that gracious, I would hate to think what life would be like for us without the hope of the cross. I pray you are able to summon the resolve to stick with it like Jesus did.

Respond in Your Relationship
Rather than React/Run Away

There is no better picture of how to reconcile a relationship than what Jesus, in faith, did for us. When Jesus's emotions yelled at Him to run the other way and to take care of Himself, He turned to God and said, "Not as I will, but as You will" (Matthew 26:39 ESV). In His pain, Jesus could have avoided the cross through several methods: sending angels to rescue him, consuming all the world's evil by fire, or even speaking the proverbial phrase "whatever!" and walking away.

How I wish it were easier for couples like Michael and Jessica, whom we met in the introduction, to take a similar step of faith toward their relationship. You may find yourself in a similar predicament with you and/or your companion experiencing intense pain. You may feel as though your pain registers close to what Jesus endured on the cross. It is so intense that you are not sure you can continue as you buckle under the weight. It hurts so deeply. Yes, relationship misunderstandings can be painful and excruciatingly debilitating. Yet, it is possible to restore the worst of relationship conditions. Hurting husbands and wives can take a step of faith toward each other even during the most difficult of experiences. That is, to try, once again, to work on the relationship even though it feels like a hopeless cause. My sincere desire is that the concepts you find in this book resuscitate your hope.

I am keenly aware that there are relationships that simply cannot be reconciled. The damage is done. Trust is broken. There is just no way to repair the relationship. But this is not because the relationship is unsalvageable. Rather, it is because one, or both, have unequivocally concluded that their pain will not diminish without permanent separation.

Please do not brush off what I just suggested. If we really believe what the Bible says about Jesus enduring the cross and becoming sin

THERE IS NO BETTER PICTURE OF HOW
TO RECONCILE A RELATIONSHIP THAN
WHAT JESUS, IN FAITH, DID FOR US.
WHEN JESUS'S EMOTIONS YELLED AT
HIM TO RUN THE OTHER WAY AND TO
TAKE CARE OF HIMSELF, HE TURNED
TO GOD AND SAID, "NOT AS I WILL, BUT
AS YOU WILL" (MATTHEW 26:39 ESV).

on our behalf, this step-of-faith thing, you know—moving toward your companion—makes complete sense. Lest we get caught up in a debate over how much pain Jesus experienced leading up to and including His death on the cross, we must remember that we are born in sin. Jesus experienced the devastation of *all sin* all at once. His pain was greater and more intense than any pain you or I could ever experience. You see, His pain was not just physical pain. Truly, His pain was "becoming sin on our behalf." This was emotional and mental anguish. In one day, He felt the searing pain of every sinful act we would ever experience and those inflicted upon us by perpetrators of abuse.

Jesus endured past, present, and future sins. He felt the pain of the innocent victims at the hands of Ted Bundy. Jesus suffered the deepest fear and incredible anxiety of the individuals falling out of the twin towers during 9/11. He held the child during the Oklahoma bombing as that innocent child took her last gasp of air and died. Yes, Jesus understands pain. But more importantly, He understands what it means to take a step of faith toward relationship rather than escape to experience relief. That is what He accomplished on the cross. He demonstrated His love for us. I love this about my Savior. He completely understands my pain.

Responsive Relationships Are Understanding

I love the ole' hymn that says, "No one understands like Jesus."[30] It's true, we can go to Him with our pain because He understands, and, quite frankly, He never leaves us to face it alone. Although there is much debate as to whether Jesus was all alone on the cross, without God's presence, we do know one thing for sure. Jesus experienced such deep pain that He cried out begging for God's presence to return. He felt all alone and weighed down with the world's sin on His shoulders. However, He helped us to see that we can embrace pain rather than run from it.

I meet so many people who tend to embalm their pain rather than cremate it. We are predisposed to hold grudges rather than to truly forgive. We often seek retribution rather than reconciliation. What a wonderful moment in therapy it is when a person can fully forgive another for deeply hurting him or her. Not just a head-sense of forgiveness, but a full body (heart, soul, mind, and strength) forgiveness.

Respect and nurture are difficult to define but you know when they are absent. All people, especially those with relationships that are in trouble, need to employ these practices. Over the years, I have encouraged the people with whom I have had the privilege of counseling to practice respect and nurture through action words like, "Yes," "Please," "Thank you," "Would you consider...?" and "I appreciate that."

Again, the first key to unlocking true intimacy—*kindness*. The initial response I get from a couple to whom I make this suggestion is, "No way; he doesn't deserve my love: that's ridiculous to ask me to do that!" Or, "My respect for her left when she did what she did. I have no more love." Attempting to resurrect or recapture lost or depleted feelings of respect or nurture can challenge the most courageous of all couples, not to mention their therapists.

However, I am always amazed at the results when a couple practices this quite simple procedure of being respectful and nurturing with their actions and words. My clients have said, "I don't know what's happened, but since we've been treating each other better, our relationship is better."

Lasik surgery on the eyes is quite common these days. I know of one person who was nearly blind before the surgery and subsequently described to me what it was like following the surgery. "I'm able to see a completely different world than what I used to see. Things look so different than before." By carefully and actively listening to another person, we are creating the opportunity for things to be seen more clearly and to *hear and see* what is being communicated rather than what we *think* is being communicated.

I MEET SO MANY PEOPLE WHO TEND TO EMBALM THEIR PAIN RATHER THAN CREMATE IT. WE ARE PREDISPOSED TO HOLD GRUDGES RATHER THAN TO TRULY FORGIVE. WE OFTEN SEEK RETRIBUTION RATHER THAN RECONCILIATION.

One person successful in listening to his wife said, "Wow, I didn't know that's what you meant all these years." Just as cataract eye surgery enables a person to see clearly, active listening sometimes takes on the form of emotional surgery. As one carefully listens to another, layer-by-layer the cataract (intense emotion) is removed from the eye until the person no longer sees through a fog but sees with clarity and clearness.

So it is when one can listen without foggy emotions and misunderstanding. Although we may think that we fully understand what the other person is attempting to express, we can be mistaken. Most marriage counselors agree that they spend a great deal of their time working on this area, helping couples listen more carefully to each other and not misinterpreting what they thought they heard.

Responsive Relationships Are Curious and Nonjudgmental

I will never forget the student who sat in the back row of my eight o'clock university class years ago. Early morning classes are not especially good times for university students who tend to stay up and do a great deal of their socializing late into the early morning hours.

This student typically gave me little, if any, eye contact. In fact, during class his eyes were almost always closed, and he rarely wrote down notes. Prompted by his apparent lack of attention and not meeting my expectations for how a *good* student should behave in my class, I formed a perception that this student could not have cared less for my class. Supported by my thirty years of experience both observing and teaching university students, I whispered to myself, "He's just plain tired from staying up late the night before." I prided myself on being a skilled listener and observer of what is really happening with people. Well, I was wrong in this case. What

I discovered was something quite different from what I initially thought.

My frustration level grew to the point where I decided to confront this student. "How dare he sleep through my class day-after-day-after day?" So, at one point in the lecture and discussion time, I called him by name in class and asked him a question. The response I received from this student was not at all what I had anticipated: he answered the question appropriately and completely. I was stunned, to say the least. I thought to myself, "How did he answer the question when he wasn't listening?"

After a little detective work, I discovered my perception of the situation was faulty. What I thought the student was communicating to me was not the truth at all. I later learned this student was not a visual learner and needed to close his eyes so he could concentrate and *picture* the information presented. My perception of what was going on was completely inaccurate. After confronting this student about what appeared to be laziness or fatigue on his part, I discovered that by closing his eyes during the lecture and discussions this student was staying connected with what was happening in the class. I learned a valuable lesson through this frustrating experience. My perception is not always reality. I suspect neither is yours.

So it is with couples and others in their attempted communications. What one perceives to be reality may not necessarily be the reality of the other person. Since so much of our communication is non-verbal and visual, it is easy to misinterpret. It is no wonder we often misconstrue what another says—especially when the physical makeup of men and women is so different and unique.

This is an area in which my wife, Robin, and I have worked diligently. I tend to get too many things going at once, believing that I can accomplish them all. During my busyness, my wife and I will be discussing the care of the children and I will sometimes sigh, which for me means I am overwhelmed with all I am attempting to accomplish. But for Robin, the sigh means something completely different. She is hearing me give her an indirect message: "Do I have to take care of the kids again?!" This is not at all what I intend to say. Nevertheless, we are often ensnared by misunderstanding.

These exchanges between Robin and me have caused us to slow our conversations down and really try to hear what is being said. This is called *active listening*. It takes effort for my wife to give me the benefit of the doubt, particularly someone like me who over-schedules and over-books his life. You can see how easily my wife could misinterpret a sigh or a groan as, "Do I have to take care of them again?" Her response could easily be, "You're always busy and don't have time for us." It is quite easy for a couple to fall into patterns of misunderstanding as illustrated in my marriage.

Finding the Good in Your Companion

So, how do you begin to appreciate and attend to your companion when there seems to be so many misunderstandings? First, find something good in the other person even if you think you cannot. One of my graduate students in counseling asked an intriguing question: "How can you find the good qualities in a very devious and abusive client?" Although the entire class discussed the question at length, someone made it more personal by asking how I manage that issue in my private practice. I responded by saying, "The question is not an easy one to answer. However, it is important to note that we all have good points and bad points regardless of who we are and where we have been."

Since each of us is born in the image of God (see Genesis 1:27), even the worst of people have something good in them. Each of us has things we like and dislike about ourselves. It is important to look for the good points in the midst of what may appear to be only bad points. Often, we will need to ask the Holy Spirit to give us eyes to see the good when all our senses tell us the person is all bad.

You may have to sincerely pray and dig deep to discover the good in your companion. One person struggling with this said, "The only good I see in him is that, regardless of not taking care of his family, he always takes care of himself by working out in the gym five times per week." Even though this man's wife may not appreciate her husband's exercise program, she could easily view commitment to an exercise regimen as a positive quality. She could consider the husband's discipline of following through on a scheduled exercise program as *good*. Therefore, thinking of something in your companion that really irritates you may be the best place to start when trying to produce something that is positive. Try it; you may be pleasantly surprised.

One person said, "Well, she's just so 'picky' about how she wants the house to look, and it drives me up a wall. I feel like she's constantly nagging at me to pick things up around the house." Although the husband may view his wife as being *picky*, another way to view her is *conscientious*. The husband may be experiencing his wife's conscientiousness as *nit-picking*. What may truly be a positive attribute of his wife comes across to him in an irritating manner, causing him to be unable to appreciate it. Yet, and at the same time, if this quality can be evaluated from a different perspective, it's possible for this man to turn what seems to be a negative quality into a positive one.

Viewing positive attributes and practicing *positive talk* takes a considerable amount of discipline. It is always easier to tear down another person than it is to build them up. But be assured, the benefits of practicing the discipline of *positive talk* far outweigh the downside of continuing the same old habits that are giving you the same old results. Many couples determine that, whether they are out in public or in private, neither one of them will say anything negative about their companion. This is a worthwhile agreement.

"We just had the pastor for lunch." This phrase may sound innocuous, if perceived as a mere report of the day's events, but it can mean much more. In my day and "neck of the woods," having someone "for lunch" could also mean pummeling them with a listing of their faults and foibles. So, in this case, "we just had the pastor for lunch" would mean discussing his negative attributes to the point where he was devalued. In a sense, we can do the same with our companion. We can devalue him or her by expressing only their negative points and holding back any statements that would encourage a brighter view of the person.

Healthy marriages are responsive while unhealthy relationships are reactive. Practicing responsive communication with phrases like, "Thank you, would you be willing to help me?" and "I'm feeling uncomfortable with your words" all create assertive relationship health. Reactive marriages are aggressive and often include statements such as, "Stop it, you never help me," and "Why do you always do that?"

Responsive marriages heal while reactive marriages destroy. Responsive relationships open conversation while reactive relationships shut down dialogue and potential healing. People desire a responsive interaction, one in which the participant's experiences are validated. These types of exchanges lead to behaving toward others responsively with a natural voice in the relationship which produces feelings of connection and understanding.

Most of us can employ responsiveness when our relationship is calm, we feel content, and things are going smoothly. It is during conflict, however, when our best efforts to maintain cordiality and civility with our companion tend to be thwarted, and we react rather than respond. It can be helpful to analyze the typical progression of escalated exchanges to see where problems first emerge. To do this, let me introduce you to the Welch Responsive Cycle.

RESPONSIVE MARRIAGES HEAL WHILE
REACTIVE MARRIAGES DESTROY.
RESPONSIVE RELATIONSHIPS OPEN
CONVERSATION WHILE REACTIVE
RELATIONSHIPS SHUT DOWN DIALOGUE
AND POTENTIAL HEALING.

Welch Responsive Cycle

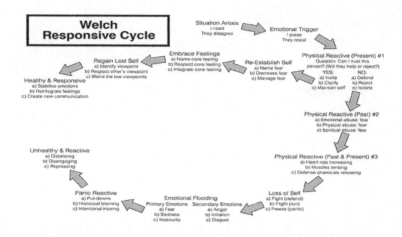

The Welch Responsive Cycle is one of the most helpful tools I have used in my counseling practice. It breaks down typical interactions between couples into component parts so the participants in the exchange can understand the decision points that lead them to either productive or unproductive places. By examining the cognitive and emotional impulses we experience during the exchange, we are in a better position to enact practical methods to steer the exchange to more responsive, and less reactive, destinations. The graphic depicts the essence of conflict. As we walk through this graphic, think about the last interaction you had as a couple in which conflict erupted and see if the sequence of events you experienced is similar.

The exchange starts at the top of the graphic with one of the participants expressing a need or expectation, either verbally or tacitly, that is confronted with some form of disagreement or resistance from the other participant. This dynamic causes the one with the need or expectation to experience an emotional trigger, a gradual or sudden escalation of anxiety and internal dissonance. The emotional trigger creates an energy source that propels the individual to press further, resulting in heightened resistance from the other.

At this point in the exchange, the triggered participant will have their first physical reaction prompting an unspoken, and often unconscious, question to percolate beneath the surface: "Can I trust this person? Will they help or reject?" The answer to this question is crucial because it determines the direction the rest of the exchange will take. Answer *yes*, and the Northern route opens for passage. Answer *no*, and the Southern route is taken.

The Northern route is the healthy route that preserves intimacy and well-being. Taking it requires intentional action to respond rather than react. On it, we name our fears, embrace our feelings, quickly regain the lost self, blend our two viewpoints, and create new connections. All these essentials we will cover in future chapters and, despite how eroded your marriage may be, you can find this path to a responsive marriage.

Unfortunately, although present circumstances activate emotional triggers, the form and intensity of them is often shaped and influenced by past hurts, trauma, or tension-filled experiences that can date back as far as early childhood. Cognitive awareness of these influencing factors from the past may be missing in the moment, but emotions never forget. Emotional triggers are often the retelling of past events, like a movie sequel, but applied to present circumstances. The more aware one is of these tendencies the more control one can exert over them to temper their untimely eruption and lessen their impact.

Nevertheless, on the Southern route, this dynamic produces a second physical reaction. Past emotional, physical, sexual, and/or spiritual abuse rushes forward into the present causing chaos and confusion. At this point, it becomes difficult to differentiate between influences from the past and circumstances of the present. It is here where the conflict often becomes muddled with off-topic and historical references that muddy the waters and make it difficult to focus on the original, precipitating need or expectation expression.

In other words, when a couple becomes hysterical they become historical. As the bewildering exchange picks up speed, the couple may wonder internally or aloud, "What were we talking about and how did we get here?" Almost immediately, physical reaction three occurs with the heart rate increasing, muscles tightening, and defensive chemicals secreting into the bloodstream from the collision of past and present influences. In a matter of seconds, the triggered participant's sense of self begins to dissolve and disfigure, forcing them into a fight-flight-freeze reaction. Their body floods with a mixture of primary and secondary emotions.

Unfortunately, in this state, we tend to be more aware of the secondary emotions than the primary ones behind them, so we easily express secondary emotions while ignoring primary ones. A form of panic occurs twisting the participants into defensive postures and the use of detrimental put-downs, blaming, and other injurious reactions. The result is distance, disengagement, and repression.

Changing Routes

Although this paints a bleak picture, at any point along the Southern route, it is possible to transfer to the Northern route. With awareness, you can stop your progression on the Southern route, back up to the fork in the road at the first physical reaction and proceed in a different direction. To do this, I recommend doing the following:

1. STOP and say, "I am experiencing emotional triggers. Please give me a moment to de-escalate."
2. Take a few deep breaths.
3. With both feet on the floor, standing or sitting, slowly move your toes or slightly shift your feet to get a sense of grounding.
4. Say, "Will you help me to process this in a more responsive and less reactive way?" This takes you back to the tacit question regarding trust at the top of the Welch Responsive Cycle. Invite your companion to be trustworthy.

5. Name your core feelings (we will cover this in chapter 6).
6. Apply listening skills to first understand and then to be understood (we will cover this in chapter 6).
7. Negotiate and problem solve together (we will cover this in chapter 9).

I want to focus you in, for a moment, on the split point in the Welch Responsive Cycle, the spot where it separates into the Northern route and the Southern route. This is the critical point in the exchange we will call the *North/South Junction*. Lots of mental activity occurs here for both parties but especially for the one triggered. The question of trust we process at the North/South Junction often hinges upon historical evidence. In a few milliseconds, our minds can replay arguments from the past and superimpose them on this new emerging conflict, thereby quickly turning us towards the Southern route. If you as a couple are more familiar with the Southern route than the Northern route, it will take earnest effort to *take the high road* and let the Northern route become your default.

One of the reasons a couple may end up on the Southern route more often is a misunderstanding of, or misconception about, what is occurring. On the Southern route we debate content and intent. We focus on what you said or did not say or what you did or did not do. We make and communicate assumptions about each other's intent or motives. Facts and motives—these are the elements attorneys introduce and emphasize as evidence when attempting to convince a jury of a defendant's guilt or innocence. Focusing on them and magnifying them for further analysis are essential for lawyers but detrimental for lovers. Doing so keeps you on the Southern route, descending further and further down the slippery slope to distance and disengagement.

To take the Northern route requires a shift in perspective, to attempt to understand what is going on behind the scenes or under the surface. The best way to do this is to view our marital interactions, including ones embroiled in conflict, through the lens of attachment.

Attachment is the innate desire and pull in all of us to connect with another human being—*heart to heart*. From the moment we took our first breath outside our mother's womb, we have desired attachment. When babies are deprived of motherly attachment, they suffer debilitating consequences. In 1945, psychoanalyst René Spitz published an article asserting that babies cared for in institutions, without maternal care or attachment, suffered from a condition he called *hospitalism* or *failure to thrive*, causing many of them to die.[31]

This need for attachment does not end with infancy. We carry it with us throughout our lives as we continue to seek attachments in close relationships, including marriage. And yes, men, you have the same need for attachment as your wife does, despite your efforts to deny it or suppress it. Men, you are just as wired for attachment as she is.

Dr. Sue Johnson, developer of Emotion Focused Therapy (EFT) for couples, postulates that the quest for attachment, and our perceptions of losing it, drive many of the negative interactions couples experience in repetitive fashion. She suggests seven conversations for a couple to engage in to "encourage a special kind of emotional responsiveness that is the key to lasting love for couples."[32] In her view, this type of emotional responsiveness is centered on three main components which she forms as an acronym—A.R.E. It can help to remember these components by asking ARE you there for me?

- *Accessibility:* Can I reach you? This means staying open to your companion even when you have doubts and feel insecure. Often, the pokes and jabs we experience from our companion while they are in distress are nothing more than attempts to reestablish attachment or connection. They are, of course, counterproductive to that goal, but amid escalating anxiety we often choose unhealthy ways to regain our sense of well-being. Despite conflict, let your companion know you are accessible to them.

- *Responsiveness:* Can I rely on you to respond to me emotionally? This means tuning in to your companion and showing them that his or her emotions, especially attachment needs and fears, have an impact on you. When conflict begins, send your companion clear signals of comfort and care.
- *Engagement:* Will you value me and stay close? This means being absorbed, attracted, pulled, captivated, pledged, and involved. It is the special kind of attention we give to loved ones. When conflict continues, stay engaged.

Through the attachment lens, we can start to see our escalated interactions differently. We can see them for what they truly are—impassioned, and sometimes desperate, pleas from our companion to reestablish connection and attachment. We can step behind the secondary emotions of frustration and anger to find and affirm the primary emotions of sadness, disappointment, and cries for connection. This simple mindset shift can be transformational.

The next time you find yourself in conflict with your companion, I hope you will picture the Welch Responsive Cycle in your mind and take the steps necessary to proceed on the Northern route. I think you will find it refreshing.

Discussion Starter Questions

- *For Couples or Groups*
  - As you read about what responsive relationships are like, what insights did you gain?
    NOTES:_____
    _____
    _____

o Describe a time recently when you were emotionally Flooded (overwhelmed by emotions). What was it like for you?
NOTES:_____

_____

_____

o During conflicts with your companion, do you tend to focus more on facts and motives or are you able to work more at the emotional level? Think about your family of origin. Did your caregivers function more at the facts and motives level or at the emotion level? What was this like for you?
NOTES:_____

_____

_____

• *For Couples Only*
o Would you say that you and your companion are moving toward each other? Why or why not?
NOTES:_____

_____

_____

o In general, do you feel understood by your companion? Why or why not? Specifically, what can your companion do to help you feel more understood?
NOTES:_____

_____

_____

o Do you feel, or have you felt, judged by your companion? Describe the circumstances and how you felt.
NOTES:_____

_____

_____

○ Talk about your last interaction where one or both of you was emotionally triggered. How did it turn out? Were you on the Northern or Southern route of the Welch Responsive Cycle? Talk about how you can help each other to take the Northern route more often? NOTES:_____

_____

_____

○ Talk together about the three components of the "ARE you there for me?" model. In general, do you feel you can reach your companion? Why or why not? In general, do you feel your companion is emotionally responsive to you? Why or why not? In general, do you feel your companion values you and attempts to remain close? Why or why not? What can your companion do to strengthen these three components for you? NOTES:_____

_____

_____

GETTING TO THE CORE ISSUE

This past week, while meeting with one of the two groups of associates (post-graduate professionals) and therapists-in-training (current graduate students) I supervise, the topic turned to couples therapy. One associate asked, "What are some tips for working with couples? Either they are fighting in front of me or they simply don't know what to say." This associate's question is essentially, "What road signs do we look for when working with couples in therapy to know where they are and where we want to lead them?" Often these road signs show up when we start working with attachment injuries from the couple's families of origin.

Individuals sometimes attract a future spouse possessing similar attachment tendencies as the individual's parents or caregivers. If you experienced distant parents, you will likely attract a distant, insecure companion. If your relationship with your parents is/was secure and close, you will likely attract someone with secure attachment.

Susan and Charlie's emotional connection is, unfortunately, insecure. Charlie expresses an insecure, protective, and commanding approach to Susan. He is rigid and somewhat suffocating with her. She is on the opposite spectrum displaying insecure and passive indifference. When Charlie doesn't feel close to Susan, he aggressively pursues her, thereby overwhelming her in the process. Her insecure attachment tendencies cause her to want distance. If Charlie gets too close and controlling of Susan, she bolts to protect herself. When she gets too distant from him, Charlie pursues her with escalating determination. This cycle repeats with bewildering regularity and intensity.

After receiving some guidance from me and others in the group, the questioning associate taught the couple techniques for lowering anxiety when they emotionally advance toward each other. The road signs became clearer. Susan learned to say, "When I experience you using these words, I feel afraid, overwhelmed, and suffocated." Charlie worked on validating her feelings, allowing Susan the space to self-regulate and come closer, and learned to recognize reactivity when it started. The couple made tremendous progress as they drew closer and developed more secure attachment tendencies.

CHAPTER 5

ROAD SIGNS

As we drive on roadways and walk on pathways, we depend upon road signs to help guide us. These signs inform us about where we are, give us clues about what is ahead, keep us going in the right direction, and help us avoid dangers and get to our destination safely. In short, road signs, when properly constructed, reduce confusion and prevent disorientation.

Road signs themselves, however, can create bewilderment. Consider these examples of actual roads signs: a sign with printed directions to "Keep Right" but with a left-facing arrow; a sign requesting that one slow down because children are present but missing crucial punctuation so it reads, "Slow Children" instead of "Slow, Children;" or one missing an essential ending letter emphatically stating, "Parking Prohibited. Illegal Parking Will Be Fine!"

As we traverse the path to a responsive marriage, we want to pay attention to the road signs, specifically those that help us avoid dangers and get to our destination safely. In this chapter, we will cover some of the challenges we may experience along the path out of reactivity to a responsive marriage that can impede our progress so we can take action to overcome them.

Emotional Trauma

In the last chapter, we described the phenomenon of emotional triggers, the escalation of anxiety and inner turmoil that occurs when past hurts collide with present circumstances. These triggers often originate from past emotional trauma. Emotional trauma is an experience that produces psychological injury or pain. That definition is broad enough to encompass all of us.

In my experience, no one is immune from emotional trauma. Some tend to apply this term only in the most egregious of circumstances, such as with sexual or physical abuse. However, the fact is that all of us are walking around with some form and degree of psychological injury or pain. In this sinful and fallen world no one can escape this inevitability.

Certainly, some are fortunate to only have minor forms of it, while others are beleaguered with debilitating injuries making it difficult to function well in life. Minor forms of it can originate from intermittent bullying experienced on the playground, the first rejection of opposite sex attraction, squabbles with siblings, inadvertent dismissal by parents, or acute health challenges.

Major forms of it occur with service in wartime, sexual abuse and violation, experiencing or witnessing violent or catastrophic events, or long and arduous battles with chronic diseases. Post-traumatic stress disorder, or PTSD, sometimes results from major forms of emotional trauma. Symptoms of PTSD can start shortly after the event, or may not appear until years later, causing significant problems in social and work situations, relationships, and daily task completion.

PTSD symptoms generally group into four categories: 1) intrusive memories, 2) avoidance, 3) negative changes in thinking and mood, and 4) changes in physical and emotional reactions.[33] Notice the last symptom category. Emotional trauma and PTSD can, and often do, contribute to reactivity in our relationships.

Spirit, Soul, and Body

God designed us with three primary components—spirit, soul, and body. These elements are described in the New Testament using the Greek terms; *pneuma* for spirit, from which our term pneumonia is derived, relating to the breath; *psuche* for soul, from which our term *psyche*, the root of psychology, is derived; and *soma* for body, from which our term psycho**soma**tic is derived, meaning a condition manifested in the body but originating from the mind. This triune construction within us is a manifestation of the image of God as the Trinity. God is Spirit (the Holy Spirit), soul (God the Father), and body (God the Son, Jesus, the divine incarnation) and this structure exists in all of us as His created beings.

Our spirit is our essence that vibrates at the inner core of our being. It connects us to the divine and to experiences that transcend the earthly realm—what we call the supernatural realm. Our soul is composed of our mind, will, and emotions. This is the element the writers of the Bible often call the *heart* within the pages of Scripture. It is our mind, will, and emotions that Hebrews 4:12 refers to when it tells us the Word of God "is able to judge the ideas and thoughts of the heart." Our body refers to the tangible components such as bones, muscles, nerves, skin, and internal organs but also denotes the mechanism that absorbs input from the outside world through our senses of sight, hearing, taste, touch, and smell.

In the beginning, God intended for our spirit, soul, and body to be in perfect union, fully integrated, and functioning in complete harmony. The introduction of sin into the mix disrupted this harmony producing fractures and fissures between, and in, the components. In other words, we became *dis-integrated* (hyphen purposeful for emphasis). Emotional trauma exacerbates this *dis-integration* pulling our spirit, soul, and body further apart. It is this *dis-integration* of spirit, soul, and body that generates the loss of self that occurs within the Welch Responsive Cycle we learned about in the last chapter.

OUR SPIRIT IS OUR ESSENCE THAT
VIBRATES AT THE INNER CORE OF OUR
BEING. IT CONNECTS US TO THE DIVINE
AND TO EXPERIENCES THAT TRANSCEND
THE EARTHLY REALM—WHAT WE
CALL THE SUPERNATURAL REALM.

Jesus came to reintegrate these elements and connect (reconcile) them back to their Creator. But this requires more than just forgiveness. It requires healing. Consequently, when Jesus first announced His ministry in the synagogue in Nazareth (see Luke 4:18), He did not say, "I have come to forgive your sins." Instead, He quotes from Isaiah 61 declaring that He had come to "preach good news to the poor, _to heal_ the broken hearted, to proclaim _liberty to the captive_, recovery of sight to the blind, to _release the oppressed_ and proclaim the year of the Lord's favor" (emphasis added).

We need healing for our fractured and _dis-integrated_ souls to be set free from the power of sin and emotional trauma. I stated before that the purpose of this book is to increase self-awareness and provide training. When the restorative power of Jesus is inserted into awareness and training, our broken hearts are healed and wounds are bound up. All three are essential for lasting change and to traverse the path to a responsive marriage. It is A.R.T.— Awareness, Restoration, and Training—that causes a different picture, a beautiful masterpiece, to emerge from the distortions of trauma that negatively impact the way we mature and attach in future relationships. This is the ART of responsiveness.

Attachment Injuries

In the 1960s, British psychiatrist and psychoanalyst John Bowlby formulated a theory regarding bond formation between a child and their primary caregiver. Bowlby observed that children need a relationship with a primary caregiver for normal social and emotional development, and when an adult is sensitive and responsive to the child's needs, the child bonds with that adult and seeks proximity to them when they are distressed. This bonding came to be known as _attachment_; what Bowlby defined as "a lasting psychological connectedness between human beings." He called this new understanding of parent/child bonding _attachment theory_.[34]

Mary Ainsworth, a developmental psychologist, expanded upon Bowlby's original work with her now famous *strange situation* study.[35] With her study, Ainsworth introduced the concept of a *secure base* as she observed infants from twelve to eighteen months seeking proximity to their mother and then venturing out in the room away from the mom to explore and play. Her study did not seek to validate whether infants attach to their mom but rather to measure the quality of the attachment.

Researchers conducted the strange situation study in a room with a one-way window for observing and filming, a door for adults to enter and leave, a collection of toys for the infant to explore, a chair for the mom to sit in, and a chair on which a research assistant would sit. Mom sat and played with the baby and was purposefully responsive to the baby's initiation and cues.

After a few minutes, a female research assistant (the stranger) entered the room, sat quietly, initiated conversation with Mom, and then engaged with the child. After this, the mother exited the room leaving the research assistant with the baby. A short time later, Mom returned to the room, pleasantly announced her arrival, and held her arms open signaling the availability of nurture for the baby. The research assistant then left the room and Mom tried to re-engage the child in play. A number of minutes passed and then the mother exited the room again, this time leaving the child completely alone. Several minutes later, the research assistant reentered the room and tried to re-engage the child in play. After several more minutes, Mom then reentered the room, pleasantly announced her arrival, and held her arms open signaling a nurturing posture.

The behavior of the infants during the two reunions with the mother was the primary focus of the experiment. From 65% to 75% of the children demonstrated confidence in the caregiver's availability and responsiveness. In these attachments, deemed *secure*, the child would possibly cry when Mom left but consistently acknowledged her return. He or she exhibited no angry avoidance or uncomfortable contact when mom returned and, after receiving comfort, soon returned to play.

In about 10% to 15% of the cases, the child demonstrated a lack of confidence that the mom was available and responsive. They were less likely to cry during the first separation and would often ignore Mom's return. If they noticed her return, they would approach her but then stop and turn away. Some would even continue playing without acknowledging her. These children had an elevated heart rate and the researchers deemed them *insecure-avoidant.*

Another 15% to 20% of the infants exhibited an *insecure-resistant/ ambivalent* attachment. They cried hard during both separations from the mother, and they either did not approach her when she returned or their approach was weak and timid. They sometimes cried to compel the mom to hold them, then subsequently struggled to be put down. When offered toys, they angrily slapped them and often did not return to play.

A few, less than 5%, exhibited a wide range of odd and out-of-context behaviors not seen with the other groups. The researchers deemed these children *insecure-disorganized.*

This study provided substantial evidence that attachment security can change with circumstances and differ from one caregiver to the next. Researchers concluded that infant attachment security is based on the infant's actual experiences. In summary, the study defined four types of child-to-caregiver attachments:

1. **Secure:** this is the most common condition where the child can depend on their caregiver. They may show some distress when separated but exhibit joy when reunited. Although they may be upset for a time, they feel assured that the caregiver will return and comfort them.

2. **Insecure - Avoidant:** children in this category tend to avoid their parents or caregivers, showing no preference between a caregiver and a stranger. This style may be the result of abusive or neglectful caregivers.

3. **Insecure-Ambivalent/Resistant:** this category is somewhat uncommon and describes children who become extremely distressed when a parent leaves but because of poor parental availability, exhibit resistance or ambivalence towards the caregiver since they cannot depend upon them for comfort.

4. *Insecure-Disorganized:* linked to inconsistent or erratic caregiver behavior, children in this category display a bewildering mix of behavior characterized by the child seeming disoriented, dazed, or confused. They may avoid or resist the parent as they view the parent as both a source of comfort and fear.

Some years after the Ainsworth experiments, further studies were done to understand the type of experience those with childhood secure and insecure styles would have as adults. Researchers found those with *secure* attachment to be *free adults*. Their world makes sense to them, and they exhibit evidence of being secure to explore and encounter their adult world without fear.

Those with the *insecure-avoidant* style would go on to be *dismissing* as adults, essentially rejecting most emotional states. They tend to be imperceptive of other's feelings and unaware of their own. Those with the *insecure-resistant/ambivalent* style would grow up to be *preoccupied adults*, often feeling flooded by their feelings. Their world feels emotionally unreliable to them. Finally, those with the *insecure-disorganized* style would struggle with unresolved trauma and loss as an adult. They are prone to exhibiting chaotic or self-injurious behavior.[36]

Parenting Impacts Attachment

To understand your own attachment experience and style, it can be helpful to review the type of parenting you received in the context of *leadership* and *nurturing*. This next graphic can help to organize and guide that review. If you are a parent, or plan to be one in the future, this graphic can also help you to design or redesign your parenting to create the most optimal environment for your children to develop secure attachments.

ATTACHMENT MATRIX					
		Leadership Styles = Structure			
		Rigid<--->Flimsy			
		COMMANDING	COLLABORATING / COACHING	CALMING	COMMISSIONING
Nurturing Styles = Emotional Support	PROTECTING (>Suffocating)	INSECURE	SECURE/ INSECURE	INSECURE	INSECURE
	PREPARING	SECURE/ INSECURE	SECURE	SECURE/ INSECURE	INSECURE
	POKING	INSECURE	SECURE/ INSECURE	INSECURE	INSECURE
	PASSING (Indifferent<)	INSECURE	INSECURE	INSECURE	INSECURE

Going across the columns are four types of leadership styles exhibited in homes. They range from rigid to flimsy and include *commanding, collaborating/coaching, calming,* and *commissioning.* These leadership styles relate to the amount of structure you experienced and are generally attributed to the father in two-parent homes. The *commanding* style is focused on strict obedience and punishment for disobedience. The parent(s) make(s) most, if not all, of the decisions for the child in an autocratic manner well into adolescence.

Collaborating/coaching is the most preferable type of leadership for a child. It honors their dignity and inherent worth. Structure exists to provide stability, and appropriate discipline is used when the child is willfully defiant. However, in age-appropriate ways, the parent asks questions, probes, and obtains input from the child to better understand any presenting issue. In this way, the parent can guide the child to the correct answer or action rather than just declaring it. This builds self-efficacy and agency in the child and has the greatest probability for creating a secure base and attachment for them.

The *calming* style attempts to avoid conflict and keep the peace. Consequently, there is insufficient structure to create stability and self-confidence in the child.

Lastly, the *commissioning* style essentially abdicates authority to the child and the parent's leadership is largely absent. The child is left to figure things out on his or her own.

As you think about each of these four styles of leadership, which one did you experience most as a child?

Nurturing is generally provided by the mother in two-parent homes and deals with the amount of emotional support the child receives in a range from indifferent to suffocating. On the suffocating side is *protecting*. This type of nurturing focuses on protecting the child from life's circumstances by removing obstacles or challenges rather than teaching the child how to manage and overcome them. Consequently, the child does not learn how to solve their own problems and often becomes debilitated or overwhelmed by them later in life when mom and dad are not around to remove the obstacles.

Preparing is the optimal type of nurturing. It focuses on helping the child learn how to effectively deal with life's circumstances. The parent uses each challenge and obstacle the child faces as a *teachable moment*. This type of nurturing has the highest probability for creating a secure base and attachment.

The *poking* type of nurturing is erratic, inconsistent, and unpredictable. Consequently, the child does not know when their need for comfort will be met, creating an insecure base.

Finally, the *passing* type is essentially devoid of active care. The child is neglected and left to themselves without active emotional support.

As you think about these four nurturing styles, which one did you experience most often as a child? The combination of *leadership* and *nurturing* experienced by the child will determine the type of attachment experience they will have as an adult. When both the *collaborating/coaching leadership* style and *preparing nurturing* style are present, parents give the child the best environment for creating a secure attachment to the parents which will then translate into secure attachments as an adult.

It is important to note, however, that with work, and sometimes with professional help, one who had insecure attachments as a child can learn to acquire secure attachments as an adult, what Dr. Curt Thompson references as "earned secure attachment" in his book *Anatomy of the Soul*.[37] He postulates that "earned secure attachment" is developed when the person is able to freely tell their story to another who listens and engages with empathy. He states it this way:

> *Transformation requires a collaborative interaction, with one person empathically listening and responding to the other so that the speaker has the experience, perhaps for the first time, of feeling felt by another... Such an encounter is necessary because we cannot change our stories without simultaneously changing the neural pathways that correlate with those changes.*

This lends further credence to the idea that marriage can be a place of healing and restoration for the wounded soul. Husbands and wives with insecure attachments formed in childhood can help each other to develop "earned secure attachment" when they learn to respond rather than react while they tell each other their stories.

Attachment Injury Example

As mentioned in previous chapters, Michael and Jessica represent many of the couples I have worked with over the years. They desire closeness, yet they interact with each other as if they are conversing with their parents. Therapists refer to this phenomenon as *attachment wounds*.

Take Michael, for instance. He could never get close to his mother. For fear of this happening in his marriage, Michael reverts to being overbearing, the same behavior Jessica was accustomed to with her parents. Jessica could not get away from her father's controlling nature until she met Michael. Out of nowhere, however, this cycle reappeared for Jessica, prompting her to seek out women friends who would listen to her without controlling her. These interactions with Michael became a vicious fight cycle, most of which was outside Jessica's conscious awareness.

It is quite common for a person to become attracted to a future mate who subconsciously replicates a parent's most hurtful ways, causing earlier childhood experiences to repeat. This tendency represents the most common therapeutic observation for most marriage counselors.

Phases and Stages

In 2001, John Eldredge, a well-known Christian author and founder of Ransomed Heart Ministries (now Wild at Heart Ministries), published a groundbreaking book titled *Wild at Heart*.[38] In the book, Eldredge describes a type of masculinity that is based on the notion that men thrive when they have a battle to fight, an adventure to live, and a beauty to rescue. With more than four million books sold, it set off a national conversation about masculinity among Christians that continues to this day. In 2005,

John Eldredge and his wife, Stasi, wrote a companion book that describes femininity for Christian women.[39]

In 2006, Eldredge released a sequel to the *Wild at Heart* book titled the *Way of the Wild Heart*. In many ways, this book was more seminal than the original as it laid out the journey of a man in six stages of life. In 2009, the book was retitled to *Fathered by God.*[40] In this book, Eldredge contends that a boy, on his way through life, must navigate six growth stages he identified as *boyhood*, from birth to about age twelve; *cowboy*, from about age thirteen to nineteen; *warrior*, generally experienced in a man's twenties and thirties; *lover*, also navigated in the twenties and thirties; *king*, from the late thirties into the late fifties; and finally *sage*, from the early sixties until death.

The central theme of the book revolved around the idea that in each stage, there are things that a boy or man must learn to be able to navigate the subsequent stages well. Eldredge further suggested that, if the core questions of that stage were either answered in negative ways or not answered at all, the eventual man would struggle later in life as he attempted to compensate for the unanswered, or inappropriately answered, questions.

This idea of life stages, and certain concepts one must learn in each, is central to our understanding of where we find ourselves today. Numerous psychologists and mental health experts have created their own versions of developmental stages. Jean Piaget is known for his four stages of cognitive development: *sensorimotor* from zero to two years old, *preoperational* from two to seven years old; *concrete operational* from seven to eleven years old; and *formal operational* from eleven years old through adulthood. Sigmund Freud is known for his five psychosexual stages of development: *oral, anal, phallic, latency, and genital.* Erik Erickson's model of psychosocial development is the most well-known. Erickson broke human development down into eight stages: *early childhood, preschool, school age, adolescence, young adulthood, middle adulthood, and maturity.*

Progressive Growth Phases of Life

One of the goals of *The Responsive Marriage* book is for you and your companion to deepen awareness of yourselves. Only when you understand yourself better can you apply methods to improve what is within your control and strengthen your relationships. Part of this deepened self-awareness comes as you explore your family of origin and early life experiences. An effective way to do this is to think about your life in stages or phases. I call this Progressive Growth Phases of Life and they are summarized in this table:

Phase of Life	Primary Focus	Approximate Age Range		Example Concept(s) to Be Learned	Core Question
		Low	High		
Beginning	Depending	0	1	Relying on mom and dad to meet my basic and core needs	Who can I trust?
Bustling	Exploring	2	2	Exploring the environment, what are the boundaries?	Is my world safe?
Blossoming	Asserting	3	4	Verbally expressing needs, speaking up	Am I heard?
Balancing	Comparing	5	11	Understanding the "hierarchy," group dynamics, and how I'm perceived by others	Am I enough?
Becoming	Developing	12	17	Self-autonomy and "separateness," sense of identity—my likes and dislikes	Am I respected?
Blasting Off	Relating	18	29	Finding a mate and/or vocation	Will I be successful?
Burgeoning	Contributing	30	59	Making a difference for others, finding purpose and meaning in life	Am I significant?
Bestowing	Transferring	60	?	Passing on wisdom and resources to my children, grandchildren, and younger generations	Do I matter?

Within each phase, there are specific concepts that are important for the person in that phase to learn and a core question that reverberates in the human soul during that phase. As we discuss these phases, you will want to think back to the previous ones you have navigated to gain clarity, consider the current phase you are in and whether you are learning the important concepts, and plan for how you might want to navigate the future phases with intentionality.

The first phase we encounter as human beings is the *beginning* phase of life. Here, we depend completely on mom and dad for meeting our most basic physiological and emotional needs. It is in this phase that our brains develop around the concept of trust without being able to form any words to explain it. Proverbs 3:5–6 encourages trust. "Trust in the Lord with all your heart and do not rely on your own understanding; think about Him in all your ways, and He will guide you on the right paths." Trust is obviously important to God.

As we have interactions with our parents and siblings, we begin to cognitively determine who is trustworthy and who is not. If this phase is fraught with inconsistent nurturing, unpredictable parental care, or episodes where comfort is not forthcoming, or magnified fear develops in this phase, we will likely have a more difficult time discerning who we can trust as adults and extending complete trust to those who sincerely care for us.

From there, we transition to the *bustling* phase of life. Here, the primary focus is on exploring our world. As we learn to crawl and then walk, our world expands and each new encounter brings fascination and wonder. It is in this phase that we are first introduced to the concept of boundaries or limits. We hear the word "no" as we reach for something that is off limits or harmful. We test the boundaries and soon our brain builds a construct for categorizing our world into "this is OK," "this is not OK." As we are developing this construct of our world, we are also learning about what is safe and what is not. If too many items in our world are categorized as off limits or fear inducing, our view of safety may begin skewing, leading us to conclude, without conscious thought, that the world is essentially unsafe.

At about the age of three, we shift to the *blossoming* phase of life as we start to assert ourselves more. We start speaking up more to express our needs and opinions. Language develops rapidly in this phase which accelerates learning and the acquisition of new skills. Unfortunately, we can tend to speak up at inappropriate moments, and in sometimes adamant ways, causing mom and dad to need to temper our blossoming spirits with some discipline. In this phase, the core question is, "Am I heard?" When I make a request or demand, am I listened to and responded to, or am I dismissed and squelched?

After the blossoming phase, we enter the *balancing* phase. This is generally when we start grade school at about age five. In this phase, through interaction with our peers at school, we naturally start to compare ourselves to others to make sense of our new school world. We learn, sometimes the hard way, about group dynamics. We start to develop our own strategies, through trial and error, to navigate the hierarchies that tend to develop within and among peer groups, and we become more conscious of how others perceive us. The core question here is, "Am I enough?"

In the book *Wild at Heart*, John Eldredge describes the question for the boy as, "Do I have what it takes?"[41] In the companion book, *Captivating*, John, and his wife, Stasi, describe the question for the girl as, "Am I lovely?"[42] Our school peers are quick to answer "no" to these questions in hundreds of diverse ways. It is essential for parents to find ways to answer the specific question for the child with a resounding "yes," in thousands of separate ways, to counteract the barrage of dissents the child will experience in school. In 1 Corinthians 15:33, we hear, "Do not be deceived; bad company corrupts good character." Therefore, good character development for the child will include the parent(s) needing to nullify the impact of negative influences.

The *becoming* phase is next as the child enters adolescence. They are becoming their own person as they develop an individual identity separate and distinct from their parents and their peers. They explore and begin to concretize their likes and dislikes. They learn to be autonomous and possess agency, the power to act on their own volition. Of course, this phase is awkward and fraught with challenges for both the adolescent and the parent as the teenager attempts to widen the boundaries and test the limits. The core question here is, "Am I respected?" In other words, "Am I allowed to be an individual within appropriate, safeguarding boundaries?" "Do my opinions and needs matter?"

The *blasting off* phase starts when the person finishes high school and goes off to college, trade school, or explores options for work and an eventual career. In this phase, the emphasis is on relating to their work, their peers, boyfriends or girlfriends, and possibly an eventual mate. The core question for this phase is, "Will I be successful?" The individual will first start developing a definition of success, perhaps different than that of their parents, and make moves to try and achieve that success. Does success, for me, mean marriage? Does it include children? What work or vocation will help me be successful in both passion and financial resources?

In the *burgeoning* phase, although the person may be working in a career and raising a family, the mindset often shifts from being successful to having significance. Questions arise in the person's mind about how they are contributing and making a difference in their world. Perhaps this will mean a career change, more volunteer efforts, grappling with the state of their marriage and family, or, for Christians, it might mean becoming more involved in the local church and/or ministry efforts.

The last phase of life is the *bestowing* phase. The person may be retired, or soon retire, from their career. The children are generally grown and out on their own. Grandchildren may be present or forthcoming. Therefore, the person's focus often shifts to passing on wisdom and financial resources to the next generation or two. In this phase, the person will often grapple with the question, "Do I matter?" Without a career, the person may question whether they have a purpose anymore. Because of this inevitable dynamic, retirement planning should include more than just financial preparation. It should also include plans for meaningful "work," which could be on a volunteer basis, to continue to feel there is a reason for getting up each morning.

Now that you have a better understanding of the phases of life we all must navigate, it would be beneficial for you as an individual, and as a couple, to review each of the phases you have already lived through to understand how, and whether, your parent(s) answered each of the core questions for you in the affirmative or in the negative.

Do you struggle with trust, safety, feeling heard, feeling adequate, feeling respected, feeling successful, believing you are significant, or that you matter? Perhaps it would help for you to go back through the phase in which the core question was either not answered, or answered negatively, and let God bring healing to those broken areas of your heart.

Then, do some planning and vision casting for the future phases of your life. Talk with your companion, and maybe another confidant, about how to best prepare for these phases so that you can navigate them successfully.

Family of Origin

The last road sign we want to be aware of is our *family of origin*. Families of origin run the gamut from wholly dysfunctional, to dysfunctional in some areas and functional in other areas, to mostly functional. It is easy to understand how a child raised in an overtly abusive or fractured home might struggle with basic life skills. However, nearly everyone experiences some type of trauma or formidable challenge in their early years that can potentially alter their development in negative ways.

No family is perfect, but some children have the blessing and fortune of a birth father and birth mother who have a great marriage and are purposeful in raising their children with values and character. Nevertheless, even children from these homes often experience some type of trauma or daunting challenge. Like a detective looking for clues to solve a case, taking the time to understand your family of origin can help to explain your reactivity, fears, and insecurities that may be hindering your current relationships.

In marriage, one's companion can sometimes be God's instrument for surfacing early childhood wounds so they can be healed by the power of Jesus. I encourage you as individuals and as a couple to be curious about the following:

IT IS EASY TO UNDERSTAND HOW A CHILD RAISED IN AN OVERTLY ABUSIVE OR FRACTURED HOME MIGHT STRUGGLE WITH BASIC LIFE SKILLS. HOWEVER, NEARLY EVERYONE EXPERIENCES SOME TYPE OF TRAUMA OR FORMIDABLE CHALLENGE IN THEIR EARLY YEARS THAT CAN POTENTIALLY ALTER THEIR DEVELOPMENT IN NEGATIVE WAYS.

1. ***Parents***
   a. Was your father physically present or absent during your early childhood and adolescence?
   b. Was your mother physically present or absent during your early childhood and adolescence?
   c. If physically present, was one, or both, emotionally absent?
   d. What was your relationship like with your father and/or your mother?
   e. Did you feel you were delighted in or did you feel more like a burden or nuisance?
   f. Did you lose a parent or parents to death, divorce, or abandonment?
   g. Did your father or mother have any addictions? (e.g., alcohol, drugs, gambling, pornography, work, etc.)
   h. Did your father or mother have any health challenges?
   i. Were you abused physically, emotionally, mentally, or sexually by your father or your mother?
   j. What was the structure like in your home? Was it rigid, stable, or flimsy?
   k. What was nurturing like in your home? Was it suffocating, caring, or indifferent?

2. ***Siblings***
   a. Did you have siblings or were you an only child?
   b. If you had siblings, what birth order were you and how did you navigate this birth order?
   c. What was your relationship like with each sibling separately and together as a group?
   d. Did you feel honored and respected as an individual or were you often compared, favorably or unfavorably, with your siblings by your father or mother?
   e. Did any of your siblings have any addictions?
   f. Did any of your siblings have any health challenges?

g. Were you abused physically, emotionally, mentally, or sexually by any of your siblings?

h. Were any of your siblings lost to death, rebellion, or traumatic separation?

3. **Other Family Members**

a. What about grandparents, uncles, aunts, and cousins? What was your relationship like with them?

b. Were you abused physically, emotionally, mentally, or sexually by any of your other family members?

The Bible contains references to the impact of our family of origin. For example, in Numbers 14:18 we read, "The Lord is slow to anger and rich in faithful love, forgiving wrongdoing and rebellion. But he will not leave the guilty unpunished, bringing the consequences of the fathers' wrongdoing on the children to the third and fourth generation." Proverbs 22:6 tells us to "Teach a youth about the way he should go; even when he is old, he will not depart from it."

These verses provide clear understanding as to why subsequent generations can suffer from the same troubles as their parents. Children of alcoholics become alcoholics. Children of abusers become abusers. Children of enraged parents become enraged. These propensities are certainly not foregone conclusions when we consider the restorative power of Jesus and the cross. Jesus came to heal the brokenhearted and bind up their wounds and, even though you may have a father or mother with egregious sins in their past, it does not mean you are forever doomed to repeat the same patterns. These tendencies are not inevitabilities. However, the Bible and science do confirm that we learn behaviors and, unless they are intentionally unlearned, they can become a person's destiny.

Human beings have always had a desire to understand their lineage and roots. The Old Testament includes many detailed records of lineage and Matthew starts his gospel account with the genealogy of Jesus starting from Abraham and progressing through

Joseph and Mary. Generational progression apparently matters to God, and it should matter to us. Not only does it provide a sense of belonging and context for our existence, but it can also help explain our current experience.

Discussion Starter Questions

- *For Couples or Groups*
  - If you feel relatively safe, share an emotional trauma you experienced as a child or adolescent? How is this trauma affecting you today?
    NOTES:_____
    _____
    _____

  - How have you experienced the restorative power of Jesus in your emotional wounds?
    NOTES:_____
    _____
    _____

  - Which of the leadership and nurturing styles did you experience most often as a child and adolescent?
    NOTES:_____
    _____
    _____

  - As you read the descriptions of the four types of attachment tendencies, which of those do you feel you experience most often?
    NOTES:_____
    _____
    _____

- Pick one of the Progressive Growth Phases of Life you have already navigated. Talk about how the core question was answered, or not answered, for you in that phase.
  NOTES:_____

  _____

  _____

- Describe your family of origin and ways in which you see the influences of your family of origin on you today. Refer to the family of origin questions in the chapter for guidance.
  NOTES:_____

  _____

  _____

- *For Couples Only*
  - Ask your companion which of the attachment tendencies they see in you and ask them to provide examples.
    NOTES:_____

    _____

    _____

  - Which of the Progressive Growth Phases of Life are you in right now? Talk about how you can help each other navigate that phase, and future phases, well.
    NOTES:_____

    _____

    _____

  - How can your companion help you to find healing for family of origin wounds?
    NOTES:_____

    _____

    _____

GOD INSPIRED INTUITION

Students frequently ask me, "How does a therapist develop a therapeutic intuition? How do I know what to say or respond to, at the right time and within the correct context, during a therapy session?" Perhaps another way of saying this is how and when do I know if I am or am not following the rules of the road? What tells me this? Instantly, I realize the answer: God.

Decades ago, I remember the first time I pondered therapeutic intuition. Working with one particular couple, Devin and Whitney, caused me to reflect on this concept. They and I were stuck. I conducted a genogram, assessed their attachment styles, tested their innate temperaments, measured their involuntary reactions, and applied other diagnostic methods. Quite frankly, I was stumped. They just weren't making any progress. Even though they were doing their homework and studying a recommended book, they sat under my therapy frozen and unable to move. I considered referring them to another therapist. But then it dawned on me. I needed to silently ask God for His wisdom. I did and God revealed to me the couple's lack of empathy—one of the major rules of the road evaluated in professional therapy. They were slow to turn toward the other, lacked eye contact, and were unable to ignore distractions.

That particular session is etched in my memory and one I will not likely forget in the foreseeable future. My number one responsibility for following the rules of the road is to include God in all I do. I've spent my career as a pastor and professor trying my best to include God in all of my life's work. On that notable, desperate day, I realized I need to live my life in utter desperation for God. This is the primary rule of the road for me as a therapist. I hope it is the primary rule of the road for you in your marriage.

CHAPTER 6

RULES OF THE ROAD

It has always been ironic to me that to operate a motor vehicle in the United States one must show proof they have gone through a specific regimen of training and demonstrate competency with a passing score on a test, but there are no such requirements for operating a relationship. Certainly, a motor vehicle possesses the power to kill and maim if not responsibly managed, but a relationship has the power to shatter hearts if the participants fail to follow certain protocols.

To learn how to operate a motor vehicle requires obtaining knowledge of the *rules of the road* and applying them consistently. Failure to do so could lead to accidents with severe consequences. We learn to stop at red lights, only go on green lights, yield to another driver when they have the right of way, drive only in the direction dictated by road signs, not exceed the posted speed limit, and signal other drivers before changing lanes. In other words, we learn to be aware of our actions and how they may affect other drivers. We learn that safety involves order. Orderly conduct on the road saves lives; disorderly conduct risks life and limb.

Good relationships have *rules of the road* as well. Failure to follow them can have troublesome, and sometimes detrimental, consequences for both parties. Relationship *rules of the road* ensure orderly communication and interaction patterns for the participants. When the flow of traffic is chaotic, people get hurt. The same result occurs when an orderly flow of communication and interaction is lost in relationships. In this chapter, we will explore this dynamic further by examining listening skills, emotional intelligence, and maintaining the self while bonding with your companion.

Listening Skills

Listening is one of the most precious gifts you can give to your companion. It is the cry of every human heart—to be listened to and receive the full attention of another. David expressed this craving numerous times in the Psalms with pleadings such as, "God, hear my prayer, listen to the words of my mouth" (Psalms 54:2), "Listen to the sound of my pleading when I cry to You for help, when I lift up my hands toward Your holy sanctuary (Psalms 28:2), and "I say to the Lord, 'You are my God.' Listen, Lord, to my cry for help" (Psalms 140:6). You can hear in these words an undercurrent of desperation, of yearning and longing beyond the superficial. When God seems silent and distant, even when we intellectually know He is always near, we crave Him to attend to our words, to *show up* and allay our fears with His presence. This same yearning is present in marriage, the most intimate of relationships. Listening creates connection. Yet many couples spend precious little time doing it or learning how to do it better.

The Myth of Multitasking

Frankly, the American preoccupation with multitasking is probably the number one reason we don't generally listen well and need focused instruction to learn how to do it. Before the advent of computers, the idea of multitasking as a desired way of working did not exist. The term first appeared in a 1965 report from IBM

(International Business Machines) to describe the capabilities of their latest computer.[43] Ironically, when personal computers first appeared on the scene in 1977, they were not primarily built for multitasking. Rather, it was the increased efficiency and reduced completion time for an individual task that made it popular.

At that time, the operating system, the core software that manages and coordinates the hardware components and programs of the computer, limited the user to interfacing with only one installed application at a time. MS-DOS (Microsoft Disk Operating System) was introduced in 1981 and soon became the standard operating system installed on all personal computers not made by Apple.[44] Those of you old enough to remember MS-DOS will remember you typed a set of abbreviated instructions on a command line to launch one program and you worked in only that program until your tasks were completed. You then closed that program before you could launch another single program to work on another set of tasks.

The introduction of the Mac OS (operating system) graphical user interface (GUI) for Apple Computers in 1984, and the Windows operating system in 1985, fundamentally changed the way users interacted with their computer programs.[45] Now you could have multiple programs (windows) open at the same time and easily transition back and forth between them.

Running concurrently with the advent of multitasking capabilities for computers was the idea that humans could *learn* to multitask equally well. Multitasking became a desired proficiency in companies wanting to increase their productivity. Soon job interviews and performance evaluations would be changed to search for this proficiency and ensure employees pursued it as a worthy goal.

We now know that our brains are not built for multitasking as we typically use that word. James Clear, the author of the number one New York Times bestselling book, *Atomic Habits*, and a consultant for major corporations, writes on numerous topics related to habits, decision-making, and continuous improvement. In *The Myth of Multitasking*, he states:

WE NOW KNOW THAT OUR BRAINS
ARE NOT BUILT FOR MULTITASKING
AS WE TYPICALLY USE THAT WORD.

*Yes, we are capable of doing two things at the same time. It is possible, for example, to watch TV while cooking dinner or to answer an email while talking on the phone. What is impossible, however, is **concentrating** on two tasks at once. Multitasking forces your brain to switch back and forth very quickly from one task to another.*

This wouldn't be a big deal if the human brain could transition seamlessly from one job to the next, but it can't. Multitasking forces you to pay a mental price each time you interrupt one task and jump to another. In psychology terms, this mental price is called the switching cost.

Switching cost is the disruption in performance that we experience when we switch our attention from one task to another. A 2003 study published in the International Journal of Information Management found that the typical person checks email once every five minutes and that, on average, it takes 64 seconds to resume the previous task after checking your email.

In other words, because of email alone, we typically waste one out of every six minutes.[46]

Numerous studies have supported this view. Researchers have concluded that our brains experience "bottlenecking" when trying to process certain aspects of tasks.[47] On the freeway, we routinely experience bottlenecks when too many cars are trying to merge into traffic. Everything slows down. Our brain experiences the same dynamic since it possesses limited attentional resources. Consequently, it attempts to sift the information and keep the *most important*. Meaning, the brain loses and does not address other information. This especially holds true for learning, one of the things we attempt to do when listening to another.

Richard E Mayer, an educational psychologist and professor of psychology at the University of California, Santa Barbara, studied the phenomenon of cognitive load in multimedia learning and concluded that it is difficult, if not impossible, to learn new information while engaging in multitasking.[48] Others have examined how multitasking affects academic success and found that students who engaged in high levels of multitasking reported significant issues with their academic work. Psychiatrist Edwin M. Hallowell went as far as to describe multitasking as a "mythical activity in which people believe they can perform two or more tasks simultaneously as effectively as one."[49]

If you are a multitasker, you may need to discard your habits of trying to concentrate on more than one thing and learn, or relearn, how to listen attentively to your companion.

Listening Must Be Learned

Adding further challenge to our attempts to listen well is the fact that listening must be learned. In one of my university interpersonal communication courses, we discuss the myths that exist about communication. One of those myths is that listening comes naturally to people, as if to suggest that we are born with the innate ability to listen. This is as far from the truth as it is that elephants can tiptoe through a flower garden.

Listening is a learned skill and not something we do naturally. Since we are born with the ability to hear noises, it would seem reasonable to conclude that we are equipped with better potential for listening than we are for speaking. However, listening becomes increasingly difficult as we gain experiences and life's challenges crowd in on us. In time, we are prone to listen less and speak more.

What, then, does it mean to listen so that we truly hear what our companion is saying? First, stop what you are doing and focus on the words of the expressed message. This is extremely important to begin correctly. Turn off the television, put down your newspaper, stop talking to one of the kids—*stop what you are doing*. Second, attempt to place yourself in the experience of that person. This is called empathy, and this is not an easy task.

I continue to reflect on the words etched on a plaque that hung on my shelf as a little boy: "Never judge a person until you have walked a mile in their moccasins." I have had reason to ponder that phrase over the years and each time I have thought about those words I conclude it is an exceedingly difficult assignment to truly listen and understand another person. The more I attempt to listen to people facing exceedingly difficult and challenging issues the more I believe that only Jesus can get it right 100% of the time and listen to another person the way in which he or she needs it. The art of listening is extremely complex and fraught with challenges.

So, what does real empathetic listening look like? Perhaps a way to think about this is the way in which my children listened to me when they were young and I would say, "Hey, do you guys want to go swimming?" Even though Savannah and Daniel might be watching the latest cartoons on TV, reading their favorite book, playing with their favorite toy, or teasing each other as only a brother and sister can do, the moment I mentioned *swimming*, their eyes got big, and they dropped whatever they were doing to attend to me.

Their body posture turned toward me rather than away from me, and they typically smiled at me with their mouths wide open. These little people then gave me a lot of eye contact inviting me to give them more information and provide the specifics of our pool adventure. Often, they would ask questions: "Tell us more, Daddy!" and "Is my floating rubber ducky invited?" They would then frequently summarize the message back to me saying, "Now, Daddy, you said that we could go the pool soon, right?"

Checking the accuracy of what they thought they heard was important to them. My children were *attending* to my communication with them; they were looking, actively listening, and tracking in response to my simple question. Sometimes, at this point in the conversation, my children would turn to each other and give out a yell saying, "Hurray!" and maybe even hug each other to acknowledge and affirm a swimming excursion in the making.

Listening with empathy is also illustrated by a couple who appears to be in love: *madly in love!* I am sure you have observed this situation. The couple is seated in a restaurant gazing into each other's eyes approximately twelve to eighteen inches apart—considered an intimate distance. They usually have an open posture (no arms folded) with each leaning forward, intent on absorbing every word uttered by the other person, as if to invite the other person to draw closer. Even the person serving them their dinner gets the hint that "this is a private party, and no one else is invited." What could better depict active listening than this?

Giving Your Companion A.I.R.

A straightforward way to summarize good listening skills is to remember that listening, truly listening, to your companion is like giving them *air*. Often, the desire to be listened to is like coming up for air after holding your breath underwater for an extended time. Cares and concerns, or perhaps simple wonderings or observations, create a desire to talk to another, to converse, to gain perspective, to express our thoughts in spoken words. Some will say, "I just need to get something off my chest" referring to the feeling of suffocation or labored breathing that the cares of life can generate. To be listened to in those times fills our emotional lungs. Giving your companion A.I.R. is an effortless way to remember how to listen well.

The "A" in AIR stands for *affirm*. This means to validate them and let them know you are for them and with them. We do this in both verbal and nonverbal ways. We can remember non-verbal ways as "a perfect *ten*"—**t**urn towards them, **e**ye contact, and **no** distractions.

When your companion wants or needs to talk, purposely turn your body so that you are fully facing them. This lets them know they, and what they are saying, are important enough for you to give them your full attention. Next, give them eye contact. Look them in the eyes as they talk. Lastly, ensure you are not distracted. Do not interrupt your attention with other stimuli such as the TV, kids, your phone, or other people walking by. Studies have proven that more than half of our communication is composed of non-verbal elements. The *ten* elements send a strong, unspoken message to your companion that they deserve, and will receive, your full attention.

The verbal ways to affirm include saying things like, "That must have been very difficult for you," or "It sounds like you were saddened by his remark," or "I am trying to understand why you would feel that way," or "I hear you saying you were pleased with the outcome." These types of statements are nonjudgmental and do not draw conclusions. They are simply observations that let the speaker know you are tracking and attempting to understand how they feel. This serves to validate their experience as legitimate. It does not require you to agree or disagree with them, try to help them interpret or evaluate events, or fix a problem. You are just letting them know you are joining them in reliving their experience.

The "I" in AIR stands for *inquire*. Ask open-ended questions grounded in curiosity. Their purpose is to obtain more information and give the speaker permission to expound on their thinking. Closed-end questions, on the other hand, require only a yes or no response. These are generally used only to confirm or deny a specific fact or assertion. They do little to encourage more dialogue.

Open-ended questions generally start with who, what, when, where, how, and *sometimes* why. Notice my emphasis on being careful with *why* questions. *Why* can sometimes carry a connotation of challenging the person. "Why did you do that?" can be interpreted as questioning the person's judgment. On the other hand, "Why do you think the person reacted that way?" could be an innocuous query. Therefore, you will want to consider possible misinterpretations when using *why* questions. We can reword, "Why did you do that?" to eliminate potential offense by saying, "How did you decide on that course of action?"

Finally, the "R" in AIR stands for *reflect* or *repeat*. Before offering your opinion or drawing conclusions, simply repeat a sentence or two of what your companion said. You can do it verbatim, or you can try to say what you thought you heard them say—in your own words. If you do the latter, you will want to quickly follow up with, "Is that correct?" to confirm the accuracy of your understanding. Do this periodically in back-and-forth iterations until both of you sense you fully understand the other's experience. If there is conflict between you regarding the subject, it may be best to repeat back every sentence they say—word for word. This helps to slow the conversation down and minimize reactivity.

A variation on this idea is to simply repeat the last several words of what they said with a questioning inflection at the end. For example, if your companion said, "My boss was really mad at me today," you might say "Mad at you today?" The question mark intonation added at the end sends your companion a subliminal message that you want to hear more.

So, in summary, listen by giving your companion AIR—*affirm* them, *inquire* of them, and *reflect* or *repeat* back to them. As simple as it sounds, this will be especially difficult for the men to implement but extremely rewarding if they do. Men, by nature, are fixers. If we hear you have a problem, we experience an overwhelming desire to fix it. "Well, here's what you need to do," we might say. We are often clueless to the fact that we have just created another problem. We have tried to fix something that she did not want fixed. She only wants to be heard, to be listened to with empathy. Guys, put your tool belt away when you need to listen to your wife. Give her AIR, not remedies.

Expressing Feelings

Why is it so difficult for men to tell their wives how they really feel? Most women will beg, plead, or cajole their husband into sharing his feelings. They are willing to do almost anything to have their man express loving feelings. It is music to a woman's ears to hear her companion say, "Wow, I feel happy or even 'sad' about that." Or even better, "Wow, that must really hurt when your best friend ignores you. I'm sorry for your pain." Is it asking too much of men to be in touch with their feelings?

Logically, men would say, "No." We [men] naturally and defensively respond with, "I'm a sensitive kind of guy." We may even go to great lengths to convince our woman that we are sensitive because we know she wants that. We purchase a greeting card or arrange for flowers at least once a year for our wives, maybe even twice, and we can use the word "feel" in a sentence. We have feelings just like women. It is just that we do not have the need to express them.

The Hallmark store pick-out-that-special-card-for-my-wife adventure is always a fun time for me. I used to wonder what the women next to me were thinking while I was searching the birthday section for the perfect sentiment. Were they thinking, *What a neat thing to witness; a man who's in love with his wife and wants to express his deepest feelings.* Why is it that we [men] applaud ourselves for the slightest amount of kindness? I guess we want to overcome being labeled as insensitive and out-of-touch with our feelings.

I could not have been prouder of myself during those card-hunting expeditions until my *pride-goeth-before-a-fall* moment happened. Until just a few years ago, it had never dawned on me that while selecting a card for my wife, I picked out cards more quickly than the other women standing around selecting their cards.

Now mind you, I was not purposely timing the task. But it did not take long for me to pick out that special card for my wife, Robin. To me, all the cards were great! I simply liked them all about the same and I thought Robin would enjoy any one of them. I did not have to select between too many since several cards said what I wanted to express to Robin. It just happened quickly. No elongated event. Just get in and get out quickly.

I can only guess what some of you women are thinking: *Hmm… another insensitive man and a therapist to boot.* Truly, I thought I was being a blessing to my wife—an extremely sensitive guy. The only problem was that I was *thinking* about which card to pick rather than *feeling* which card to pick.

That's where the problem lies. Most men do not have a clue as to what they feel. I learned this early on during my pastoral days when I would look at the couple sitting in front of me and ask, "So, John, now that we've heard how your wife feels, could you tell your wife about how you feel?" He would give me that look that males will rarely share with another male. It's the look that says, *Pleeease don't make me try and answer something that I have absolutely no knowledge about.*

We men certainly know what we think: we can explain it with precision and accuracy. It is second nature for us to tell you the right way to clean a gun or the appropriate car washing maneuvers. We are eager, for the most part, to tell you what we think. But the feeling part, that's miles from where we experience life. Men know who they respect, not how they feel about that person. It needs to be factual, reasonable, and sometimes quantifiable for it to make logical sense to a male. That's it: logical sense *feels* good to a male.

One man said it well, "Why 'feel,' it only gets you into trouble?!" After exploring that idea further, I realized this man equated feelings with vulnerability, and vulnerability leads to being hurt. Basically, *feeling* means that you are placing yourself in a one-down position. Why would anyone, on purpose, choose to make themselves vulnerable (get in touch with their feelings) only to feel defenseless?

Grasping for Control

Most men choose to remain in control. Any logical human being would agree with that—even with a therapist like me. One men's Bible study leader linked this feeling of control with not praying with their wives. "All of the men with whom I meet want to but can't pray with their wives." Men universally accept the idea that to pray with our wives makes us feel too vulnerable and out-of-control.

It is true that sharing your feelings with another creates vulnerability. Yet, being vulnerable is "manly" because it requires courage. David—a man after God's own heart—the shepherd boy who fought off a lion and a bear, the young teenager who downed the giant with a stone and a sling, the warrior who led Israel in numerous bloody battles and conquered nations, the king who governed a kingdom—was vulnerable.

He and others filled the Psalms with the expression of deep emotion and intense feelings. In Psalms 6:2–3, David lays his heart open with these words expressing *fear*, "Be gracious to me, Lord, for I am weak; heal me, Lord, for my bones are shaking; my whole being is shaken with terror." Later in that same chapter he expresses *sadness* with, "I am weary from my groaning; with my tears I dampen my pillow and drench my bed every night" (Psalms 6:6–7). In Psalms 13:2, we hear of his intense *anxiety* when he says, "How long will I store up anxious concerns within me, agony in my mind every day?" In Psalms 51, he expresses *remorse* and *regret* when he laments, "Be gracious to me, God, according to your faithful love; according to your abundant compassion, blot out my rebellion. Wash away my guilt and cleanse me from my sin. For I am conscious of my rebellion, and my sin is always before me" (Psalms 51:1–3).

I dare say that, next to Jesus, David is likely the most courageous man who ever lived. Yet, he was vulnerable as well. He could wield a sword and share a feeling. He epitomized godly masculinity, the optimal blending of strength and vulnerability. Exactly the attributes of masculinity that Jesus displayed.

IT IS TRUE THAT SHARING YOUR FEELINGS
WITH ANOTHER CREATES VULNERABILITY.
YET, BEING VULNERABLE IS "MANLY"
BECAUSE IT REQUIRES COURAGE.

So, men, it is acceptable to be vulnerable, especially with your wives. But you likely need more than permission. You also need instructions. Although we are born with feelings, we are not born with the ability to express them appropriately. For that, we need training.

But women, you may also need training on how to express your feelings. Because although women have an easier time identifying and naming them, they can struggle with appropriately expressing them without overwhelming their husbands.

Using "I" Statements

The method I am about to share with you has positively changed the communication patterns of hundreds of couples I have counseled. It is both simple and profound. The basis of this method is turning *you* statements into *I* statements.

When spouses communicate, especially in the midst of conflict, we resort to expressing our observations or evaluations of the other. We say things like, "You never put your dishes in the dishwasher," "You always leave your dirty clothes on the floor," or "You hurt me." All these statements are accusatory and result in the receiver of those statements taking a defensive position. This elevates anxiety, shuts down productive problem solving, and creates emotional distance. When in a dispute or dealing with any controversy, starting your sentences with *you* is akin to picking a fight. Furthermore, doing so keeps the conversation focused on processing each person's perspective on the facts which is a sure way to *pour gas on the fire*.

Debating the facts plunges a couple into *intellectualization* which is a flight into reason (utilizing only cerebral thinking and arguing with your companion), one of the classic negative defense mechanisms. The couple fights over their perception of the experience rather than validating feelings. If you remain stuck on your perception, you and your companion will likely disagree and never truly understand each other's actual feelings.

Persons in a relationship most likely always view the situation differently. All college psychology textbooks illustrate this with the classic example of three people witnessing the same vehicular accident. Three police officers arrive on the scene, separate the three witnesses, and individually interview them. Each describes a different story of the accident based on their unique perception and processing filters.

A 2008 movie titled *Vantage Point* portrayed this phenomenon well. The plot involves the investigation of an assassination attempt on the president of the United States in Salamanca, Spain. Investigators must piece together clues provided by multiple individuals who witnessed the shooting but all from different vantage points or perspectives. Each of the witnesses think their conclusions are the complete story. But for the investigators, each witness's story has troubling gaps. Only when the investigators blend the accounts together does the full picture emerge thereby allowing them to solve the case.[50]

In every situation, each person's perception will be unique. Perception is often closely tied to a person's central nervous system and their personal history. Let's say during your childhood you despised soccer and were forced to practice on your backyard lawn. You may have associated the smell of cut grass with your dislike of soccer. To this day, you do not like the smell of cut grass. Today, the smell of cut grass causes an involuntary and *autonomic* dislike or sickening feeling in your stomach.

If a couple neglects the feelings behind the tense discussion they will automatically default to a flight to intellectualization and perpetuate the fight. Trying to understand the other person's feelings positions the couple to resolve the conflict. It is essential to validate feelings rather than debate perception or experience if increasing intimacy is the goal.

To avoid accusing the other and debating perspective, I recommend you employ a different method, the "I feel _____ when I experience _____" method. To help you identify and define your feelings, the following table lists common feelings within the five primary emotion sets of happy, sad, angry, scared, and confused.

HAPPY	SAD	ANGRY	SCARED	CONFUSED
Admired	Burdened	Abused	Afraid	Ambivalent
Appreciated	Condemned	Betrayed	Alarmed	Awkward
Assured	Crushed	Disgusted	Appalled	Baffled
Cheerful	Defeated	Displeased	Apprehensive	Bewildered
Confident	Dejected	Enraged	Defensive	Bothered
Determined	Demoralized	Exploited	Desperate	Constricted
Ecstatic	Depressed	Fuming	Dreadful	Directionless
Elated	Deserted	Furious	Fearful	Disorganized
Encouraged	Devastated	Hateful	Frantic	Distracted
Energized	Distraught	Hostile	Horrified	Doubtful
Excited	Drained	Humiliated	Insecure	Flustered
Exuberant	Empty	Incensed	Intimidated	Foggy
Grateful	Exhausted	Jealous	Overwhelmed	Hesitant
Gratified	Grievous	Outraged	Panicky	Immobilized
Joyful	Helpless	Patronized	Petrified	Misunderstood
Jubilant	Hopeless	Rebellious	Shaken	Perplexed
Justified	Humble	Repulsed	Shocked	Puzzled
Loved	Miserable	Resentful	Skeptical	Staggered
Marvelous	Pitiful	Ridiculed	Startled	Surprised
Optimistic	Rejected	Sabotaged	Suspicious	Torn
Proud	Sorrowful	Seething	Swamped	Trapped
Relieved	Terrible	Spiteful	Tense	Troubled
Resolved	Uncared For	Strangled	Terrified	Uncertain
Respected	Unloved	Throttled	Threatened	Uncomfortable
Terrific	Unwanted	Used	Tormented	Undecided
Thrilled	Worthless	Vengeful	Uneasy	Unsettled
Valued	Wounded	Vindictive	Vulnerable	Unsure

Upon consulting the feelings list, instead of saying, "You never put your dishes in the dishwasher" say, "I feel displeased when I experience seeing dirty dishes on the counter or the sink." Instead of saying, "You always leave your dirty clothes on the floor" say, "I feel incensed when I see dirty clothes on the floor." Instead of saying, "You hurt me" say, "I feel hurt when I experience your angry words." Of course, the receiver of those words needs to employ active listening skills to keep the dialogue productive—*affirm*, *inquire*, and *repeat/reflect*. An exchange like this comprised of *I* statements and AIR listening will provide you, as a couple, with the opportunity to problem solve together rather than debate which allows intimacy to flourish and grow.

Maintaining the Self

The last *rule of the road* we will cover deals with the paradoxical nature of *two becoming one*. Recall that our definition of intimacy from chapter 1 is "a close relationship that does not operate at the expense of the self, with a self that does not operate at the expense of the other, and in which each is fully known and faithfully loved." This definition emphasizes the importance of the participants, in this case husband and wife, maintaining a separateness of identity at the same time they are *becoming one* in the closest of relationships possible.

We often overlook this essential aspect of marriage. In attempting to make *us*, we sometimes lose the distinctness of *you* and *me*. One may act in ways that causes the other to diminish the size or volume of themselves. In other words, the relationship is operating at the expense of the self, provoked by one operating at the expense of the other. The healthiest marriages allow for each companion to maintain autonomy with separate interests, friendships, activities, and opinions while at the same time merging the two into one. I depict this goal in the *Me-You-Us* graphic:

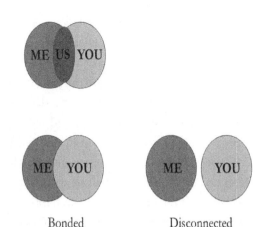

Enmeshed   Bonded   Disconnected

In order to maintain a healthy relationship, a couple needs to navigate the complexities of merging their separate lives into an *us* without falling into the pit of enmeshment on one extreme or disconnection on the other extreme. Notice that on the enmeshment side of the graphic, the *me* and *you* have hazy borders and the *me* is mostly hidden and crowded out by the *you*. This occurs when one or both companions mistakenly believe that for the two to become one, one must reduce to zero, or at least something less than one.

Although we are called to lay down our lives for others, this does not mean we must lose our distinctiveness. If God required this, He would not have included "loving our self" within the two greatest commandments passage in Matthew 22: 37–38. Furthermore, Paul would not have combined looking out for our own interests with looking out for the interests of others in Philippians 2:4 after he instructs us to consider others as more important than ourselves in the preceding verse.

Barriers to Maintaining the Self

The concept of *codependency* contains the dynamic of losing the self. You may be familiar with this term in relation to alcoholism, drug addiction, domestic violence, or chronic and debilitating illness of a loved one. Codependency occurs when one becomes overly dependent upon the other for emotional support and the one depended on feels they have no purpose without the other.[51] In other words, the caregiver needs to be needed so much they are willing to endure excessive personal cost and self-sacrifice. The dependency becomes unhealthy and transitions into codependency.[52]

Codependency can occur in contexts other than those previously referenced (i.e., alcoholism, drug addiction, domestic violence, and chronic, debilitating illness). It can happen in marriage without any of those conditions when one simply becomes dependent on the other to define them. The result is loss of a clear and distinct self.

Loss of self also occurs when dominance exists. If one personality tends to overpower the other, as can be the case with a reactive *Director* temperament, the overpowered one will, over time, lose parts of themselves. It can be beneficial for the couple to examine their current relationship dynamics to determine if there are signs of one or both losing their sense of self.

An uncomplicated way to do this examination is for each companion to draw a large square on a piece of paper to represent their entire marital environment or emotional space. Then each companion, on their own paper, draws or fills in the portion of the emotional space they feel they inhabit and the portion of the emotional space they feel their companion takes up. Finally, compare the drawings. A healthy marriage is one in which both companions take up roughly equal emotional space in the drawing. If one of the inhabited spaces is significantly larger than the other on either of the companion's drawings, *codependency* or *dominance* could be occurring. Couples should discuss this either together or with a counselor.

Voice and Choice

When there is healthy bonding and an optimal balance of *Me-You-Us*, there is also an abundance of choice and voice in the relationship. As previously mentioned in chapter 1, choice is freedom of decision; voice is freedom of opinion. Both are essential elements for an intimate relationship. Lack, or inhibition, of choice or voice leads to loss of self. A marriage with the appropriate amount of choice is one in which permission questions are asked.

For example, "Do you have a moment to talk?" or "Would you be willing to help me with the dishes?" or "Is it OK if I go out with my buddies tonight?" are questions that extend choice. But, to have genuine choice, the asker must be OK with a *yes* answer or a *no* answer. If any punishment, *cold shoulder*, or other shunning or dismissive type of reaction awaits the one who chooses to say no, then choice does not really exist.

For voice to exist, the couple must implement the listening skills I described at the beginning of this chapter consistently. Poor listening translates into lack of voice for the speaker. Without good listening skills, we dispute and dismiss opinions and desires before we completely understand them. The one with the opinion or desire is effectively silenced, eliminating their voice in the relationship.

Peter and Tiffany, a couple I counseled whose names have been changed to protect confidentiality, provide an excellent illustration of what can happen when choice and voice are compromised. Peter wanted a divorce from his wife of fifteen years and was having an affair. Tiffany did not want the divorce. She was willing to reconcile even though her husband expressed that he no longer loved her and was not sure that he wanted to continue in the marriage. Although many factors contributed to the demise of their marriage, money seemed to be a key factor in draining the emotional strength of this couple. Peter explained that he did not want to live this way any longer. "I don't enjoy the relationship anymore, and I want out."

As we began to explore this couple's history, it became evident that Peter had never felt any emotional control in his relationship with Tiffany. Peter's business was not growing at the rate they had hoped, and Tiffany was bringing in most of the income. A deeper look into Peter's emotional status revealed he was emotionally spent. He could not focus on things; he was numb, depressed, and found little joy in life.

He had one too many emotional withdrawals related to *their* money. The harder Peter tried to be successful in his company, the worse the situation became. He had lost any hope that he would gain ground. So, whenever Tiffany asked him to help around the house, Peter already felt like a failure. It was like he was a *paid hand* without any say in the family's future. Peter's emotional bank account was slowly and steadily depleted over fifteen years of marriage.

It is important to note that this type of emotional depletion does not happen in a vacuum. While constructing a genogram (an expanded family tree diagram), Peter revealed that while he and his siblings were growing up, his father was relentless about demanding things from them that were oftentimes unreasonable. His father would never give Peter or his siblings the opportunity to negotiate on tasks around the farm. In other words, they had no choice. Peter's father was the authority and there was no room for discussion. His words were final in all situations—the *commanding* leadership style. Therefore, Peter never learned how to negotiate with another person. You could say that this grown man was developmentally an infant when it came to negotiating issues of life.

So, you can probably guess what happened to Peter in his marriage. From the very beginning of his marriage to Tiffany, her demands whittled away his self-esteem. Tiffany came from a lengthy line of strong women, and she knew how to assert herself. She could negotiate with the best of people. Peter perceived Tiffany's negotiation tactics as authoritarian and demanding rather than negotiating and compromising. Without realizing what was going on, Peter was relating to his wife as he had related to his father.

Although Peter did not enjoy his wife's antics and demanding way, her style of communicating (being rather straightforward) and his style of acquiescing (giving in and just going with the flow as he had done with his father) felt familiar or comfortable to him. Since childhood, Peter had practiced neglecting his own feelings. Therefore, during his marriage to Tiffany, he did what came naturally to him consistent with his self-talk. "Don't express your feelings, people are not really interested in them." And that is exactly what he did during his marriage. Hence, Peter had no voice in the relationship. He was not only clueless about Tiffany's feelings, but he was completely unaware of his own.

Their marriage worked for a while until Peter became completely bereft of emotion. Rather than self-destruct, he tried to self-medicate through another relationship. Thus, the affair with his colleague at work. Although there was much more to Peter and Tiffany's problems than money, there was no question that the lack of control over finances and reduced choice and voice were the catalysts to his emotional destruction and, subsequently, the demise of their marriage.

The all-telling statement expressed by most people in similar circumstances is what Peter said. "If I do not get out of this relationship, I will die." Perhaps a more enlightening way to express those sentiments is to say, "I am depleted. My emotional bank account is empty. Unless there are some emotional deposits for me in this relationship, I will retreat, or worse, connect with someone who understands me."

Couples must be careful to ensure each has adequate choice and voice to allow intimacy to flourish and grow. A good place to start is for each to rate the level of choice and voice they feel they have on a scale from one to ten, with one being little or no choice and voice, and ten being an abundance of choice and voice.

Hierarchy of Needs

Another related aspect of choice and voice to consider is the degree to which each companion feels emotionally safe in the relationship. In the 1940s, American psychologist, Abraham Maslow, postulated that there are five levels of needs each person possesses that undergird their motivation and decision-making.[53] These needs, he asserted, were to be understood as a hierarchy which he visualized as a pyramid. Because of the hierarchical nature of these needs, one could not seek satisfaction of the needs near the top of the pyramid if the needs at the base of the pyramid were unmet.

In Maslow's system, human needs progress from *physiological* (i.e., food, water clothing, shelter, and sleep), to *safety* (i.e., protection from violence and theft, emotional stability and well-being, health security, and financial security), to *love and belonging* (i.e., friendships, family bonds, social groups), to *esteem* (i.e., self-respect, self-esteem), and finally to *self-actualization* (i.e., education, skill-building, refining of talents, caring for others).

So, according to Maslow, one must have their *physiological* needs met first before they can have any chance of having their *safety* needs met. *Physiological* and *safety* needs must be met to be able to pursue the fulfillment of *love and belonging* needs. *Physiological, safety,* and *love and belonging* needs must be met in order for the individual to have their *esteem* needs satisfied. Finally, the fulfillment of *physiological, safety, love and belonging,* and *esteem* needs are prerequisites to the individual being able to participate in *self-actualization* activities.

Notice that *safety* needs must be met before *love and belonging* needs can be pursued. Safety is essential to close relationships. Without it, one or both will be unable to risk and be vulnerable. How safe do you feel in your relationship? Use the following scale to plot your current sense of feeling emotionally safe with your companion:

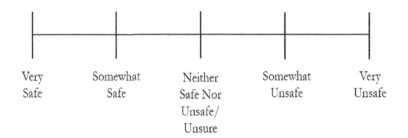

| Very Safe | Somewhat Safe | Neither Safe Nor Unsafe/ Unsure | Somewhat Unsafe | Very Unsafe |

To sum up where we have traveled so far on our path out of reactivity to a responsive marriage, let's review the elements that comprise what I call The Responsive Marriage Equation.

The Responsive Marriage Equation

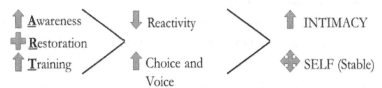

When we increase awareness and training, then add the restorative power of Jesus, it leads to reduced reactivity and increased choice and voice, thereby increasing intimacy while maintaining stable and distinct selves.

Discussion Starter Questions

- *For Couples or Groups*
  - As you read about the concept of listening well, what grade would you give yourself in this skill from *A* to *F*? NOTES:_____
  _____
  _____

○ How easy or difficult is it for you to express your true feelings and why?
NOTES:_____

_____

_____

○ Setup a role-playing scenario. Have one person describe their day while the other person uses the AIR method to listen well.
NOTES:_____

_____

_____

• *For Couples Only*
○ Give each other a grade, from *A* to *F*, on listening. Tell your companion what you are going to do to improve your listening skills.
NOTES:_____

_____

_____

○ Pick a recent event you and your companion experienced together that DID NOT have any conflict. Use the "I feel _____ when I experience _____" format to describe the feelings you had about the event while the other uses AIR to listen well. Then switch roles and let the listener be the speaker and the speaker be the listener. After this, describe how this process was for you.
NOTES:_____

_____

_____

○ Separately, take a piece of paper, draw a large square to represent your marriage environment and entire emotional space, then fill in the portion of the square you feel you take up and the portion of the square you feel your companion takes up. Compare your drawings and discuss the implications and differences using "I feel _____ when I experience_____" statements and the AIR listening method.
NOTES:_____

_____

_____

○ Using a scale from one to ten, with one being little or no choice and voice, and ten being an abundance of choice and voice, how much choice and voice do you feel you have in your relationship? What can you and your companion do to increase choice and voice for each other?
NOTES:_____

_____

_____

○ Using the scale provided in the chapter, assess the degree to which you feel emotionally safe with your companion separately and then come together to discuss the results. What can each of you do to increase the level of emotional safety in your relationship?
NOTES:_____

_____

_____

○ As you examine the *Me-You-Us* graphic together, does your relationship have any signs of enmeshment or disconnection? Discuss ways you can move to more of a bonded relationship.

NOTES:_____

_____

_____

FINDING TIME FOR EACH OTHER

Victor and Connie live a jet-set life of travel and excitement. They are the envy of their friends and family: rich, young, talented, with a bright future. Nothing can get in their way except for each other. Their marriage is on the rocks—no love and no hatred, just indifference. Their stares resemble those of the San Diego Zoo alligators with no visible movement yet ready to pounce if the observer were to step into their world. Victor is at the top of his class in his particular field, while Connie pursues her preferred career path with vigor. They are a stunning couple and, by all worldly standards, set on a trajectory toward success. They are preparing to purchase a second home in southern California where most only dream of owning a single, modest residence.

Everything about Victor and Connie screams success—but at what cost? My curiosity gets the best of me during our first session. I quickly ask, "Tell me about how you rest." Victor flippantly replies, "What do you mean by that? We rest all the time: in planes, in fancy restaurants, in airports around the world. We get lots of rest. I'm up on the current literature comparing good sleep to nutrition." With no hesitation, I ask the question in a different way. "How do you 'rest stop' in your busyness or find a moment of reprieve?"

The number one challenge for a couples' therapist is the two not finding time to do their therapy homework. Even if they do the homework, many don't take the time to apply the homework concepts to their relationship. Most couples under my therapeutic care can't seem to locate five minutes a day to read a book together or apply proven tools for relationship improvement. For Victor and Connie, and similar couples with time management troubles, I ask them to complete the Time-Margin Calculator. This simple tool allows a couple to analyze their daily/weekly activities and purposely allocate time for "rest stops" and relationship enhancement.

Well, what happened to Victor and Connie? They applied their business acumen to their marriage. Upon completion of the Time-Margin Calculator, Victor realizes he spends far too much time playing video games. Connie discovers her Instagram use is overpowering other important pursuits. They commit to reallocating their time slots to open up ten minutes per day for investment in their marriage. This results in marriage rejuvenation for them.

CHAPTER 7

REST STOPS

Driving long distances is not one of my favorite things to do. Traveling the highways of certain states in certain areas can subject you to long stretches without any signs of civilization. In Utah, there is a 110-mile segment of Interstate 70 where there are no motorist services, no gas stations, no bathrooms, and no exits. This can challenge even the most seasoned long-distance driver. Travelers need rest stops, someplace to get out, stretch their legs, and empty their bladders.

In marriage, we need rest stops as well. Marital rest stops allow us time for playful and relaxed interaction. They keep us refreshed and rejuvenated. They brighten our spirits and draw us closer together. Unfortunately, if we are not purposeful, the frenzy of everyday life causes us to miss the rest stops and just keep going. While this may be great for reducing travel time, it is detrimental to marital intimacy.

Enjoying the Moment

One priority often neglected in marriage is carving out time so that the couple can nurture and expand their emotional intimacy and connection. Soccer practices, piano lessons, and youth events at church pull families in many directions these days. Either a couple can learn to be intentional and manage their schedules, or these activities will control their life.

Just this week, I once again heard another couple bemoaning their frantic schedule, "What do you mean time for each other—we can barely get our child to the next event!" There is no doubt we reside in a busy society too often running from one responsibility to the next. However, a healthy couple engages in intentional behavior. The age-old question that is worth asking ourselves is, *Are we doing the right things or are we just doing a lot of good things?* Soccer, music, school functions, and church activities are all exceptionally good, but are they the right activities for this time?

My wife, Robin, and I plan how many meals we will have together and, within reason, the time of day we will experience them. It may sound a bit contrived, but current research indicates mealtimes together can be one of the best ways for couples to create and sustain intimacy. Decide how many meals you plan to enjoy together per day and per week. You will find greater opportunities for intimacy building. It is simple math, if *you* don't decide your mealtimes together, your schedule will crowd them out.

Then plan how many date-moments you would like per month or per week. Typically, Robin and I have thought of date-moments in terms of an outing—leaving the kids with a sitter and taking time away from the home for just the two of us to be together. This activity is vital and couples should not neglect it.

However, we often miss short moments during the day when we, as a couple, can *date* one another. These moments can be utilized in purposeful ways to genuinely enjoy one another. They may range from short interactions with devotional readings and prayer to discussing current events. The important thing to remember is that you, as a couple, decide when these times will be. Otherwise, life's responsibilities will decide for you causing them to never occur.

During a recent couple's seminar, I asked those participating what creative things they do for fun, which is simply a way to continuously date one another. I was amazed at the couple's creativity. I heard, "We read books together," "Pillow fights are our number one date night event," "We go bird watching," "Water gun fights are delightful after a hard week," and "We love the mornings when we can read a short devotional and pray."

Believe it or not, one couple said, "Well, we have this mud pit in our backyard. One day we slipped into it accidentally and found ourselves mud wrestling. We've kept the backyard mud pit and periodically make it one of our date moments." I kept my eye on this couple during that weekend seminar. They were extremely playful and energetic with each other. Their mud wrestling events topped the chart as the best idea for *dating* your companion.

Barriers to Enjoying the Moment

Perhaps the most important word in a couple's vocabulary is *no*. The ability to say no to things and events that do not nourish the marriage is imperative. The famous line used in drug education curriculum, "Just say no!" may be worth considering here as you become more intentional in your marriage. You may need to practice this by standing in front of a mirror from time to time and saying, "No!" so that you have time to say *yes* to each other. Saying yes to each other means learning to enjoy the moment together.

Enjoying the moment, however, can be an unreachable expectation for couples with children. Most parents seeking marital counseling have no time to enjoy the moment. They need more time to spare. Is it possible to remain grounded, calm, and present when children demand your attention 24/7?

Many mothers of young children have turned their bathrooms into retreat centers to get a momentary reprieve. But little voices and tiny fingers find their way under the bathroom door of Mom's retreat center, asking for one more thing from the frazzled mommy needing just a few minutes alone. From the needs of a diaper change to the

PERHAPS THE MOST IMPORTANT WORD IN A COUPLE'S VOCABULARY IS NO. THE ABILITY TO SAY NO TO THINGS AND EVENTS THAT DO NOT NOURISH THE MARRIAGE IS IMPERATIVE. THE FAMOUS LINE USED IN DRUG EDUCATION CURRICULUM, "JUST SAY NO!" MAY BE WORTH CONSIDERING HERE AS YOU BECOME MORE INTENTIONAL IN YOUR MARRIAGE.

soccer shoes left at home, from spending money for school events, financial support for college, and young adult weddings, to help with housing costs and grandchildren's needs, most parents struggle throughout adult life trying their best to manage their schedules but finding precious little time for each other. Enjoying the moment is the elusive dream of most parents.

Early in my therapy practice, I contemplated whether to allow parents to bring their new infant into their couples' therapy sessions. My three decades of teaching developmental theory at the university level taught me that the infant should be out of earshot of their parents' negative emotions. Having the infant in the counseling session would no doubt undermine that goal. From the gestation time of infancy to about six years of life and beyond, children absorb emotion as the brain develops abstract thought. Nevertheless, I decided to allow each couple to make the decision.

My colleagues giggle a bit when I share with them that I request all parents who choose to bring their infants into the therapy office to sign a release of responsibility form for their infant. Although less than ideal, a side benefit of having the infant in the couples' session is observing the couples' handling of interruptions, often revealing the couple's inability to enjoy each other. This became a great starting point for discussing ways for them to enjoy the moment together.

Being Self-Reflective

However, enjoying the moment can be a more daunting task to accomplish than parenting itself. From the beginning of parenting to later seasons of life, we teach our children to think about others instead of themselves. We tell them to consider the feelings of others over their own, be polite, eat with their mouth shut, sit up at the dinner table, don't slouch, and on and on it goes. We focus on behaviors more than promoting self-reflection. We are, of course, teaching correct behaviors for good character development. But if

I have one regret in my parenting, it would be that I did not take enough time to encourage our two children to self-reflect. Having spent my career assisting university students and patients in growing their self-reflection skills, I often ask myself if I fell short in assisting my children to enjoy the moment and learn the art of *being* rather than *doing*.

I remember our first attempts to try and teach our oldest child, Savannah, how to be self-reflective. I asked her which dress she would like to wear to church, blue or yellow. As a three-year-old, Savannah was not sure which dress to pick since she liked both. Her first response was to ask me which one I liked. I responded, "I'm happy to share my favorite after you decide the one you most like." Savannah looked around with uncertainty. Peering out the window and noticing the blue sky she turned back toward me and boldly blurted out, "The blue one. I like the blue sky; I like the blue dress." We were off to a good start encouraging Savannah to self-reflect and make her own decisions.

Self-reflection is a valuable tool, not only for learning more about yourself but also for learning to enjoy the moment. Another helpful method for learning to enjoy the moment is to increase awareness of your five senses.

To better understand how this can help you train yourself to enjoy the moment, let me walk you through my morning routine as I take an early morning jog with Sadie, our family dog, and describe the ways my five senses are stimulated.

Tuning into Our Senses

Sadie is an Australian shepherd who loves to guide me and everyone else as if we are a member of her herd. It is part of her instinctual nature. Since we live on the coast, I run by the bay and the ocean with her. Sometimes, she leads us off the beaten path to explore the landscape and surrounding beauty where we experience new moments of enjoying our five senses.

The first sense I notice during preparation for our adventures together is sight. At approximately 5:15 a.m. each morning, my alarm wakes me and I quietly prepare for the jog trying not to awaken my wife, Robin. I begin by thanking God for another day of health and vigor and for all of His many blessings as I briefly look at my wife resting in our bed.

Next, I begin the process of preparing Sadie and me for the jog by noticing how quiet everything is throughout our home. I walk to Sadie's *condo*, a more endearing name for her dog kennel. She is always happy to see me as evidenced by her backside wiggling in anticipation of our run and outside adventures. You may be aware that Australian shepherds have a recessive gene for a shortened tail. Instead of Sadie's tail wagging, her bottom naturally wiggles when displaying delight and happiness. You can watch YouTube demonstrations of Aussie wiggles that are quite hilarious.

I glance out the back sliding doors of our condo at the lights shimmering in the distance. I observe the nearby lights of our community mirroring off the smooth glasslike quiet bay waters that form a channel through my neighborhood. I find myself thanking the Lord for the opportunity to view such beautiful surroundings. I love the outdoors and God's exquisite creation. I especially enjoy early mornings and the calming effect it has on me.

In the winter I bundle up and place Sadie's collar on her. She patiently waits for our daily ritual. I look into Sadie's brown eyes, noticing her excitement for the upcoming run. I observe how quiet the streets and sidewalks are this time of morning. Most occupants of surrounding homes have not yet awakened, so interior lighting is absent. I see flowers blooming here in San Diego County, even in the wintertime.

One area I run through has an abundance of bougainvillea vines. One of the first photos of Robin and me captures us standing next to a bougainvillea bush with its bright red leaves. On occasion, light winds create movement in the surrounding palm trees. If I am focused on the channel bay water along the run, I often see fish jumping which creates a familiar swirl of water that takes me back to my childhood. My best friend, David, and I were avid anglers. On most Saturdays, we would walk in the dark to a farm lake close to my home in San Luis Obispo, California to enjoy a day of fishing. We loved watching the fog burn off the glassy-like pond as the sun appeared above the horizon.

Touch is another sensory experience I notice each morning. I feel my feet on the ground, my socks, the running shoes with soft soles, the solid asphalt street, and the cement sidewalk. My feet feel spongy, light, and a bit free to move. Touch is essential to well-being.[54] Touch lowers breathing and heart rate and calms the limbic system, the part of the brain where anxiety starts. When I open the little dog bag to pick up Sadie's deposited morning business, I focus on the texture of the bag. Often I must moisten my fingers and apply a bit of pressure to get the bag open. As the sun is peaking over the mountains in the east, I feel the warmth of its touch. I turn toward the sun without thinking.

Sadie and I turn west as we enter the part of our jog where we deposit Sadie's plastic bag into the trash canister. I feel the texture of the lid as I open the canister and drop the bag inside. As we continue jogging westward, we lean on the brick fence and begin our half-mark stretch. As Sadie begins her usual sniffing of the fifteen-acre park's grassy area, I am looking out over the Pacific Ocean remembering how Robin and I played with our kiddos on that exact beach. We taught them to surf, built sandcastles, played catch with a football, and much more. For a brief moment, I am there with Robin, Savannah, and Daniel with our feet feeling the caress of the Pacific Ocean that spans part of the globe and connects us to other parts of the world.

I feel satisfied, proud, and deeply connected to those I most love. I take off my shoes and socks here. The constant ocean movement over my feet and sand give me a calming sensation unmatched by any other experienced sensation. I look above the ocean to the distant west which ignites a thought that there is no end above the horizon.

I enjoy the tactile sensation of the waves rushing in on my lower legs as the water's power removes portions of the sand underneath my feet with the undulation of the tide. I am moving—yet not really. The dissipating sand under my feet creates a sense that I must refocus to maintain my balance. I focus on that touch sensation. Multiple memories are rushing back and forth in my mind throughout this sensory-laden moment. Touch is a remarkable way to de-escalate anxiety, fears, and doubts.

Noticing smells is another way to enjoy the moment. The saltwater is powerfully aromatic when the ocean is calm, especially in the early mornings. I involuntarily take a few deep breaths of the salty ocean air. Without realizing it, my body begins relaxing in the memories of growing up in San Luis Obispo, some three hundred miles north of San Diego, where, at the beach, many of my church's youth events occurred. I remember laughter, hot dog roasts, s'mores, and Pastor Mel Rich leading us with his guitar in the all-time favorite song, *Kumbaya*. I feel safe, connected as part of a community, and loved.

On other occasions, Pastor Mel and I would, independent of the youth group, make our way to the beach to surf some of California's best waves. Those memories flood my mind as I jog along the beach. I feel essential, believed in, and meaningful. The lead pastor of my church viewed me as important enough to spend many a late afternoon surfing alongside me while we experienced the smells of beautiful Southern California.

Back on my jog, I am feeling more relaxed in the present moment in San Diego but also reminiscing about past years as a young adolescent. I need to find the soft-cut grass so Sadie can continue her early morning business. We are now jogging along the bay in the park near us. The cut grass reminds me of happy moments playing soccer, baseball, softball, football, basketball, flying kites, and wrestling on the green grass park with our two children, Savannah and Daniel. That park is directly across from Savannah and Daniel's childhood home.

The sense of smell has a powerful way of connecting us to long-term memory. Scents go directly to the brain's smell center, the olfactory bulb connected to the amygdala and hippocampus, bypassing the thalamus that acts as a relay station for the other four senses. The hippocampus and amygdala enable a person to experience intense emotions and memories when they smell something. More than any of the other four senses, smell *immediately* links us to emotions and memory. This is why people who have lost a loved one will often lament that they miss the sweet scent of the one who passed. Some of my patients have shared with me that they cannot dispose of their deceased loved one's clothing. Each day they will hold up the clothing—once worn by that loved one—to their face to remember them by the smells of their wardrobe.

As I smell the cut grass on my morning jog, I remember the weekly lawn care I performed as a kid. I maintained the front and backyards of my childhood home. Annually, my dad and I removed the old lawn and replanted an entirely new crop of green, lush grass. We rented a tiller to remove all elements of the old grass, including its roots, before spreading seed for the new lawn. Since San Luis Obispo borders Northern California, nighttime can cool significantly, causing frost to engulf the city during a good portion of the winter. We placed transparent plastic tarps over the newly seeded front and backyard grass to prevent freezing of the tender shoots.

While my current experience takes me back to that memory, I feel like a farmer awaiting the harvest. I remember the first signs of newly sprouting grass buds. I feel proud, influential, and successful. My dad, a respected college professor, allowed me to experience these moments from early childhood which formed and shaped my connection to nature. When fully blooming, the soft, succulent grass would undergo its first trimming event. I would push the hand mower blades across the lush grass while taking in the aroma of fresh-cut lawn. "We did it," I say to myself. In later years, the push mower became a gas-driven mower. I feel proud, capable, and self-reliant, believing my family, especially my dad, is proud of my efforts.

Pausing for Perspective

Let's pause for a moment to emphasize what is occurring here. As I am experiencing this present moment jog with Sadie along the beach, I am purposefully noticing the stimuli that is bombarding my five senses. I take time to process it internally, in my mind, and allow the sensory experience to also take me back to fond memories.

Notice also, that as stimulus is activating my senses I am labeling the feelings I experience. Most of the time, due to our busy schedules and constant motivation to *get to the next thing*, we miss the enjoyable moments that are right in front of us. As an American and a multitasker, you will have to retrain yourself to stay in the present moment, consciously process the sensory input, allow pleasant memories to bubble up, and label the feelings the sensory input and memories elicit.

On my run, my surroundings also heighten my sense of hearing. The streets, sidewalks, and park near our home are quiet. The ducks, American white pelicans, reddish egrets (a large heron), and seagulls, create a symphony of bird calls and a wonderfully soothing environment. I consider them my friends. I listen to each of the birds' distinct sounds. Some are abrupt, loud, and ostentatious, while others are soft and contemplative. The American white pelican is particularly boisterous. They are like a friend who forewarns you of danger. They announce their arrival with rambunctious squawking and their flight is a remarkable sight. With a wingspan of 95 to 120 inches, I can hear their mighty wings flap in the air. With the second largest wingspan of any Northern American bird and weight between 7.7 and 30 pounds, this bird demands attention. It is much larger than a bald eagle but smaller than a California condor.[55]

I genuinely admire birds and continue appreciating their unique sounds. As a kid, I often attempted to mimic their vocalizations. Except for recent years, I have always had a pet parakeet. Our daughter, Savannah, has carried on this tradition with her current parakeet named Tweety Bird. I would sit for hours trying to communicate with our pet birds. We would occasionally let Perkie, my childhood bird, out of her cage to fly around the house. She and I developed such a rapport that I could whistle to her from across my childhood home and she would fly to my shoulder.

Lest you think my experience with birds and bird calls is all in vain, this past week while working with a six-year-old patient and his mother, the child asked if I could whistle. I rarely hear that question from a patient. Taken by surprise, this exchange became one of those delightful play therapy moments a therapist can rarely engineer. I asked him to listen to my whistle which contained two sounds emitted simultaneously. My *skill*, if you can call it that, developed over many years trying to mimic bird sounds. I started by whistling one tone and then continued with that sound while overlaying it with another. My six-year-old patient's eyes brightened, and an inquisitive smile enveloped his face.

I responded, "When we carefully listen, we can hear unusual sounds. This can quiet us until we are focused." My patient laughed, and we quickly moved onto another topic. Listening to sounds can be a calming experience.

Then there is the sense of taste. During my run, I can taste the salt in the air. It has quite an unusual taste. Sadie regularly sniffs and randomly picks up things with her mouth but does not necessarily swallow everything. She is only interested in what seems like a treat to her. For years, the sound of the word *treat* sent Sadie's limbic system into high alert. She has never found a treat she did not like. On occasion, when I reach down to pet her and my face is too close to hers, I catch some of her hair in my mouth—not a pleasant sensation or likable taste. Australian shepherds are notorious for shedding. Sadie is quite a normal Aussie and regularly loses her hair. The piece of hair in my mouth becomes uncomfortable, so I immediately attempt to spit it out.

Incidentally, one of my best times for prayer is during my daily jog. I suspect while running, my diaphragmatic breathing enables my brain to fully oxygenate, assisting me to focus on listening to

God while enjoying His created beauty. The combination of physical exertion, heightened awareness of my five senses, and encountering the beauty of God's creation all around me causes me to replay memorized scripture and meaningful statements from others about the presence of God as I run with Sadie.

As I am writing this chapter on the five senses and how to de-escalate anxiety and enjoy the moment, our dog, Sadie, is in her last few days. She has cancer at age six—a devastating blow. We are within a week or two of her impending death. If you have ever lost a pet, you probably know what my family and I are experiencing.

Shortly after Sadie arrived at our home as a puppy, my wife, Robin, began a challenging cancer season, which I describe a bit more in chapter 9. During this time, Sadie grew remarkably close to Robin, sensing Robin's pain and suffering. When opening a can of Sadie's food during Robin's cancer battle, I was completely unaware that my brain was beginning to associate Sadie's food with Robin's cancer pain. Sadie's food smell seemed to take on a negative taste for me. Fortunately, I have never actually tasted Sadie's food. However, to this date, my paired serving of Sadie's food and Robin's suffering gives me a negative sense of *pseudo-tasting* Sadie's food. It is quite an unusual experience.

Stop and Smell the Roses

I challenge you to begin noticing and mentally processing input from your five senses in a more purposeful fashion. Take the time to notice what you see, hear, touch, smell, and taste at various times during your day. Try this when you and your companion are together and see if you can learn to hone the skill of enjoying the moment.

We hear the suggestion to *enjoy the moment* whispering from various maxims or adages that may routinely come across our social media feeds including:

- "Stop and smell the roses." (re-phrasing from the 1960s of a sentiment found in a 1956 autobiography by golfer Walter Hagen, born 1892, died 1969, who said, "You're only here for a short visit. Don't hurry. Don't worry. And be sure to stop to smell the flowers along the way.")[56]
- "Living in the moment means letting go of the past and not waiting for the future. It means living your life consciously, aware that each moment you breathe is a gift." (Attributed to Oprah Winfrey, American talk show host, television producer, and philanthropist born 1954.)
- "Mix a little foolishness with your serious plans. It is lovely to be silly at the right moment." (Attributed to Horace, Roman poet born 65 BC, died 8 BC.)
- "Live in the present, launch yourself on every wave, find eternity in each moment." (Attributed to Henry David Thoreau, American naturalist, essayist, and poet, born 1817, died 1862.)
- "The great science to live happily is to live in the present." (Attributed to Pythagoras, Greek philosopher born 570 BC, died 495 BC.)

As captured in a few of these maxims, the idea of enjoying the moment is inextricably linked with the notion of *staying present*. When we let our minds wander to ruminate on past frustrations or predict the future, we fail to stay present and enjoy the moments we are currently experiencing. The buildup of anxiety is one notable obstacle to enjoying the moment that we will cover in the next chapter.

For this chapter, I want to focus on three other obstacles that you as a couple will need to overcome to enjoy the moment together. They are *Family Overtaking Marriage*, the *Tyranny of the Urgent* and *Lack of Margin*.

Family Overtaking Marriage

Did you know that the word *priorities*, as a plural word, is a new idea in history? The term *priority*, meaning "the first or prior thing," was only used in a singular context for over five hundred years from its origination. In his bestselling book *Essentialism*, Greg McKeown explains:

> *The word priority came into the English language in the 1400s. It was singular. It meant the very first or prior thing. It stayed singular for the next five hundred years.*
>
> *Only in the 1900s did we pluralize the term and start talking about priorities. Illogically, we reasoned that by changing the word we could bend reality. Somehow, we would now be able to have multiple "first" things.*[57]

One must wonder, then, about the quantity of our priorities. Rather than adjusting the order of our priorities, do we just have too many creating a need to trim down the list? Do we have too many *firsts*?

This could be a place to start as a couple. For example, some Christians may recall being admonished to put "God first, then family, then church." This can be helpful to remember if attending church and church-related activities are getting confused with putting God first and, in the process, starting to crowd out time with your family. It can also be helpful in conveying the truism that if you do not put God first, your tendencies to let the flesh rule (your selfish desires) will escalate and throw the ranked order of other essential elements of your life out of alignment.

What I think is unhelpful about the "God first, then family, then church" adage is it says nothing about where marriage ranks in relation to other *family* priorities. This would be an important conversation for you as a couple to have. For example, where does your marriage rank in priority to your children?

Many couples mistakenly believe that putting their children first will improve their family. Nothing could be further from the truth. If you are married with children, the quality of your family is directly proportional to the quality of your marriage. If your marriage is not solid, like a rock, and your kids do not experience you as being genuinely honoring of, respecting of, affectionate with, and enamored by, each other, all the benefits they receive from your attendance at their soccer games, baseball games, gymnastic meets, and cheerleading competitions will unravel. Your kids need your marriage to thrive and succeed.

And, by the way, you can't fake that with kids. Kids have an amazing way of separating fact from fiction. Any toxicity or reactivity in your marriage will spill over onto them no matter how hard you try to hide it from them. If you want to set them up for success in life, spend less time focused on their academic achievement or sporting prowess and more time on learning how to love their mom or dad well.

As children or teens, they certainly will not admit, or even understand, that they need your marriage to be solid more than they need your collective or individual attention. Nevertheless, I dare say that if the adult children of divorced or estranged parents were asked, in retrospect, which was more important to them, receiving more attention from their parents or happily married parents, they would pick the latter.

I am certainly not suggesting you neglect your children for the sake of maintaining a happy marriage. There is a stark difference between shifting the primary focus of your attention and neglecting your children. When you and your companion love and honor each other well, in consistent fashion and in full view and earshot of your children, they will thrive. That is the best legacy you can pass onto them.

MANY COUPLES MISTAKENLY BELIEVE THAT PUTTING THEIR CHILDREN FIRST WILL IMPROVE THEIR FAMILY. NOTHING COULD BE FURTHER FROM THE TRUTH.

Tyranny of the Urgent

I love the phrase "Tyranny of the Urgent" because it encapsulates in four simple words the devastation that occurs on our ability to effectively manage our time when our priorities get jumbled. The phrase was first used by Charles E, Hummel in an essay he wrote in 1967 published as a booklet by InterVarsity Press with that title. During his lifetime, Hummel was president of Barrington College in Rhode Island and director of Faculty Ministries at InterVarsity Christian Fellowship in Madison, Wisconsin. The booklet was an instant success in both Christian and business circles because it contained sage advice for improving personal effectiveness by managing time in more purposeful ways. Over the years, business management gurus have used Hummel's original concept, including Steven Covey in his book titled *First Things First*.[58]

Hummel starts his work in defining the Tyranny of the Urgent with an interesting premise based on Jesus's pronouncement in John 17:4, "I have finished the work which Thou gavest me to do" (KJV). This statement may seem a bit bewildering to some of us. Jesus's ministry only lasted about three and a half years and He is now done. There were certainly more people who needed physical and emotional healing, others who needed release from demon oppression, and many who still had not heard the *good news*. Yet, Jesus could, in perfect calm and peace, say that His work was finished. How can this be?

Hummel points out that Jesus worked extremely hard while He was here on earth. There are points where the four Gospels confront us with the sheer exhaustion that Jesus must have experienced as He went about doing good. Mark records in his gospel, "When evening came, after the sun had set, they began bringing to Him all those who were sick and those who were demon-possessed. *The whole town was assembled at the door*, and **He** *healed many* that were sick with various diseases and *drove out many demons*" (Mark 1:32-34, emphasis added). In another chapter, Mark records how Jesus was so exhausted after a strenuous day of teaching that He falls asleep in a boat and a severe storm cannot awaken Him (Mark 4: 37–38).

Yet the Gospels also depict a lack of frenzy in Jesus's interactions and journeys. He could spend hours talking to one person, such as the Samaritan woman at the well, and state emphatically to His brothers who wanted Him to go to Judea and reveal Himself as a miracle worker in Judea, "My time is not yet come" (John 7:6a KJV). According to Hummel, in Mark 1:35, we learn the key to Jesus's ability to accomplish a lot of remarkable things but not be undone by a frenzied pace. "Very early in the morning, while it was still dark, He got up, went out, and made His way to a deserted place. And He was praying there." In short, Jesus waited for His Father's instructions before proceeding. Hummel concludes, "By this means He warded off the urgent and accomplished the important."

Future adaptations of Hummel's assertions divide the time of a leader into four quadrants intersecting *important and not important* on the vertical axis and *urgent and not urgent* on the horizontal axis. Advice givers then accompany this division with advice to spend more time in the *important-not urgent* category and not be deceived and distracted by the *urgent-not important* quadrant.

	Urgent	Not -Urgent
Important		
Not-Important		

For our purposes here, I simply want to use this graphic to encourage you, as a couple, to wisely distinguish between the important and the urgent. There are many priorities, good things, which compete for your limited time and attention. But your marriage is hugely important, and you may need to ignore, or at least postpone, more urgent matters to give it the attention it needs and deserves.

Lack of Margin

Margins, in writing, are the space between the words and the edges of the page. When sitting down to write using a word processing software program, it is one of the first things you deal with—setting the margins. By default, most software programs set the margins as one inch at the top, bottom, left-side, and right-side. If you want to fit more words on each page you reduce the margins. Imagine for a moment how unusual it would feel to read a book with absolutely no margins, where the sentences extend across the entire page from the very edge on the left to the very edge on the right. In word processing programs, it is not possible to set the margins to zero. If it were, doing so would cause the printing on the edges of the paper to bleed and smear.

Yet, many of us set our margins at zero when it comes to our schedules. There is absolutely no margin, or space, for one single minute of unplanned events or rest stops. Every minute is filled with work, chores, appointments, to-do list items, church, driving the kids here and there, attending their events, helping them with, or ensuring they do, homework, and a myriad of other activities—none, or little, of which help or improve your marriage.

This lack of margin was the premise of a book first written in 1995 by a medical doctor titled *Margin: Restoring Emotional, Physical, Financial, and Time Reserves to Overloaded Lives.* In the book, Richard A. Swenson, M.D., provides alarming accounts from his own practice of the devastating impacts on the physical body of margin-less living. The opening paragraphs of the book describe the condition this way:

> *The conditions of modern-day living devour margin. If you are homeless, we send you to a shelter. If you are penniless, we offer you food stamps. If you are breathless, we connect you to oxygen. But if you are margin-less, we give you yet one more thing to do.*
>
> *Margin-less is being thirty minutes late to the doctor's office because you were twenty minutes late getting out of the bank because you were ten minutes late dropping the kids off at school because the car ran out of gas two blocks from the gas station—and you forgot your wallet.*
>
> *Margin, on the other hand, is having breath left at the top of the staircase, money left at the end of the month, and sanity left at the end of adolescence.*[59]

In my counseling practice, one of the common refrains I hear when I suggest a couple carve out more time for each other is, "We don't have time for that." I certainly understand their frustration with my suggestion but, the truth is, if they do not purposely make time for each other, it will never happen. The urgent will always eject the important. The more productive response to my suggestion would be, "Our current schedule doesn't include time for us." This acknowledges the truth but also highlights the culprit—your schedule—which is, by the way, within your control.

Examining Our Schedules

To provide rest stops for your marriage, it is imperative that you both examine your schedules closely and be purposeful about incorporating what I call "marriage enhancement activities." These are things you do together as a couple, just the two of you, to strengthen your relationship. Here are a few examples:

- Sit down facing each other and have a conversation with no interruptions and no distractions.
- Go out and get some ice cream or coffee.
- Go out on a date.
- Have sex.
- Give each other back rubs.
- Play a game together.
- Pray together.
- Read a daily devotional together.
- Take a walk together.

I suggest you aim for at least one hour per day for these activities.

The other important purpose of examining your schedules together is to ensure your schedules have margin. When you add up all you do in any given week, including marriage enhancement activities, and subtract it from the 168 hours per week that every human being on the planet must operate within—no more, no less—there should be some remaining time. If there is not, you are living a margin-less life and are susceptible to the ramifications, including heightened anxiety and many physical ailments too numerous to mention.

Here is a simple tool you can use to help you realign your schedule to incorporate marriage enhancement activities and build in personal margin. I call this the Time Margin Optimizer and you can find an on-line, interactive version at http://www.welchtherapyinstitute.com/margin-calculator

TIME MARGIN OPTIMIZER			
Activity	Hours Per Day (To Nearest Qtr Hr)	# of Days Per Week	Hours Per Week
Total Time Available	24.00	7	168.00
Sleeping	8.00	7	56.00
Working at a Job or Vocation	9.00	5	45.00
Food Preparation and Eating	2.00	7	14.00
Personal Care/Prep	1.00	7	7.00
Household Chores and Responsibilities	3.00	1	3.00
Attending Church	2.00	1	2.00
Ministry or Volunteer Activities	2.00	3	6.00
Prayer, Bible Reading, Time with God	0.50	7	3.50
Exercising/Fitness Activities	1.00	5	5.00
Personal Education/Attending School			0.00
Activities with Children/Teens/Grandchildren	1.00	7	7.00
Friendship Development Activities	1.00	2	2.00
Extended Family Activities	2.00	1	2.00
Marriage Enhancement Activities	1.00	7	7.00
OTHER:			0.00
OTHER:			0.00
Personal Margin (Time Remaining)		5.06%	8.50

Laughing to Connect

One last piece of advice for visiting rest stops together in your marriage. Laughter exchange is the first behavior couples enjoy and the first to go when they are under stress. Daily laughter is critical to the health of a couple. The American Lung Association compares laughing to cardio-type exercising for improving cardiovascular, respiratory, and pulmonary function. More specifically, while laughing, the diaphragm, abdomen, and chest muscles tighten, causing the lungs to work harder, pushing air out and allowing new air to enter.[60] If your daily laughter is, for some reason, sidelined, consider making laughter part of your daily interaction.

Early in my therapy sessions with couples, I ask, "When was the last time you laughed together?" At first, when asking this question, it stunned me when so many couples responded to my simple question with a pregnant pause. They were speechless. Other couples would blurt out, "We've never laughed together," or "He (or she) is boring, lacking any sense of humor." Of course, we know this cannot be an entirely true statement. No one is *always* or *never* all the time.

Robin and I have learned some tools we consistently apply to create room for laughter in our marriage. Since the birth of our children, I have been self-elected to be the family scribe. When our children would say or do something of note, I would quickly write the words, events, or behavior in a journal on my laptop. I have pages and pages of funny sayings, hilarious behaviors, and atypical interactions; all written down verbatim to capture the memory. Over the years, we have often read and reread those events and laughed to exhaustion.

Here are a few excerpts from my memory log. On January 10, 2004, as I was putting the kids to bed and singing Christmas songs, Savannah and Daniel wanted to sing the songs individually. As Daniel sang *We Three Kings*, he said, "We three kings who travel from Mars."

On another occasion, we attended Savannah's singing program at school when she was four years old. We videotaped her and watched her up front with the other kids. Savannah did not sing at all. After the event, my wife, Robin, asked Savannah why she didn't sing. She said, "I didn't want to because I was having my quiet time."

These, and many other pages of childhood experiences with our kids, create laughter for Robin and me. You too have moments of laughter with little children. Your children, or a nephew or niece, may be saying these funny quips, and you will soon forget them unless you write them down.

The point is to purposefully incorporate laughter into your marriage. You may read or watch a funny show or movie when life gets too serious. We really like *I Love Lucy* reruns. Your favorite show or movie may be much more recent. Finding what ignites laughter between you is the important piece. Laughter equals connection. And connection is what a couple desires, and needs, the most.

Discussion Starter Questions

- *For Couples or Groups*
  - How good are you at enjoying the moment? What prevents you from enjoying the moment?
    NOTES:_____
    _____
    _____

  - How good are you at being self-reflective?
    NOTES:_____
    _____
    _____

  - Explain a time when you felt like you were intensely aware of your five senses.
    NOTES:_____
    _____
    _____

  - Do you feel like you might be a victim of the Tyranny of the Urgent? Why or why not?
    NOTES:_____
    _____

o How much margin do you think you have in your life right now? How much would you like to have?
NOTES:_____

_____

_____

• *For Couples Only*
  o Do you feel like your family life has overtaken your marriage in terms of importance? What can each of you do individually, and collectively, to raise the level of importance for your marriage?
  NOTES:_____

  _____

  _____

  o Work on the Time Margin Optimizer separately and then come together to discuss the results. How much time are you going to devote to marriage enrichment activities each week? How are you going to help each other create more margin in your schedules?
  NOTES:_____

  _____

  _____

CONSTANT ANXIETY

William and Emma are a well-put-together, attractive couple yet anxiously disconnected from what they want most: *each other*. Each routinely expresses significant anxiety emanating and accelerating from dreadful anticipation. Their anxiety has no speed limit. They seem to be wound tight, always full speed ahead, and always anticipating what may happen next. Emma's anxiety-producing thoughts center around their finances. She runs her own company and finds it difficult to take breaks. She complains that she and William never seem to have enough money. They are always one dollar short. Emma's constant mantra of never having enough is captured in John D. Rockefeller's infamous saying, "How much money does it take to make a man happy? Just one more dollar." Emma experiences constant anxiety to make one more dollar in pursuit of the seemingly elusive dream she has for William and her.

William's anxiety is a bit different but in many ways aligns with Emma's. His work is hands-on and solo. As is usually the case, the couple is opposite in temperament. Emma is much more extroverted expressing outwardly before turning inward, whereas William is introverted processing internally before expressing verbally. The complementarity of their temperaments creates a significant bond between the two as they balance each other's weaknesses. Yet anxiety troubles their marriage and becomes the focus of our work together.

Each session I experience the couple's anxiety engulfing the room. I even find myself a bit anxious during the sessions. I can sense my lungs tighten and my breathing become shallower as the couple transports their anxiety into the therapy room. As is often the case, a couple with shared anxiety brings the dynamics of their childhood homes into the marriage. As far back as William can remember his parents constantly battled and they now sleep in separate rooms and regularly exchange spiteful comments. Emma grew up poor with her mom and dad both working extra jobs to make ends meet. Emma remembers often feeling embarrassed by her hand-me-down clothing. "No way am I going to ever experience this again. Our children are going to have the 'best money can buy'," says Emma.

I call Emma and William my couple without any speed limit. Over time, though, they learn to manage their anxiety, using some of the tools you will learn in this chapter, thereby allowing their relationship to thrive.

CHAPTER 8

SPEED LIMIT

Many will no doubt agree with me on this next assertion. Seeing the flashing lights of a law enforcement vehicle in your rearview mirror generates a sickening and sinking feeling in the pit of the stomach like no other sudden event in life. I hate that feeling. It feels as though you have been caught stealing. You suddenly feel small and diminutive wanting to hang your head in shame. Anxiety rushes up your torso with lightning speed as you look down at your speedometer and see the evidence: you have been caught speeding!

Some husbands and wives could be caught speeding in their marriages. Recall when we learned about the Welch Responsive Cycle in chapter 4, we contrasted the Northern and Southern routes and discussed the dynamic that occurs on the Southern route when escalating events emotionally trigger you. This route is a downhill one that is characterized by high speed. Things happen very quickly on this route in nearly simultaneous fashion. The triggered companion has several physical reactions in rapid succession and quickly propels toward loss of self, emotional flooding, and reactive panic. In a few brief moments, the couple is moving so fast it becomes nearly impossible to pause the momentum. We start saying things we do not really mean and soon it's like a tennis match with two players at the net trying to return each other's *kill shots*. This speeding effect is caused by anxiety.

In order to have healthy expression (responsiveness) in our temperament, we must be in a relatively calm state. When we are in an agitated state, reactivity abounds and the interaction picks up speed. Therefore, to reduce our reactivity we must learn how to manage our anxiety in the moment. To manage it, we need to understand it so that we can apply effective methods and create the possibility for taking the Northern route on the Welch Responsive Cycle.

Understanding Anxiety

Anxiety is common to all. Everyone experiences anxiety because it is a universal reaction to a perceived threat. It is our brain's method for signaling to us that *something is wrong*. It is a productive mechanism that God created for our well-being. Without it, we would not be motivated to take action to extricate ourselves from perilous circumstances. It is the precursor to the fight-flight-freeze response. It is a gift. But it can also feel like a curse.

The prevalence of anxiety in our society has increased dramatically over the years. More people are being diagnosed with Generalized Anxiety Disorder than ever before, and the prevalence of it among children and adolescents has grown dramatically.[61] In 2022, after the disruptions of the COVID-19 pandemic subsided, schools across the nation and around the world reported a significant increase in the number of children experiencing anxiety and aggressive behaviors. At the time of the writing of this book, federal and state governments are spending billions of dollars to try to address what experts are calling a *mental health crisis* for school-aged children in the United States.[62]

Anxiety falls into three categories based on intensity and severity. The first type is *episodic anxiety*. This is the normal, routine type that occurs in response to a particular identifiable event or trigger. It has a distinct starting and ending point bounded by the start and end of the triggering event. This type of anxiety does not tend to be debilitating and does not normally interfere with everyday functioning. It is our body's natural fight-flight-freeze response to what we perceive as a threat.

This type of anxiety would be what you feel if you were walking in the woods and came across a mountain lion. Your brain would go on high alert, adrenaline would be dispensed into your body, your heart rate would increase, your breathing would become shallower, all responses that prepare you to deal with the danger by either fighting, running (not recommended when encountering a mountain lion), or simply freezing in place.

It is also the type that occurs when you must give a speech in front of an audience. Depending on your experience with public speaking, your level of anxiety may be high, moderate, or low, but you would, nevertheless, have anxiety. This is because the outcome is uncertain. They might like you, they might not. Those who do well in these circumstances are those that do not ignore the anxiety or try to suppress it. They merely use it to their advantage to sharpen their senses and ensure they are well prepared.

Generalized anxiety is a more debilitating type because, rather than being acute, it becomes chronic, pervasive, and persistent. The unease and apprehension continue after a precipitating event or trigger has ended. It can interrupt sleep and distract the person from being able to accomplish normal or routine tasks. Anxiety originates from the limbic system in the center of the brain and, in a heightened state, this system uses an excessive amount of mental resources causing the frontal lobe, which houses the thinking, reasoning, and analytical structures of the brain, to have fewer resources available. Our attention shifts from reasoning to survival.

This is the type of anxiety that many experience after traumatic events. This can be trauma experienced as a child or trauma experienced as an adult. Trauma overloads and overwhelms the brain. And it is not just physical, emotional, or sexual abuse that causes trauma. Traumatic stress is a normal reaction to an abnormal event. This could be a natural disaster, war or brutal conflict, a pandemic, a health crisis, an unexpected death, or a school shooting. And when these events occur in succession, it elevates our feelings of uncertainty and a sense of impending peril to a debilitating level. Millions of Americans, including increasing numbers of children and adolescents, are currently suffering with *generalized anxiety disorder*.[63] The good news is there are ways to manage anxiety and eliminate its detrimental effects.

It is important to understand that *episodic* and *generalized* anxiety can both be at play in our interactions with our companion. Anxiety then leads to reactivity which shuts down productive dialogue.

The third type of anxiety is the most debilitating. *Panic attacks* are a severe form of anxiety that erupt in sudden and intense bursts and cause substantial interference with basic human functioning. People with panic attacks report extreme difficulty in breathing with an almost suffocating type of reaction, extreme agitation, and an intense desire to run or flee. *Panic attacks* often occur without warning or signals. Suddenly, within a matter of seconds, the body is flooded with cortisol heightening a sense of dread and gloom. Many times they occur at night when a person is sleeping, waking them suddenly in panic.

Managing Anxiety

Now that we understand the types of anxiety we may experience, let's learn how we can manage anxiety in any form to bring calm and reason to anxious moments. *Mindfulness* is a topic that has gained much notoriety in the last decade due to its effective use in managing anxiety. Unfortunately, the word is closely associated with the eastern religion of Hinduism that promotes the concept of *emptying yourself* and *transcendental meditation*, both of which are practices we are admonished in Scripture to avoid. While the Bible

THE GOOD NEWS IS THERE ARE WAYS
TO MANAGE ANXIETY AND ELIMINATE
ITS DETRIMENTAL EFFECTS.

does refer to meditating on God's Word (see Joshua 1:8), it is the *transcendental* part that is unscriptural as the meditator attempts to transcend this earthly realm into an altered state of consciousness. The Bible is clear that this type of practice opens the door to satanic influence and activity.

Nevertheless, *mindfulness*, when used in its literal sense, is nothing more than attempting to *stay in the present moment.* Unhealthy anxiety, depression, and other mental health disorders occur when a person is in a state of mind focused on the past or the future. We perpetually ponder the past and frightfully fret about the future. This hinders us from fully experiencing the present—the here and now.

Philippians 4:6 commands us to be "anxious for nothing." Although it seems quite impossible to not have anxiety, God would not tell us to do something that is impossible to do. We obtain further guidance in the subsequent verses as to how to be anxious for nothing.

First, we are supposed to, in everything, transfer our cares to God through prayer and supplication and let His supernatural peace guard our hearts and minds in Christ Jesus. Next, we are to focus our thoughts on what is true, honorable, just, pure, lovely, commendable, of moral excellence, and praiseworthy. Those words all encompass things that are presently occurring. Hence, these scriptures tell us to stay in the present.

So, let's explore some practical ways we can stay in the present and avoid ruminating about the past and fretting about the future during our interactions with our companion. First, it is important to understand that trying to ignore or suppress your anxiety will perpetuate it, especially when we experience generalized anxiety or panic attacks. Trying to turn away or run from anxiety is a signal to your amygdala that the anxiety itself is to be avoided. This can lead to a *fear of the fear* response causing anxiety to quickly spin out of control. To avoid this, it is best to merely let the anxiety occur. Turn and face it mentally while employing techniques to soothe and

UNHEALTHY ANXIETY, DEPRESSION, AND OTHER MENTAL HEALTH DISORDERS OCCUR WHEN A PERSON IS IN A STATE OF MIND FOCUSED ON THE PAST OR THE FUTURE. WE PERPETUALLY PONDER THE PAST AND FRIGHTFULLY FRET ABOUT THE FUTURE. THIS HINDERS US FROM FULLY EXPERIENCING THE PRESENT—THE HERE AND NOW.

assuage it. It may help to think of anxiety as a bee landing on your shoulder. If you try to swat it away, it can cause the bee to become angry and aggressive. Just acknowledging the anxiety but letting it be (pun intended), will result in the bee eventually flying away. This is what we will learn how to do next.

Anxiety Management Techniques

Anxiety management techniques fall into four main categories:

- *Deep breathing* which means breathing from the diaphragm at a slow, deliberate pace, fully in and fully out
- *Grounding* which involves using the five senses of sight, hearing, touch, taste, and smell to re-engage the body in connection with our present surroundings
- *Progressive muscle relaxation* which involves tensing and relaxing a targeted muscle group, in succession, while focusing on the feelings of tension and calm
- *Visualization* which involves retrieving mental images of a relaxing and calm place while describing the details of it in your mind.

All of these techniques involve using the body in various ways to stay in the present. Anxiety originates in the brain and circulates in the mind. Some who experience panic attacks will say they feel like they are having an *out of body* experience. This is because the amygdala has *hijacked* brain cells and escalated survival-based activity. By engaging the body and its five senses, we can calm the amygdala down and signal the parasympathetic nervous system to take over. With repeated practice in a non-threatening environment, we can train the mind and body to work in tandem to create *muscle memory*, allowing us to invoke these techniques automatically when we feel threatened in a dialogue with our companion.

Deep Breathing

The most essential type of anxiety management technique is *deep breathing*. This involves two changes: 1) breathing from the diaphragm rather than the chest and, 2) slowing the breath cycle down. One of the first reactions to occur when anxiety starts is for our breathing to speed up and become shallower as our heart starts beating faster. Purposely slowing our breathing down will counteract this reactivity and slow our heart rate, both of which signal the onset of calm to the brain.

To practice this, you can either sit in a chair with both feet on the floor and your back straight, or you can lie down on your back on a couch or the floor. I like to close my eyes when I am doing this, but you can leave them open if you like.

Put your left hand on the center of your chest and your right hand on your stomach. Start to breathe in through your nose but purposely try to let the breath build from your gut rather than your chest. Your right hand should move up and down while your left hand stays still. Do this for three breaths.

Next, we want to slow our breathing down to a deliberate pace with the outbreath being twice as long as the inbreath so that we get all the air out before we start to breathe in again. So, with your right hand still on your stomach and your left hand still on your chest, breathe in through your nose to a count of four and breathe out through your mouth to a count of eight, then pause for a count of two. Do this three times for practice.

I recommend you practice this exercise several times per day for a week. Then, when you are in dialogue with your companion and conflict arises, be aware of your breathing. When anxiety begins to escalate, purposely slow your breathing down and breathe deep from the diaphragm.

Grounding

The second category of anxiety management techniques, *grounding*, involves engaging your five senses of sight, hearing, touch, taste, and smell. Focusing on tangible things we sense is a way to get out of our heads and re-engage the body's awareness of its present surroundings. I gave you an example of this in the last chapter when I took you with me on my morning run with Sadie. This time, we will use a method called *5-4-3-2-1*. You can do this while seated or standing.

Start by naming, in your head, five things you see. For example, "I see a chair," "I see a plant," "I see a pillow," "I see a lamp," "I see a door." Then name four things you touch (e.g., your forearm, a table, a piece of paper, your shirt). Then name three things you hear (e.g., the air conditioning fan, traffic outside, the snap of my fingers). Then two things you smell (e.g., your hand, flowers) or two scents you like (e.g., lavender, rose). And finally, one thing you taste. Maybe it's the coffee you had this morning (or a taste you most like).

Another type of grounding technique is to focus attention on your hand for a minute or two. Look at the palm and notice the lines, notice the fingers. Touch the palm of your hand and describe how it feels in your head. Turn it over and look at the back of your hand. What do you notice? Touch the back of your hand and your fingers.

A variation on this is to focus on your feet. Take off your shoes and stand up. Close your eyes and feel your feet anchored to the floor. Slowly sway back and forth several times continuing to feel your feet grounded on the floor. Lift your heels to flex your toes and feel them pressing into the floor. Do this for a minute or two.

The final type of grounding technique is called a *full-body scan*. You can do this while seated or when standing. If seated, put both feet on the floor and sit up straight. Close your eyes and begin to mentally scan your body from top to bottom.

Start with the top of the head. What do you feel there? Is it tingling or pulsing? Linger there for a few seconds. Then shift your mental focus to your face and jaw. What do you feel there? Is your face tight or relaxed? Is your jaw tight or relaxed? Try to loosen them a bit and let them relax. Then shift to your neck. **(NOTE: If you have structural bone challenges or any other physical aberrations, consult your medical doctor before proceeding.)** Move your head slightly in a swivel to heighten the sense of your neck. What do you feel there? Is it tight and can you relax it?

Shift your focus to your shoulders. What do you feel there? Are they tight or loose and can you loosen and relax them a bit? Now to your upper arms. What do you sense there? Any pulsating or tingling feelings? Then shift focus to your lower arms, wrists, and hands. Do you feel any pulsating or tingling sensations there? Linger for a few seconds with your attention on your lower arms and hands.

Now shift focus to your chest. Can you sense your heart beating and your lungs filling with air? Shift attention now to your stomach area. Are you hungry or full? Any rumblings in your tummy? Can you feel your stomach rise and fall as you breathe from your diaphragm? Now shift to your back. Do you feel any tension there? If so, can you relax your back and release some of the tension?

Now move to your pelvis and buttocks. Can you feel the chair or floor under you holding you up? Moving down now to your thighs. What do you feel there? Do they feel tense or loose? Are you able to relax them? Then shift to your lower legs, shins, and calves. What do you feel there? And finally, your feet. Move your toes a bit to heighten awareness of your feet. Do you feel any tingling or pulsing? Can you relax your feet? And now expand your focus so you can sense your whole body and linger there for a few seconds.

The full-body scan can be a great activity to do in the morning before you start the normal routine for your day. It helps begin your day with some purposeful relaxation and grounding. During your day, if you are feeling a bit stressed, find a quiet place and do the full-body scan for three to five minutes to create a calming effect.

Progressive Muscle Relaxation

The third category of anxiety management techniques, *progressive muscle relaxation*, is a bit like the full-body scan except you start from the bottom of your body and work up and you purposely tense and relax a targeted muscle group in succession.

It is often best to do this while lying on your back, but you can also do it in a seated position. You are going to tense a targeted muscle group, hold it for ten seconds while you focus on the tension, then release and relax for ten seconds focusing on the calm. The sequence is as follows:

1. *Feet*: Begin by pulling your feet up so only your heels are on the floor, flexing your toes upward and outward. Feel the tension and hold this for about ten seconds. Then relax and feel the sense of looseness and calm for about ten seconds. Describe the feelings to yourself in your mind.

2. *Shin/Calves*: Tense your shin and calves, hold for ten seconds, release, feel the relaxation for ten seconds. Describe the feelings to yourself as you do this.

3. *Thighs*: Tense, feel the tension as you hold for ten seconds, release, feel the relaxation for ten seconds.

4. *Pelvis/Buttocks*: Tense, feel the tension as you hold for ten seconds, release, feel the relaxation for ten seconds.

5. *Torso/Stomach/Lower Back*: Tense, feel the tension as you hold for ten seconds, release, feel the relaxation for ten seconds.

6. *Chest/Upper Back*: Tense, feel the tension as you hold for ten seconds, release, feel the relaxation for ten seconds.

7. *Upper Arms/Biceps/Triceps*: Tense, feel the tension as you hold for ten seconds, release, feel the relaxation for ten seconds.

8. *Hands/Lower Arms*: Clench your fists, feel the tension as you hold for ten seconds, release, feel the relaxation for ten seconds.

9. *Shoulders*: Pull your shoulders up towards your ears, feel the tension as you hold for ten seconds, release, feel the relaxation for ten seconds.

10. *Neck/Face*: Tense, feel the tension as you hold for ten seconds, release, feel the relaxation for ten seconds.
11. *Full Body*: Mentally scan your body from the top of your head down to your feet feeling the relaxation all over.

Again, this is something you can practice in the morning before you start your day and do during the day when you can find a quiet place to be alone.

Visualization

The last type of anxiety management technique, *visualization*, involves using your mind's eye to generate images of a relaxing and peaceful place for you. It could be a beach, a secluded mountain top, some place in nature, a cozy coffee shop, or a favorite vacation destination. Close your eyes and imagine this place in your mind, describing the details as you mentally scan the images. Ideally, you should linger here for two to three minutes so you can fully take in the scene and feel relaxed and serene.

To ingrain these techniques into muscle memory so you can invoke them when anxiety occurs it is best to practice them daily in a calm state for at least a week. As you are practicing the grounding, progressive muscle relaxation, and visualization techniques, try to also concentrate on deep, diaphragmatic breathing.

Then, when you are in a dialogue with your companion that begins to escalate your anxiety, consciously think about your breathing and purposely slow it down and deepen it. Try also touching the palms and back of your hands or feeling your feet on the floor to provide some grounding. As Christians, we can also call on Jesus to help us calm ourselves down so we can remain present with our companion and stay on the Northern Route of the Welch Responsive Cycle.

Discussion Starter Questions

- *For Couples or Groups*
  - Which of the three types of anxiety have you experienced?
    NOTES:_____
    _____
    _____
    _____

  - Describe the physical sensations you have when you are anxious. What thoughts float through your head when you are experiencing anxiety?
    NOTES:_____
    _____
    _____
    _____

  - Read Philippians 4:4–9. Describe the responses or reactions you have to the instructions in these verses.
    NOTES:_____
    _____
    _____
    _____

  - Have you used, or do you use, any of the anxiety management techniques described in this chapter? How successful have they been for you?
    NOTES:_____
    _____
    _____
    _____

- *For Couples Only*
  - ○ Work together to create a plan for both of you to separately practice some of the anxiety management techniques each day over the next week. Come back together again at the end of the week to discuss how it went.

    NOTES:_____

    _____

    _____

    _____

A MOMENT OF SILLINESS

Earlier this afternoon, it dawned on me that as much as I enjoy the California Hume Lake Christian Camps and the Sequoia National Park giant trees, my most enjoyable scenic destinations occur looking into my precious wife's eyes as she and I curiously reflect on our life together. In each of these precious moments I'm reminded of what it must be like in heaven. Marriage points me to heaven. My wife's curiosity about me mimics heaven. I feel fulfilled when my precious wife takes that much interest in me. Jesus not only takes that much interest in me (and you!) but also continues this curiosity through eternity. That's difficult for me to comprehend if it were not for my happy marriage.

May I be more specific? One of these scenic moments happened this very afternoon. In preparation for this book, we needed updated photos. We hadn't spent this much time on photos since our wedding decades ago. The photographer wanted to get some humorous photos and asked Robin and me, "What is something Don does that Robin appreciates?" Robin piped up and said, 'I really appreciate it when Don takes our new puppy, Gracie-Anne, out for her duties." The photographer said, "Good. Look at each other and start talking about this kind act Don does for Robin that is so meaningful." We looked at each other and I think my inner child saw an opportunity for another, unplanned scenic destination. I began by saying, "Gracie loves to poop. She does it when I take her out at 5:15 a.m. each morning, and she sometimes does it in the evening when I take her out. And, sometimes her business gets on my running shoes and sometimes it doesn't...."

Robin and I started laughing together talking about dog poop while the photographer snapped photos of Robin. Immediately following that portion of the photo shoot, the photographer showed us one photo with Robin and me laughing and carrying on about our new little puppy's poop. She commented, "This one shows sheer love for each other." Robin and I looked at each other and nodded in unison. Yes! Robin then retorted, "I think Don and I were about to give each other a big kiss." The photographer said, "I could sense you were about to kiss each other and was hoping to get it on camera." This is a scenic destination for Robin and me that we thought we would share with you. The silliest moments in your marriage can create a brand new scenic destination. Enjoy a bit of heaven together.

CHAPTER 9

SCENIC DESTINATIONS

Besides relaxation and unplugging from our normal routines, one of the reasons people vacation is to view scenic destinations. God's creation brims with beauty. Our spirits ignite when we observe the grandeur of the Grand Canyon; sail along the Na Pali coastline in Kauai and see the spectacular waterfalls and emerald-hued cliffs accenting gorgeous beaches; hear the cacophonous rush of water and view the colorful, magnificent displays of Niagara Falls; or observe a herd of wild gazelle wandering across the plains of the Serengeti. This world we inhabit is a tapestry of beauty weaved and woven together by our magnificent Creator. Our hearts yearn for beauty, especially when they are weary of the grind and routine of everyday life. The human heart can only endure so many arduous or mundane experiences. At times, we need relief from the difficulties of human existence and familial challenges. In this chapter, I want to offer you some ways to visit more scenic destinations in your marriage, figuratively speaking, so that you can experience each other's beauty and thrive rather than just survive.

Welch Relationship Model

First, it is important for a husband and wife to spend time establishing and pursuing relationship goals. Having a common set of goals is important when embarking on any endeavor. Things go awry in new initiatives, as well as relationships, when one companion is working towards goals that are dissimilar or incongruent with the other companion's goals. Uniting around a common set of goals creates synergy and stability.

In my years of counseling as a pastor, professor, and licensed psychotherapist, I have found the four goals in this graphic to be the most important and beneficial for a thriving relationship. They are for companions to be *comfortable, creative, close,* and *clear.*

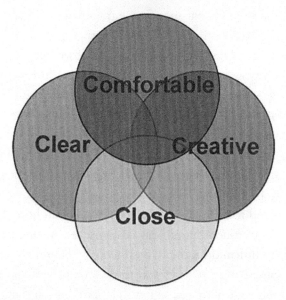

Comfortable: Empathy-exchange, kindness, soft-hearted, active listening

Creative: Originality, imaginative, curious, collaborative problem solving

Close: Responsive, trusting, even-tempered, regular time spent together

Clear: Conscientious, well-organized, honest, transparent, no secrets

Being *comfortable* implies feeling secure in the relationship. There is an abiding calmness and lack of chronic anxiety. To achieve this, each companion should focus on exchanging empathy, trying to get inside the other's experience and really understand it. It involves being kind, considerate, and soft-hearted toward each other.

Being *creative* means there is room for new ideas and suggestions. Each companion is free to imagine possibilities and, when there is conflict, each approaches it with a collaborative problem-solving mindset rather than as a battle of wills.

Being *close* means each is endeavoring to be responsive to the other rather than reactive. There is mutual trust and stability in the relationship. While escalation may occur, overall, each is working on being even-tempered rather than explosive or unstable. There is regular time spent together in conversation or mutual activities.

Being *clear* means communicating expectations, needs, and desires with clarity and being honest and transparent with each other. It means admitting mistakes, taking responsibility, and ensuring there are no secrets.

To accomplish these goals, some foundational prerequisites are essential. There must be *trust*, *choice*, *negotiation*, and *flexibility*.

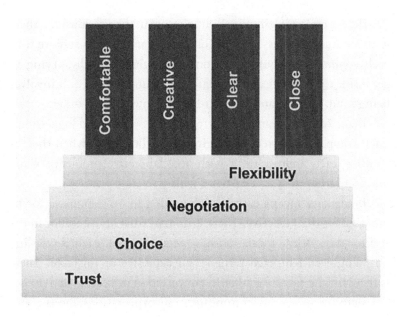

Let's explore each of these individually.

Developing Trust

Trust is the currency by which close relationships are maintained. Without it, relationships go bankrupt. Trust is defined as the capacity to rely on the integrity, strength, ability, and surety of another person or object.[64] When we trust in another, we are confident in them being there for us when needed. Similar to how people handle money, each of us may handle the extension of trust differently.

With money, some are *savers*, and some are *spenders*. When given a choice, savers will typically opt to not spend money on something, preferring to *put it away* instead to see it grow and/or use it for a future, planned or unplanned, expense. Spenders, on the other hand, when given a choice, will typically opt to spend their money now to obtain some benefit other than growth or saving for a future expense. This does not mean they are necessarily wasteful or irresponsible. They just approach the use of money differently than savers.

These dual patterns are similar to how people may extend trust. Some are *savers*, preferring to wait to extend trust until the other person proves themselves trustworthy. Others are *spenders*, preferring to give people the *benefit of doubt* and extend trust right away, but with the option of retracting it if the person proves themselves to be untrustworthy in some way.

The type of trust extender you might be is often the result of prior experience and/or temperament. Those who have had trust broken by caregivers early in life may learn to distrust by default. Those who are high *C*, the Contemplators, may be more prone to distrust since they tend to be more skeptical and pessimistic. Those who are high *I*, the Influencers, on the other hand, tend to be more trusting since they are generally more optimistic and accepting of others.

Stephen M.R. Covey, son to the Stephen R. Covey who wrote *Seven Habits of Highly Effective People*, also wrote an insightful and impactful book titled *The Speed of Trust*.[65] In this book, the author outlines thirteen behaviors that one must consistently and genuinely exhibit in order to engender trust.

Covey suggests that trust exists when there is a stable combination of *character* and *competence*. Character means there is a consistency between who you are on the outside and who you are on the inside. Furthermore, there is an alignment between what you say and what you do. If you say it, you do it. If you do not say it, you don't do it. Trust is undermined when you say you will do something and you do not do it, or you say you will *not* do something, and you do it. This point is understood. What is often overlooked, however, is when you do not say something about what you are planning to do, and then you do it. Depending on what it is, this can create surprise for your companion and introduce unpredictability into the relationship. Unpredictability can undermine trust, just like not following through on your commitments.

As a couple, you may want to take some time to assess the level of trust that exists in your relationship. Ask each other something like, "On a scale of one to ten, with ten being the highest amount of trust and one being the lowest, how much do you trust me?" Then discuss what may be contributing to an assessment of less than ten that, if improved, could move the score higher.

Expanding Choice

The next foundational element to accomplish the four relationship goals is *choice*. We referred to the importance of this element in chapter 1 when we defined intimacy. This is because it is one of the most essential elements needed in any intimate relationship. In fact, one can argue that when choice is absent intimacy does not exist. It is fascinating to me that God himself infused choice into His relationship with humans. When we observe suffering in our fallen world, one of our first gut-wrenching cries is, "Why doesn't God intervene?" "Why does He allow school shootings, sex trafficking, and slave trade to occur?" The answer to that question is the same answer we must wrestle with when we read the creation story. "Why did God even have a tree of the knowledge of good and evil in the Garden?" "We could have avoided all this if Adam's and Eve's culinary choices didn't include the infamous apple." "And why didn't God intervene *before* Eve took a bite of the forbidden fruit?"

The answer to all these questions is the same—*choice*. God knew that, without choice, there would be no intimacy with His creation—no *love*. So, He took the risk of introducing choice with *limits*. Every tree was available to Adam and Eve for nourishment, *save one*. There must have been hundreds, if not thousands, of trees in the Garden. Nearly unlimited choice, but there was a limit, nevertheless.

So, we want our intimate relationships to have choice as well. Certainly with limits since unlimited choice can prove harmful to those possessing a selfish nature like we do. But lack of essential choice in an intimate relationship breeds resentment. This is because

GOD KNEW THAT, WITHOUT CHOICE, THERE WOULD BE NO INTIMACY WITH HIS CREATION—NO LOVE. SO, HE TOOK THE RISK OF INTRODUCING CHOICE WITH *LIMITS*.

we violate the very definition of intimacy when we remove choice. Remember, an intimate relationship does not operate at the expense of the self and does not overly expand the self to operate at the expense of the other. Losing choice means you lose self.

To give choice means we ask rather than declare, command, or insist. "Would you be willing to empty the dishwasher for me?" gives choice, while "I want you to empty the dishwasher" or "Empty the dishwasher please" removes choice. "Would it be possible for you to not go shopping today?" provides choice, while "You better not go shopping today" or "I hope you're not planning on going shopping today" eliminates choice.

Employing Negotiation

The next important foundational element for intimate relationships is *negotiation*. Negotiation is an art, not a science. It requires active listening, finesse, mutual respect, and the ability to adapt to changing circumstances.

At its core, negotiation is figuring out how each party can get some, or all, of what they desire or need. It involves an exchange of things of value. Each has something the other wants and each is willing to give something of value to get something in return. The outcome of negotiation is either an impasse, meaning the parties cannot or will not agree, or a negotiated agreement. Negotiations occur everywhere and in all walks of life. Those who are successful as leaders have learned how to negotiate—and those who are successful in relationships have learned the same.

Let's start with an understanding of the two primary methods for negotiating. One method is called *positional bargaining*. This means that each party comes to the table with their position(s) fully developed. They already have in mind the outcome they want, so they each present their *solution* for a negotiated agreement and hope the other party will *see it my way*. Then they commence negotiating, looking for areas of agreement and disagreement. For the areas of disagreement, they look for ways to compromise but each tries to get more value than they relinquish. In the end, if there is a negotiated agreement, the result is getting some of what I want but not all. Depending on the process that ensued during negotiations, the parties may walk away feeling victorious, defeated, or just moderately satisfied. Often, this type of negotiation results in *win-lose* scenarios. One party wins while the other loses.

A better, and more productive, approach to negotiations is called *interest-based bargaining*. In this type of negotiation, the parties agree not to establish an initial position but rather to explore together each person's interests. In other words, rather than starting with what may be a proposed solution, they start with clearly identifying needs. This is like using "I feel ____ when ____..." statements rather than "Here is what I want you to do" or "You need to" declarations. Interest-based bargaining invites exploration. Often, negotiations can quickly deteriorate when there is no clarity around the needs of each party. Take the time to discuss needs without opposing judgments or conclusions. List them down and see where there is common ground. Then work toward a *win-win* solution where each can get what they want.

Of course, even with the best of intentions and use of the best method, there may be times when a couple will just need to *agree to disagree*. However, these events can be more palatable if there are more events where a negotiated agreement is achieved than events resulting in impasse.

Developing Flexibility

The last foundational element in the Welch Relationship Model is *flexibility*. Companions need to be flexible with each other. This means being willing to bend or yield. It requires truly considering and regarding the other's perspectives and opinions. Those who are flexible recognize and honor each other's differences and find ways to compromise.

We often discover wisdom for our relationships in the simplest form. *Veggie Tales*, the original animated series for children, contained some beautifully simple theology regarding flexibility. My family and I loved these entertaining characters. If I were having difficulty lifting my children out of a bad mood, I would resort to singing Larry the Cucumber's song *Oh Where Is My Hairbrush*. After modulating and repeating the song with vigor, my children would finally begin their giggle and beg me to stop singing.

During one *Veggie Tales* episode, Larry is robbed by some bandits, and they force him face down in a hole. Since cucumbers do not have arms, well, let's just say—Larry can't get himself out of the hole. The thing I always appreciate about Larry's personality is that he tends to remain flexible. After advocating for help from several people passing by, Larry finally entices the *good Samaritan* to help him out of his predicament. Although the good Samaritan is really the focus of the story, His ability to remain calm and flexible created the possibility for Larry to extricate himself from his troublesome situation.

Flexibility, the ability to adjust one's thinking and behavior while maintaining a good attitude, is one of the most essential qualities to possess in marriage, and in life itself. Recent research reveals that those who maintain and express a cheerful outlook (flexibility) improve their quality of life and wellbeing.[66]

The importance of this quality became evident to my wife, Robin, and I during our university work and several witness-team trips. Early on, we discovered that the success of leading a trip with thirty students to a developing nation depended upon the team's flexibility quotient. I remember one trip where the word *flexibility* became a mantra during breaks, mealtimes, and even devotional moments. As I recall, this turned out to be one of the more successful trips.

The "Full" Life

When we pursue the relationship goals and install the relationship foundations of the Welch Relationship Model in marriage, we can experience the fuller life Jesus describes in John 10:10. Our target is the center of this diagram—*a full life.*

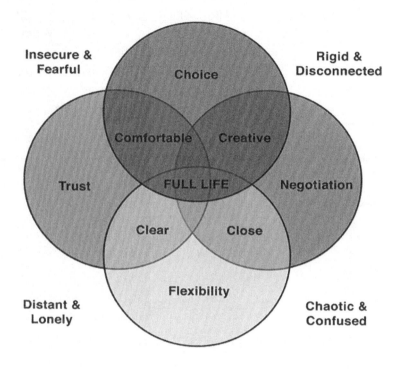

When we infuse *trust, choice, negotiation,* and *flexibility* into our relationship, we create the environment to achieve the four goals of being *comfortable, creative, close,* and *clear.* This leads to a thriving relationship and a full life for you and your companion. When we operate the relationship outside of this optimal range, we risk creating a relationship that is insecure and fearful, rigid and disconnected, chaotic and confused, or distant and lonely. If those phrases characterize your current relationship, it is likely that one or both of you are reacting rather than responding to each other.

Let us bring this all together. Adhering to the principles of the Welch Responsive Cycle I introduced you to in chapter 4 allows you and your companion to be in a better position to create the foundations of *trust, choice, negotiation,* and *flexibility* necessary to achieve the relationship goals to be *comfortable, creative, close,* and *clear.*

The complete graphic below depicts these essential elements. Since this graphic encapsulates not only scientifically verified practices for improving marital communication but also sound biblical principles, I have included a table following the chart that summarizes the scriptural underpinnings:

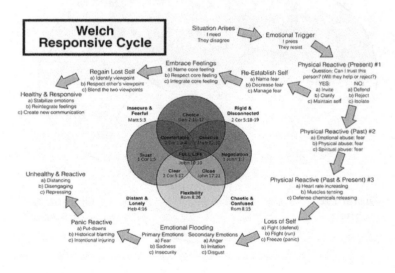

WELCH RESPONSIVE CYCLE SCRIPTURES		
Section	Element	Scripture Reference
Relationship Goals	Comfortable	2 Corinthians 1:3–4
	Creative	Matthew 22:30
	Close	John 17:21
	Clear	2 Corinthians 5:17
Relationship Foundations	Trust	1 Corinthians 1:5
	Choice	Genesis 2:16–17
	Negotiation	1 John 1:7
	Flexibility	Romans 8:26
Undesirable Relationship Results	Insecure & Fearful	Matthew 5:3
	Rigid & Disconnected	2 Corinthians 5:18–19
	Chaotic & Confused	Romans 8:15
	Distant & Lonely	Hebrews 4:16
Desirable Relationship Result	Full Life	John 10:10 (NIV)

Sexual Responsiveness

No marriage book would be complete without a chapter, or at least a section, on sex. I can almost hear the husbands saying, "Well it's about time. What took you so long?" In fact, if you are like most husbands, after your wife told you about her desire to read this book together, you probably went right to the table of contents to find the chapter on sex. Sorry to disappoint you men with no chapter dedicated to the subject, but I do want to cover the topic in this chapter since there is probably no more scenic of a destination in marriage for men, and perhaps some women, than sexual encounters. Furthermore, I do not want my Board Certified Sex Therapist credential to go to waste.

The Bible has plenty to say on the subject of sex both inside and outside of marriage. It cannot be overstated, however, that sex between a husband and wife in covenantal marriage is the only type labeled *undefiled* when marriage is respected as it should be (see Hebrews 13:4). All other forms are, by extension, impure or *defiled*. This is not my opinion, it is God's unequivocal mandate clearly stated and referenced throughout the Bible, both Old and New Testaments. There is no other conclusion any reasonable person who believes in the authority of all Scripture as God's instructions to us can draw.

The Enemy's Assault on Sex

That being said, as a counselor, I have experienced first-hand the brokenness, devastation, turmoil, and deep wounds that sex, both inside and outside of marriage, can wreak on otherwise beautiful children of God. I dare say there is no other function in human existence that receives more attention from our adversary, the Devil, than this one. I am convinced that Peter could have appended "especially in their sexuality" at the end of his alarming proclamation in 1 Peter 5:8 without violating scriptural accuracy. "Be serious. Be alert. Your adversary the Devil is prowling around like a roaring lion looking for anyone to devour **[especially in their sexuality]**" (bracketed words mine).

Satan hates marital sex because it reminds him of the *image of God*. He knows that God stamped His image in our gender. He also knows that the act of the *two becoming one flesh* is the merging of the separate male and female attributes into one, more complete, representation of God. So, hell launches its full assault against the act of sexual intercourse between a husband and wife every day. We see it in sex trafficking of minors; we see it in rape. We see it in sexual abuse and child molestation. These brutal attacks on the sanctity of marital sex continue to escalate year after year as more reports surface of sexual trauma inflicted by those in positions of power over others.

SATAN HATES MARITAL SEX BECAUSE
IT REMINDS HIM OF THE IMAGE OF
GOD. HE KNOWS THAT GOD STAMPED
HIS IMAGE IN OUR GENDER.

Our sexuality, as God originally designed it, is also bombarded by hellish assaults in our marriage. Do you really think the incessant conflict you both have regarding the frequency of sex, the type of sexual acts permitted, the lack of desire, the sexual dysfunction, and the anguish of past sexual trauma that keeps coming up, are just random occurrences or only caused by your acts or omissions? Your enemy has a personal stake in causing the demise of sexual intimacy in your marriage because, in doing so, he mars the image of God that is carried in your gender and, by extension, your sexuality.

So, if you want to experience the type of marital sex described in the Song of Solomon, you are going to have to fight for it—both of you. Sex can be the most exhilarating, pleasurable, satisfying, and connecting act on planet Earth. But it can also be the most painful, destructive, disastrous, and separating act on planet Earth as well. The transition from the latter to the former is possible, but it will take purposeful action, dedicated effort, and courage to fight the enemy. As Dr. Clifford and Joyce Penner suggest in their book *Restoring the Pleasure,*

> *Emotional barriers and conflicts are the source of sexual dysfunction. These emotional factors keep individuals from freely abandoning themselves to the sexual experience and thus interfere with the creativity designed sexual response cycle. Many of God's sexual beings have never allowed themselves the joy in delighting in each other's bodies as did the lovers described in the Song of Solomon.*[67]

Sexual Ground Rules in Marriage

As we discuss the difference between responsive and reactive sex, I will lay out some ground rules for how sex should be treated in marriage from a scriptural perspective. As I stated earlier, there are numerous Bible passages and verses providing insight and guidance into human sexuality. I am going to focus on only three to create a framework that couples can build upon. This framework is composed of three principles:

1. Marital sex should be *essential and integrated* rather than *discretionary and modular.*
2. Marital sex should be *unburdened and adaptable* rather than *restricted and rigid.*
3. Marital sex should be *liberating and uninhibited* rather than *guarded and subdued.*

Principle number one is contained in 1 Corinthians 7:5 which says, "Do not deprive one another sexually—except when you agree for a time, to devote yourselves to prayer. Then come together again; otherwise, Satan may tempt you because of your lack of self-control."

Unfortunately, husbands sometimes misuse this verse by making it into a hammer verse rather than an encouragement verse. Paul is describing a principle here that is based on the human condition and the intensity of the sexual drive. Several human urges are prone to self-control challenges, especially when there is a perception of deprivation, the most notable being sex, eating, and drinking. Deprive someone of these essential elements and the need for more focused and purposeful self-control goes up.

God embedded sex in the definition of marriage in Genesis 2:24 by saying, "And the two become one flesh." Marriage cannot be separated from this act. It is an essential component and should be integrated into the marriage, a normal and regular occurrence. Certainly, there are physical barriers that may prohibit sexual intercourse, either temporarily or permanently, but wise is the couple in this category who finds alternative ways to connect sexually/sensually and continues to integrate sexual activities in their marriage as an essential element.

Unfortunately, the cares of life, raising children, emotional conflict, or past sexual traumas can cause us to relegate sex to a *discretionary and modular* status. It becomes something that the couple does "if we have time" or "when things settle down a bit." Or it might be treated as an *add-on*, like an optional software module that is not talked about or invoked until *it just happens.* I encourage you to work together to ensure your sex life is *essential and integrated.* This will require intentionality.

Principle number two is contained in 1 Corinthians 7:4 where we are told, "A wife does not have the right over her own body, but her husband does. In the same way, a husband does not have the right over his own body, but his wife does."

Just like verse five of that same chapter, many a husband has abused and distorted this verse for his own selfish desires to get his wife to do some sexual act she is not willing to do. Using this verse to justify coercing or cajoling your wife into doing something against her will would be a violation of numerous other scriptural commands, the most notable being to, "Consider others (your wife) as more important than yourself and look out not only for your interests, but the interests of others (your wife)" (Philippians 2:3–4).

There is a principle here in 1 Corinthians for marital sex, though, that will improve sexual intimacy. Namely, sex, in marriage, should be *unburdened* and *adaptable* rather than *restricted* and *rigid.* This does not mean there are not appropriate boundaries, and it doesn't mean that *anything goes,* even if one partner is unwilling. The idea here is that both the husband and wife approach sex with a mindset of flexibility and openness. There should be a mutual give and take and willingness to explore and adapt to each other's desires, as appropriate. When one is too restrictive and too rigid, sexual intimacy suffers. Unfortunately, a husband or wife with sexual abuse in their background may attempt to make the sexual experience restricted and rigid to control the event so they can feel *safe.* There may be times when restrictions are needed to allow a companion to heal, either physically or emotionally. But the goal should be to

THERE IS A PRINCIPLE HERE IN 1 CORINTHIANS FOR MARITAL SEX, THOUGH, THAT WILL IMPROVE SEXUAL INTIMACY. NAMELY, SEX, IN MARRIAGE, SHOULD BE *UNBURDENED* AND *ADAPTABLE* RATHER THAN *RESTRICTED* AND *RIGID*.

transition to more of an *unburdened and adaptable* environment as soon as possible. Otherwise, having a sexual playing field the size of a postage stamp will eventually cause the other to feel as if they are wearing a straitjacket in bed.

Principle number three comes from Genesis 2:25 which reports, "The man and his wife were naked yet felt no shame." God made this pronouncement *before* the fall, so it refers to a time when sin was not present. But we should also view it as God's original design for marriage.

This speaks to sex being *liberating and uninhibited* rather than *guarded and subdued*. With sin came shame, and shame may now be the primary reaction a husband or wife experiences when they are first naked together. God intends for the husband and wife to feel no shame, to have no negative reaction, when they are naked in each other's presence. Being naked together as husband and wife should be a wholly positive experience. But sadly, this is not always the reality. One, or both, may feel inhibited and subdued as they grapple with the notion of being completely exposed, both physically and emotionally, to their spouse. Poor body image can exacerbate this condition. As we learned in chapter 3 when we reviewed gender differences, poor body image is more common with women than men. The husband needs to be extra careful in this arena to not say anything or do anything that the wife could perceive as critical of her body.

A word now about biblically allowable sexual activity. This is probably the most frequent and common question asked by couples during Q&A time at marriage retreats, seminars, and conferences. Attendees usually pose the question this way, "Is it OK to _____ (fill in the blank)?" This is certainly an important question for Christians since we want to always honor God in our actions. So, let me use Scripture to fully answer the question, in a general sense.

The first evaluation criteria of any sexual activity should be its *lawfulness*. In other words, does it violate a specific precept or command of God? Romans 2:23 is the scriptural reference for this criterion. "You who boast in the law, do you dishonor God by breaking the law?" If it violates a specific command of God, it is off limits—period.

If criterion number one is passed and there is no specific command or precept prohibiting it, the second evaluation criteria for any sexual activity should be its *helpfulness*. In other words, is it helpful—physically, spiritually, and mentally—for me *and* my spouse? This criterion is found in 1 Corinthians 6:12a. "Everything is permissible for me, but not everything is helpful." If it's not helpful and doesn't draw the both of you closer together, then the option should be discarded.

If both criteria number one and number two are passed, the next evaluation criterion is the *addictiveness* of the sexual activity. 1 Corinthians 6:12b provides the basis for this criterion. "Everything is permissible for me, but I will not be brought under the control of anything." Pornography would be an example here that would fail to meet this criterion. Unfortunately, some couples believe that viewing pornography together will *spice up their sex life*. Nothing could be further from the truth. Pornography is addictive, especially for men, and creates the opposite effect.

Wife, your husband is stimulated visually. God made them that way. His intention is for your husband to bond to you visually as sex hormones flood his brain during arousal and orgasm. The visual image(s) he sees during sexual activities sear into his memory with great intensity by the action of neurotransmitters in the brain. Introducing other provocative images into this process disrupts this natural, God ordained, bonding mechanism for husband and wife. Furthermore, it subjects him to addiction-provoking material with destructive capabilities. Couples should allow no other participant, including those on media, their marriage bed if sexual intimacy is the desired goal.

If criteria number one, number two, and number three are passed, the last evaluation criterion to consider is the activity's *fruitfulness*. In other words, will it result in good fruit or bad fruit?

The basis of this criterion is found in Matthew 7:16 when Jesus tells His disciples, "You'll recognize them by their fruit. Are grapes gathered from thornbushes or figs from thistles?" In other words, a good tree (activity in this case) produces good fruit while a bad tree (activity) produces bad or no fruit. Growing and deepening sexual intimacy produces good fruit. Bad fruit is produced if anyone is hurt in the process, either physically or emotionally.

Sexual Reactivity

On a warm summer day in San Diego, Noah and Olivia (not their actual names) sat across from me with battle-fatigued faces like those you might see on sailors leaving a Navy ship with Post-Traumatic Stress Disorder (PTSD). Olivia and Noah's dream of the return of sexual intimacy was waning. Their one-year-old daughter, Sophie, was a source of contention in their marriage, or so they thought. Experiencing sleep-deprived nights, irritation with each other, and harsh judgments, they sat in front of me joyless with sadness in their eyes. They had lost their passion for each other, and their sexual intimacy was dissipating. Instantly, I felt empathy and compassion for this couple. Neither Noah nor Olivia met the criteria for PTSD. We ruled out several diagnoses except for one—adjustment disorder with mixed anxiety and depressed mood. Their emotional, physical, and spiritual pain from lack of sexual intimacy was palpable.

Before our first therapy session, Olivia and Noah had taken all my required intake assessments providing in-depth insights into their sexual symptoms. As a certified sex therapist, I have a set protocol for those undergoing sex therapy, including several questionnaires and delineation of medical history. Noah and Olivia were desperate to connect sexually—a once vital and regular part of their marriage they now missed.

Sophie was their third child. According to Olivia, all previous births went well. However, the couple lost a child through miscarriage between their second and third child (Sophie) and something went awry. They had lost the ability to discuss their pain with each other. Before moving forward, I directed the couple to their primary medical doctor for further tests, since it is always important to separate biology (i.e., body function, hormones, etc.) from psychology, especially when conducting sex therapy. If the psychotherapist is not super careful, they may unintentionally harm a patient by trying to treat a biological issue with a mental health remedy. Unless the therapist rules out biological issues, psychological treatment remains a guessing game and results in treating symptoms rather than the real causes of dysfunction.

We were successful in eliminating biology as a contributor to their sexual problems which left us to focus on their psychological issues. We began exploring their adjustment disorder (anxiety) first. During and after the loss of their third child (before Sophie), the couple could not nurture each other. Dr. Rayna Markin says, "Following the loss of pregnancy, women often experience anguish and desperation, as well as the feeling of shame and inadequacy."[68] A buildup of reaction between the couple created continuous misunderstanding and intensifying, destructive interactions.

Although Olivia and Noah's sexual problems do not mimic all couples' sexual challenges, their symptoms are standard, especially after carefully analyzing them with a team approach that included the family physician and a mental health professional. Noah and Olivia were facing unusual levels of stress and anxiety, which caused them to have negative, sexual reactions: loss of desire, lack of response, and lackluster connection.

After experiencing a miscarriage and the arrival of their third child, Noah and Olivia, but particularly Noah, felt the stress of financially providing for the family. They decided Olivia would resign from her ten-year job to be a full-time mom at home with their three children. She would also take on the homeschooling responsibilities. Their income decreased by 40%, while Noah's anxiety increased exponentially. His anxiety exceeded his ability to maintain his self-worth, leading to a decline in his self-confidence. Olivia's self-worth was devastated by the miscarriage, as her value as a mom diminished. Noah also began questioning his abilities in many areas of his life including his ability to be sexually intimate with his wife.

With Olivia's feelings of shame, discomfort, and self-doubt, the couple lost the ability to communicate and be close through vulnerable interactions—the number one ingredient for sexual intimacy. Without the couple sharing openly, they became disconnected, discouraged, and frustrated. They needed a dose of appropriate vulnerability, but they were exhibiting reactivity instead. We discovered this when they took the Welch Responsive Assessment (WRTA) and we analyzed results for Dimension 4: Assertive vs. Vulnerable. When one is reactive in the *vulnerable* section of this dimension, they become submissive, conforming, and passive. Their self-image tends to plummet. This low ego might stem from childhood events that led them to self-doubt. They will be shy and have strong feelings of discomfort in social settings, even feeling like a doormat. Both Noah and Olivia's WRTA reports revealed high reactivity in this area.

Unfortunately for Olivia and Noah, the pregnancy loss of their child unleashed crashing waves of anxiety. Poorly managed anxiety will only increase over time. With most people tending to avoid anxiety rather than embrace it, the anxiety inflames and becomes more pronounced and debilitating. Anxiety is the number one killer of sexual intimacy. This was the case with Olivia and Noah. Their relationship had reached a point where anxiety was overwhelming, causing them to shut down sexually and emotionally.

Facing Loss

Several years ago, my wife, Robin, and I faced a loss that quickly turned into monumental anxiety. Late one evening, a night now permanently etched in my memory, Robin discovered a lump in her breast. In psychology, we call it a flashbulb memory, a sudden event blinding you completely for a second or two while the image becomes emblazoned in permanent storage. With my wife in tears and me no longer breathing, time seemed to stop as panic erupted. Unaware that our future life compass was now set on Robin's physical survival over the next year, our journey began with the next day's mammogram news alerting us to a five centimeter tumor (the size of a lemon) with rapidly growing cancer that had already spread to her lymph nodes.

Unfortunately, this life-changing event was immediately before Thanksgiving weekend (2018), and we would have to wait three weeks before the oncologist could meet with us. Those weeks felt like years with little ease of anxiety throughout the entire excruciating period. I had never experienced the type of agonizing fear I did during those three weeks of waiting. We cried together as a family and continuously prayed for God's miraculous intervention.

During those first few days, God gave us an epiphany-filled-moment when in the emotional mix of fear and anxiety, I remember suggesting to Robin, "We are desperate and in need of God to help us with this intense fear and anxiety. I don't know how to embrace my anxiety and get it to a manageable level. How about if we begin writing down God's many miracles from the past?"

We both agreed and it did not take us long to realize God's numerous miracles in our family were more than we had initially remembered. Each time we focused on God's miracles, we were more able to lean into God's miraculous power, and the anxiety faded. Although the pain of Robin's cancer journey remained, we were in a better place to endure the anxiety.

Robin carefully followed the treatment protocol, and the miraculous indeed took place. San Diego's Scripps MD Anderson Cancer Center protocol was chemotherapy first, followed by surgery, then radiation. By the time the doctor scheduled surgery, the large tumor was no longer visible. The surgeon said, "This is quite unusual as you should still have cancer, but there is no sign of it. The tumor is gone." Robin said, "Many of our family and friends are praying for us." The surgeon responded, "Well, keep them praying."

We did, and after the surgery, the doctor pronounced Robin "completely clear of cancer." The radiation oncologist happened to be a Christian, and he met with us and said, "Well, good news. We cannot detect any cancer. You are clear. In my twenty-five years practicing medicine, I have not experienced this before. Your results contradict biology, yet as Christians, we know it is a miracle. Let's pray and thank God for your miracle."

Talk about a moment in time etched in one's memory forever. The words of that kind radiation oncologist were exhilarating and the presence of God was palpable at that moment. I remember thinking that the absence of anxiety is the presence of God. Now a few years with cancer in our rearview mirror, when I am sitting with people in the therapy office experiencing the agony of anxiety, I believe with my entire being that God's presence is the absence of anxiety. My favorite childhood song says, "Jesus loves me this I know, for the Bible tells me so…I am weak, but he is strong…yes, Jesus loves me."

As Olivia and Noah began leaning into Jesus, they were learning how to experience God's presence and decrease their anxiety. They were talking to each other in this new season of life. Olivia began feeling more confident and amorous toward her husband. Noah was finding new ways of expressing his love and compassion for his wife. God's amazing grace often humbles me while working with a couple like Olivia and Noah.

Once Olivia and Noah strengthened their skills and applied tools to understanding the other's sexual needs, their relationship improved. It is sad to report that the top need for any couple struggling with their sexual relationship is the ability to talk—to be candid—for each to express their spiritual, emotional, and physical needs, to speak and be heard, and to listen to each other. This sounds quite simple, but it is, nevertheless, profoundly complex.

Are you working on this with your companion? How is your communication? Do you pray with your companion during meals and before you fall off to sleep at bedtime? Do you take at least ten minutes during each day to discuss with your companion: 1) three emotions you felt today, 2) one or two things you appreciate about your companion, and 3) one or two things you are learning in your walk with God?

Sex is one of the greatest gifts given by God to humankind. But we must nourish and protect it. Anxiety and violation of scriptural principles in its application can have lethal consequences for sexual intimacy and responsiveness. The wise couple will work together to ensure their sexual experience is *essential and integrated, unburdened and adaptable,* and *liberating and uninhibited.*

Discussion Starter Questions

- *For Couples or Groups*
  - Which of the four relationship goals resonates the most for you and why?
    NOTES:_____

    _____

    _____

  - Would you say that you and your companion negotiate well or negotiate poorly in your relationship?
    NOTES:_____

    _____

    _____

- Do you tend to use *positional bargaining* or *interest-based bargaining* when you negotiate?
  NOTES:_____

  _____

  _____

- On the continuum between *flexible* and *rigid*, where would you place yourself?
  NOTES:_____

  _____

  _____

- ***For Couples Only***
  - As you review the Fuller Life graphic together, where would each of you place your relationship in the graphic currently? What can you do separately and together to have a relationship that is *comfortable, creative, close,* and *clear*?
    NOTES:_____

    _____

    _____

  - On a scale of one to ten, with ten being the highest amount of trust and one being the lowest, ask your companion how much they trust you? Discuss what may be contributing to an assessment of less than ten that, if improved, could move the score higher.
    NOTES:_____

    _____

    _____

  - Would you describe your sex life as *essential and integrated* or *discretionary and modular*?

NOTES:_____
_____
_____

○ Would you describe your sex life as *unburdened and adaptable* or *restricted and rigid*?
NOTES:_____
_____
_____

○ Would you describe your sex life as *liberating and uninhibited* or *guarded and subdued*?
NOTES:_____
_____
_____

○ What steps can you take together to make your sex life more *essential and integrated, unburdened and adaptable,* and *liberating and uninhibited*?
NOTES:_____
_____
_____

○ Ask your companion if there is any element of your sex life they feel is violating one or more of the four criterion for permissible activities for them. Discuss how you will resolve this conflict.
NOTES:_____
_____
_____

CHAPTER 10

FOOTPRINTS

I love the poem *Footprints in the Sand*. It is prominently displayed in our family cabin where Robin and I spent summers with our children absorbing God's beauty all nestled in California's Sequoia National Forest. I often stop and reread these wonderfully, comforting words. It is a great synopsis of the way God relates to us. There is some dispute about who authored the poem originally and there are several versions found on the Internet. Nevertheless, the basic premise of all versions is consistent: God walks with us through life, and he sometimes carries us when we feel like we cannot go on. The last several lines of one version reads:

> But I have noticed that during the most troublesome
> times of my life,
> there is only one set of footprints."
> "I don't understand why, when I needed You the most,
> You would leave me."
> The Lord replied, "My son, My precious child, I love
> you and I would never leave you,
> During your times of trial and suffering
> When you see only one set of footprints,
> It was then that I carried you.[69]

We never walk this life alone. Scripture tells us, "He is near to the broken-hearted and saves those who are crushed in spirit" (Psalms 34:18). What a great assurance that although we traverse some difficult paths, God is always there to guide us and care for us, sometimes literally scooping us up in His arms when our weary souls cannot continue the journey without relief.

The Marriage Triangle

This is an essential aspect of our marriage to remember. As Christ-followers, our marriages are not a two-person arrangement. We are not relegated to figuring things out on our own. The Creator of marriage is an active member of our marital union if we let Him be. I recall someone telling me at one time that it would be best to consider my marriage relationship as an equilateral triangle rather than a line connecting only my wife and me. With the application of triangular geometry, if both my wife and I are moving closer to God, we naturally reduce the distance between each other and become closer as husband and wife.

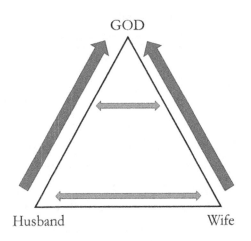

Of course, despite our best efforts to grow in our walk with Jesus, the path out of reactivity to a responsive marriage can still be difficult at times. My wife and I have had to work at reducing reactivity and increasing responsiveness in our marriage. We still do not get it right all the time. Sometimes, we must remind each other to be quick to listen, slow to speak, and slow to anger.

Although our reactivity has significantly lessened over the years, we can still experience anxiety and emotional triggers that threaten to divert us to the Southern route of the Welch Responsive Cycle and put us on a trajectory to arrive at an unhealthy place. But we can, and do, repair quickly. The key is awareness. We are each more aware of our tendencies and anxiety patterns. Awareness provides the opportunity to choose to stop, turn around, and divert to the Northern route to find a healthier destination.

This is where training is essential. Robin and I have trained ourselves with practical tools and techniques that increase the opportunity for us to choose responsiveness. I have used these same tools and techniques with my clients who have sought out my counsel as a last resort before divorce. Most in this quite hopeless condition have been able to assimilate the responsive relationship concepts I have laid out in this book and transform their fractured merger into a thriving marriage. And you can too.

Where to Start

Perhaps you are now intuitively aware that reactivity troubles your marriage. This is a great and essential first step—awareness. But general awareness is insufficient to enact an improvement plan. In the medical field, a general awareness that a patient is experiencing pain is hardly helpful. Awareness prompts further analysis and a search for answers. It creates opportunities to choose among alternatives. Doctors must conduct a physical examination, order diagnostic tests, and research the symptoms of various conditions to locate the

AWARENESS PROVIDES THE
OPPORTUNITY FOR CHOICE.

root cause of the pain and develop an action plan for healing and restoration. This is where we must start and proceed as well in our search for the responsive marriage.

Let me first give you a few suggestions for diagnostic tests. The Welch Responsive Temperament Assessment (WRTA) can help you to diagnose reactivity in your marriage. As mentioned earlier, it first provides you a picture of your temperament, your natural personality that God, your Designer, "knit together in your mother's womb" (Psalms 139:13). Learning that you are a *Director*, an *Influencer*, a *Stabilizer*, or a *Contemplator* by design (see chapter 3), coupled with knowing your natural strengths and reactive weaknesses, can be empowering. Although past events and experiences may have distorted the expressions of your intrinsic temperament, the natural ways you interact with and filter your world are God ordained. Your companion's natural temperament is God ordained as well, even though it is likely opposite from, and different than, yours.

The most empowering aspect of the WRTA, however, is the insight it provides you about the expression of your temperament within the nine dimensions of expression. The measurement of these dimensions reveals the areas where reactivity may lurk. You will learn whether you are primarily outgoing or primarily reserved and whether you self-regulate to be self-controlled or whether anxious episodes impede self-regulation. Are you mostly upbeat and positive or too sullen and unhappy? Does assertiveness characterize your personal interactions or are you overly vulnerable with others? Are you primarily engaging and connected in your relationships or do you tend to withdraw and remain aloof when anxiety occurs? Are you mostly agreeable or do you become aggressive when conflict erupts? Do you exhibit and experience a confident and controlled demeanor or do you become tense and frantic as your responsibilities grow? Are you caring and concerned when others express needs or is ambivalence your first reaction? Do you approach tasks in a resolved manner or does a sense of overwhelm envelop you?

The WRTA can help you assess the degree of reactivity present in your marriage. It is accompanied by the *Responsive Relationship Handbook* which provides practical tools and resources for overcoming reactivity and increasing responsiveness. It is important to recognize, however, that I created the WRTA after conducting extensive scientific research. It is, therefore, a scientifically based diagnostic tool and not a harmless novelty.

For this reason, I designed the WRTA to be used in consultation with a mental health professional, a pastor providing counsel, or in a small group setting, where the results of the WRTA can be processed and interpreted in a safe and supportive environment. This is essential so that someone who takes the WRTA does not misinterpret or misapply the outcome. For more information on the WRTA and its use, see the end of the Epilogue at the end of this book.

Another method for gauging reactivity in your marriage is to review the various concepts we have covered in this book with an eye towards assessing the presence of reactive tendencies. Here is a simple outline to follow using a series of yes/no questions in the form of a General Reactivity Questionnaire:

1. Does the erosion survey in chapter 2 indicate a moderate or substantial degree of erosion in your marriage?
    ____YES ____NO

2. Are the *works of the flesh* outlined in chapter 3 present more often in your interactions with each other than the *fruit of the Spirit*?
    ____YES ____NO

3. Are any of the four relationship horsemen of the apocalypse enumerated in chapter 3 present in your relationship?
    ____YES ____NO

4. Do you, as a couple, take the Southern route of the Welch Responsive Cycle, described in chapter 4, more often than the Northern route?

____YES ____NO

5. Does one or both of you sense a *dis-integration* between your spirit, soul, and body or does one or both of you experience a soul fracture from severe emotional trauma described in chapter 5?

____YES ____NO

6. When you review the Attachment Matrix in chapter 5, was the leadership style you experienced in the home in which you spent the most time as a child and adolescent primarily *commanding, calming,* or *commissioning*?

____YES ____NO

7. When you review the Attachment Matrix in chapter 5, was the nurturing style you experienced in the home in which you spent the most time as a child and adolescent primarily *protecting, poking,* or *passing*?

____YES ____NO

8. As you review the Progressive Growth Phases of Life described in chapter 5 through which you have already passed, were any of the core questions of those phases left unanswered or answered negatively for you?

____YES ____NO

9. As you review the family of origin questions in chapter 5, did you answer 1.a "absent," 1.b "absent," 1.c "yes," 1.e "burden or nuisance," 1.f "yes," 1.g "yes," 1.h "yes," 2.d "compared to siblings," or "yes" to 2.e, 2.f, 2.g, 2.h, or 3.b?

____YES ____NO

10. Are your interactions with your companion comprised of mostly *you* statements rather than *I* statements as described in chapter 6?

_____YES   _____NO

11. As you draw the emotional space you occupy and the emotional space your companion occupies in your relationship, as described in chapter 6, does one of you take up significantly more space in the relationship than the other?

_____YES   _____NO

12. When you review the Me-You-Us graphic in chapter 6, is your relationship defined more as *enmeshed* or *disconnected* rather than *bonded*?

_____YES   _____NO

13. When you both self-assess the degree to which you feel emotionally safe with the other, do you or your companion feel somewhat unsafe or very unsafe?

_____YES   _____NO

14. As you think about how you manage your schedules and prioritize your marriage, are your children or other endeavors being treated as more important than your marriage?

_____YES   _____NO

15. Do you suffer from the Tyranny of the Urgent or from lack of personal margin described in chapter 7?

_____YES   _____NO

16. As you think about your typical anxiety patterns from those described in chapter 8, do you sense that the prefrontal cortex (reasoning center) of your brain shuts down or

diminishes regularly when you experience conflict with your companion?

_____YES _____NO

17. As you review the Welch Relationship Model in chapter 9, are any of the foundational elements *(trust, choice, negotiation, flexibility)* missing or deficient in your relationship?

_____YES _____NO

18. Is your relationship operating outside of the *full life* circles described in chapter 9?

_____YES _____NO

19. Would you describe the sexual aspect of your relationship as *discretionary and modular, restricted and rigid,* or *guarded and subdued*?

_____YES _____NO

If you answered yes to any of those questions, it is possible that reactivity is present in your relationship. The more yes answers you have, the more likely it is that reactivity is hindering your ability to create and sustain intimacy.

What to Do

Now, if the WRTA reveals reactivity or you have yes answers to any of the questions in the General Reactivity Questionnaire, what is your improvement plan? Recall, in chapter 5, I said that, to invoke the command of James 1:19–20 and be quick to listen, slow to speak, and slow to anger—in other words, less reactive—we need to remember the ART of responsiveness. We need to deepen *awareness*, let Jesus *restore* us, and *train* diligently.

The WRTA and General Reactivity Questionnaire provide the *awareness* piece. When we surrender the mess of our lives to Jesus, He starts the *restore* part and He never quits. 2 Corinthians 3:18 (NIV) tells us that we "are being transformed into His image with ever-increasing glory." This is the restoration process Jesus alluded to in Luke 4:18 when He refers to "healing our broken hearts and binding up our wounds."

In other passages, Scripture refers to this process as "sanctification," the on-going renewal of our souls. While you have an active part to play in the restoration process, you are not the primary protagonist in that story. As you confess your sins, admit your faults, and surrender to His will, you allow Jesus the freedom to enact restoration in your heart. In other words, "It is no longer I who live, but Christ who lives in me" (Galatians 2:20 ESV).

Now, let's talk about the *training* element. This is your primary part. Lasting change never occurs with inactivity. Navy Seals do not just read books and study manuals to learn elite fighting techniques. They must do them, over and over and over again, until muscle memory takes over and they no longer need to think about the decisive actions they will take when faced with tremendous adversity. They simply *flow* into the moment and let their training dominate.

This is where we want to get to as we traverse the path to a responsive marriage. We want our training to take over when the adversity of anxiety confronts us. We want *muscle memory* to engage quickly when emotional triggers fire and divert us to the well-worn Southern route of the Welch Responsive Cycle. *Muscle memory*, or *training*, can get us off the Southern route and onto the Northern route to repair quickly and end up at a healthier destination together, with our *self* and our intimacy intact.

Action Plan

Let's create an action plan together.

Action #1: Implement Anxiety Management Techniques

I recommend you implement and practice the anxiety management techniques described in chapter 8. Anxiety is what generates reactivity so we must learn to manage it. We will, of course, never eliminate it. Anxiety is a fact of life and a God-given mechanism for mobilizing our mental and physical resources to deal with impending threats. But we must learn how to manage and mitigate it. When anxiety overwhelms us, we become flooded with emotions that shut down our reasoning. Anxiety management techniques help to restore reasoning power so we can effectively deal with conflict and resolve differences.

First, you should learn to control your breathing, slow it down and breathe deeply. Practice this for at least seven consecutive days, multiple times per day, when you are in a calm state. Refer to chapter 8 for instructions. Then, when you are engaged in an interaction with your companion and you sense your anxiety escalating, remember to slow your breathing down and breathe deeply. You have my permission, and hopefully your companion's permission, to pause the interaction to gain composure and calm.

Next, review the list of grounding techniques in chapter 8 and become adept at one or two of them, again practicing them for a week in a calm state. Then, when conflict erupts and anxiety builds, take a moment to feel or sense your hands, your feet, and your body position. This can help to keep you in the present and prevent you from ruminating on the past or predicting the future.

If you struggle with *generalized anxiety*, it would also be helpful to practice the progressive muscle relaxation techniques for a week by yourself. Then, when tension emerges with your companion, perform a condensed version of this by tightening and loosening your hands and feet. Notice where tension is building in your body and purposely stiffen then relax those parts.

Action #2: Slow Things Down

Speed is the enemy of intimacy. Rushing things or letting conflict accelerate are ways to ensure you stay on the Southern route of the Welch Responsive Cycle. To take the Northern route requires purposeful deceleration. Brakes are required on the Northern route but missing on the Southern route. Anxiety tends to speed things up and expand the number of topics in the conversation letting reactivity burst onto the scene.

You must both commit to pausing the interaction if anxiety starts to crowd out reason and civility. Simply say, "Can you give me a moment to compose myself before we proceed?" or "I would like to take _____ minutes to think more about my responses. How about if we come back together again at _____ to continue? Is that ok with you?"

Notice that these questions contain both voice and choice for you and your companion. During this pause time, you may want to review the feelings list in chapter six. Then, write down your feelings and form them into "I feel _____ when I experience _____" statements that you can verbalize to your companion when you reconvene.

Action #3: Conceptualize Your Reactivity Patterns

In my counseling practice, I often work with men who have anger problems. Anger is only one of many reactive ways of interacting. One of my first questions to them is, "When do you first notice you are angry?" Their answers both perplex and disturb me. They inevitably say something like, "You mean when I pull my fist away from the person's face I just hit?" or "You mean when I pull my fist out of the hole in the wall I just created?"

SPEED IS THE ENEMY OF INTIMACY.

These replies are indicative of the dynamics of reactivity. Because reactivity occurs in the limbic system rather than the cerebral cortex, we react first and then awareness comes. We are not usually aware of our reactivity until it has already occurred. Consequently, it can be helpful to map out your reactivity to identify points along the way where conscious intervention can help. We provide several useful worksheets at the end of the *Responsive Relationship Handbook* to guide individuals through this process. You receive the handbook when you take the Welch Responsive Temperament Assessment, or you can obtain it separately. See the Epilogue at the end of the book for more information.

I will simply summarize the Reactivity Processing Instructions provided in the handbook here in the following steps:

1. Identify an incident when you were reactive. You might ask your companion for an example.

2. Write down a brief description of it using a *who, what, when, where, how* format.

3. List the primary feelings you experienced just before and during the incident.

4. Rate the intensity of each feeling listed using a scale from zero to one-hundred with zero being no feeling and one-hundred being the most intensity possible.

5. Identify core beliefs you have about you, others, and the world associated with those feelings. These are conclusions you have drawn, or agreements you have made, and can be thought of in the form of "I am...," "Others or you are...," and "The world is...."

6. List automatic thoughts originating from your past that went through your mind just before you experienced the feelings. These might be related to the core beliefs you identified, or they could be in other forms such as perceptions. For example, if you felt *afraid*, an automatic thought might be, "I'm all alone."

7. Circle one of the automatic thoughts that you believe is the *hot thought*. This will be the one that seems most prominent, intense, and impacting.

8. List elements of the reactive incident that tend to reinforce the *hot thought*. What happened that tends to make the *hot thought* credible or believable in your mind?

9. Develop one, or a few, responsive behaviors you could exhibit that would diminish the *hot thought* and lessen its intensity. For example, if your *hot thought* is "I'm all alone," a responsive way to address this *hot thought* might be to ask your companion to hold your hand or sit closer to you.

10. Write down an alternative thought to replace the *hot thought* ("Replacement Thought"). For example, for the "I'm all alone" *hot thought*, the Replacement Thought might be "I am married, and my companion is with me."

11. Rate how much you believe the Replacement Thought from 0% to 100%.

12. Say the Replacement Thought to yourself three times aloud multiple times a day over several days.

13. After reinforcing the Replacement Thought, again rate how much you believe the Replacement Thought from 0% to 100%. Hopefully, your belief is growing as you remind your brain of it in repetitive fashion.

14. Re-rate the intensity of the feelings you wrote down in step number three, and any new ones you identified during this process, using the same 0% to 100% scale. Hopefully, you see a decline in the intensity of your feelings.

The goal of these focused intervention efforts on your reactivity is to reduce the intensity of your feelings, mitigate anxiety, and promote an environment where responsiveness can live.

A Word to the Men

I would like to spend the last part of this chapter and the book talking specifically to my male readers. Women, you are certainly welcome, and encouraged, to listen in but this will be primarily a call to action for husbands. I am going to be rather blunt because I know, as men, you can handle it.

Men, God created you for action and accomplishment. The creation story makes clear that God intended men to be the initiators and women to be the responders. As we learned in chapter 3, Genesis 2:15 reports that God created Adam outside the garden and then God placed him in it to "work it and watch over it." We can summarize this verse as, "Take action and tend to what needs to be done." In verses sixteen and seventeen of Genesis 2, we discover that, prior to the existence of the woman, the man was given the specific instructions for how to handle the various trees in the garden. All could be eaten, except the tree of the knowledge of good and evil. God further described the horrific consequences to the man that would ensue should he disobey this singular command.

The very next verse (Genesis 2:18) records God's proclamation that it was "not good for the man to be alone." Adam needed help to act and tend to what needed to be done, so God extracted female attributes from him and made the separate and distinct woman to be his *complement*. There is no record of how Eve learned of the tree command she recites to the serpent in Genesis 3:2–3 during the serpent's deceptive interaction with her, but I think it is safe to assume that Adam informed her of this requirement. He initiated the passing down of the instruction to her.

What is fascinating to me is that the primary reason for the infamous Fall, when Eve took a bite from the fruit of the knowledge of good and evil and allowed sin to enter the world, was the passiveness of her husband. Adam failed to initiate, to take decisive action. He sat on the sidelines observing the whole event and did absolutely nothing. Genesis 3:6 records the devastating passivity of her

ADAM FAILED TO INITIATE, TO TAKE DECISIVE ACTION. HE SAT ON THE SIDELINES OBSERVING THE WHOLE EVENT AND DID ABSOLUTELY NOTHING.

husband. "Then the woman saw that the tree was good for food and delightful to look at, and that it was desirable for obtaining wisdom. So, she took some of its fruit and ate it; _she also gave some to her husband, who was with her_, and he ate it" (emphasis added). God gave the instruction directly to Adam and adequately apprised him of the detrimental consequences for disobedience. Yet, Adam stood by and watched the whole diabolical episode unfold with the serpent and took no action, other than to silently accept his wife's offer of the fruit. I don't know about you, but as a man, I want to scream, "Step up man!" "What happened to your masculinity?!"

Yet, this is the same question we scream today. "Where are the men? To where have they disappeared?" A crisis of masculinity has swept this country by storm. According to the National Fatherhood Initiative, the census bureau reports 18.4 million children, which is one in four or 25%, live in a home _without_ a biological, step, or adoptive father. That's enough children to fill New York City twice or Los Angeles four times.[70] If we add to that statistic the number of homes with a father who is emotionally disengaged from his children and somewhat oblivious to their needs (the _commissioning_ leadership style in the Attachment Matrix from chapter 5), I'm quite certain we will have included much more than half the children in this country.

These are the homes where boys may never learn what it means to be a man, to be masculine, to have a paradoxical blend of strength and vulnerability, to treat all women with the utmost respect and dignity, and to understand that men run to the battle not away from it. Consequently, the crisis of masculinity continues to expand in severity and careens our society and culture toward the cliff of utter chaos. The statistics on divorce and counseling offices filled with women pleading for their husbands to engage add further credibility to the notion that we are currently experiencing a crisis of masculinity.

Prisons are populated mostly by men growing up without fathers. Where true masculinity is absent, selfishness abounds and crimes are committed to satisfy that selfishness. True men are sacrificial, giving up their rights for the sake of others. These are the men who fight oppressors wherever they are in the world, run into a burning building to save others, take their teenage daughters out on "dates," engage them in conversation even though they don't completely understand them, stop working to play catch with their boys, or turn off the football game on TV when their wife says those four scary words, "We need to talk." False men, posers, as John Eldredge calls them in his book *Wild At Heart*,[71] live for self-aggrandizement, to heap ever-expanding pleasures on themselves while ignoring the chaos around them they have either caused or perpetuated with their failure to engage.

As we learned in chapter 3, men tend to error on one side of the assertiveness spectrum or the other. They can be either *passive* or *aggressive*. Adam was passive and failed to initiate. Other men may shift to the opposite end and become aggressive. Both of those extremes are detrimental to a marriage. Your wife needs you to initiate and resist *passivity*. She also needs you to manage your temper, stubbornness, and dominance to avoid *aggressiveness*. These are exemplary goals of manhood that Jesus fully displayed as an example to us as men. We would do well, men, to courageously confront our tendencies for *passivity* and *aggressiveness* in our marriage and parenting, and work diligently to stay centered in genuine assertiveness.

One reason we are experiencing a crisis of masculinity is because the definition of manhood in our society is hazy. Young boys need to be taught what it means to be a man. They need initiation into the fellowship of men. They require a more compelling definition than "one who brings home the bacon" or "one with strong muscles" or "one who plays sports well." One of the best definitions I have heard for godly masculinity comes from the Men's Fraternity program authored and conducted by Robert Lewis. In the *Quest for Authentic Manhood* video series, Lewis describes the authentic man as one who *rejects passivity, accepts responsibility, leads courageously,* and *expects the greater reward* (heaven and God's favor rather than superficial accolades).[72] Now that is a compelling definition, one to which we all, as men, can aspire.

A straightforward way to evaluate the current condition of your masculinity in your marriage is to ask yourself, and if you are courageous enough, your wife, whether you are primarily a *provider* or a *consumer*. A *provider* does his best to meet the needs of others, not just financially but also emotionally, spiritually, mentally, and physically. A *consumer*, on the other hand, seeks to gratify and promote his own needs and desires. A *provider* considers others first—a *consumer* considers himself first. A *provider* improves the situation—a *consumer* complains about the situation. A *provider* gives—a *consumer* takes. A *provider* sacrifices—a *consumer* demands.

An essential element for restoring authentic and God-centered masculinity is for men to realize they must be vulnerable with other like-minded men. Proverbs 18:1 describes the peril that awaits a man who believes he is a "self-made man," and he can "do it all on his own." The writer sternly warns us in this verse that, "One who isolates himself pursues selfish desires; he rebels against all sound judgment." When left to themselves, men can convince themselves of anything. These are the men who discard their careers, reputation, and family for momentary sexual pleasure. These are the men who embezzle from retirement funds and financially devastate hard-working Americans. These are the men with influential ministries who corrupt the name of Christ with their selfish choices.

To counteract this tendency in men, Proverbs 27:17 tells us, "As iron sharpens iron, so one person sharpens another." This is what a small group of men meeting regularly can accomplish. Every man needs other like-minded men to encourage him in his masculine journey, to let him know he is not alone with his feelings of inadequacy or his struggles to maintain sexual purity, and to hold him accountable for doing the things necessary to secure his family, strengthen his marriage, support his children, and sustain his spirit.

In short, men need other men with whom they process their life and give it meaning. Think about it, the worst possible condition for a warrior is by himself in enemy territory. What makes Navy SEALs so effective is their ability to work together to accomplish the mission. A lone SEAL can certainly be a menacing force. But link him with other SEALs, and you have a powerhouse able to invade impenetrable fortresses, take out oppressors, and rescue captives. This is what it will take for Christian men to reestablish authentic masculinity and walk with their wife on the path to a responsive marriage.

One Last Word

My last words to you, both husbands and wives, are to stick with it. Your marriage is worth it, and your companion is worth it. Few are the couples who experience a smooth marriage. My counseling experience has taught me that the majority of couples struggle to maintain intimacy and oneness in their marriage. Marriage is not easy. If it were, licensed marriage and family therapists like me would be unnecessary.

The marriages that last, that stand the test of time, are those in which perseverance and endurance are exhibited. While I would not say that marriage is an affliction, the wisdom of Romans 5:3–4 is nevertheless applicable to marriage as much as to our walk with God, because both come with tremendous obstacles. As you work together to reduce reactivity and increase responsiveness in your marriage remember that, "Affliction produces endurance, endurance produces proven character, and proven character produces hope."

We have spent considerable time in this book focusing on the benefits to you, as husband and wife, of developing a more responsive marriage. There are, however, substantial benefits that extend beyond the two of you. The title of this chapter is significant, not only to convey the notion that God carries you through the rough times, but also to remind you that traveling the path out of reactivity to a responsive marriage creates footprints for your children, grandchildren, younger family members, and other future generations to follow. The ripple effect of your efforts will be monumental.

God often told the Israelites to tell their children about how the Lord delivered them from various troubles. In Joshua 4, God instructs Joshua to direct one man from each tribe to retrieve a stone from the Jordan river and place the twelve stones where they were spending the night. When they reached Gilgal to camp for the evening, they set up the twelve stones as God had commanded. Joshua 4:23 records the reason for doing this. Joshua tells them, "In the future, when your children ask their fathers, 'What is the meaning of these stones?' you should tell your children, 'Israel crossed the Jordan on dry ground'."[73] Use this biblical example to remind you to tell your children and grandchildren what God has done in your marriage when you committed to being more *responsive* and less *reactive*. Show them the path to a responsive marriage as well.

I sincerely pray that this book has given you hope for a thriving and fulfilling marriage. *The Responsive Marriage* is within your reach as you walk the path and faithfully follow the principles contained in it and within the inerrant, infallible, and immutable word of God to you. I pray God's richest blessings over you as you traverse the path to a responsive marriage.

Discussion Starter Questions

- *For Couples or Groups*
  - How close or distant do you feel you are with God right now? What is contributing to the closeness or distance? NOTES:_____
    _____
    _____

○ How would you rate your *awareness* level before reading this book and after reading this book?
NOTES:_____

_____

_____

○ How would you rate your *restoration* level currently? What specific areas of your life do you need the restoration of Jesus in? How can others be praying for you?
NOTES:_____

_____

_____

○ How would you rate your *training* level before reading this book and after reading this book? What is your plan to continue training?
NOTES:_____

_____

_____

○ What were your thoughts after reading the *A Word to the Men* section of the chapter?
NOTES:_____

_____

_____

○ What were your thoughts after reading the *One Last Word* section of the chapter?
NOTES:_____

_____

_____

- *For Couples Only*
  - Take the General Reactivity Questionnaire together and discuss the results. What can you do separately and together to generate more *no* answers in the areas you have control of? (i.e. questions one, two, three, four, five to some degree [seeking and receiving restoration], ten, eleven, twelve, thirteen, fifteen, sixteen, and seventeen)
  NOTES:_____

  _____

  _____

  - Follow the Reactivity Processing Instructions alone for a selected incident. Then come together to discuss what you discovered.
  NOTES:_____

  _____

  _____

EPILOGUE

The path out of reactivity to a responsive marriage is a continuous journey to discover the fulfilling and deeply satisfying marriage you both desire. You and your companion will traverse through valleys of disappointment and experience mountaintop exhilaration along the way. This is the nature of human relationships. We do not always get it right. In our quest for enduring intimacy, we make mistakes, we misinterpret, and we say things we do not mean. We are flawed individuals with proclivities for self-protection that sometimes interfere with relationship advancement. Consequently, our marriages may stagnate or seem completely unfulfilling at times.

But the difference between lasting, fulfilling marriages and those that die is not predicated on perfection. If that were the gauge, we would all receive a failing grade. What makes the difference is perseverance, what current social research calls *grit*. Dictionary. com defines *grit* as, "Firmness of character; indomitable spirit."[74] In the educational field, researchers have studied this characteristic extensively. Many teachers today lament the lack of grit they observe in their young students, and much of the significant turnover of employees being experienced in corporations and businesses today, like never before in history, can be attributed, at least in part, to the inability or unwillingness of employees to persevere when they experience challenges, obstacles, or disagreements. Rather than exhibiting tenacity, increasing numbers of people these days just "throw in the towel" in hopes of finding "greener pastures" elsewhere.

Developing Grit

A Forbes magazine article published in 2013 provided some interesting insight into the topic of grit.[75] The author outlines five characteristics of grit that are applicable to many environments where the quality is beneficial, including marriage. The first characteristic he identified is *courage*, the ability to manage the fear of failure. Those with grit use failure as teachable moments for themselves rather than as supporting evidence for continuing discouragement. Teddy Roosevelt captured the essence of courage best with his speech delivered in Paris on April 23, 1910:

> *It is not the critic who counts; not the man who points out how the strong man stumbles, or where the doer of deeds could have done them better. The credit belongs to the man who is actually in the arena, whose face is marred by dust and sweat and blood; who strives valiantly; who errs, who comes short again and again, because there is no effort without error and shortcoming; but who does actually strive to do the deeds; who knows great enthusiasms, the great devotions; who spends himself in a worthy cause; who at the best knows in the end the triumph of high achievement, and who at the worst, if he fails, at least fails while daring greatly, so that his place shall never be with those cold and timid souls who neither know victory nor defeat.[76]*

You will need *courage* to continue walking the path out of reactivity to a responsive marriage.

The second characteristic of grit espoused by the Forbes author is *conscientiousness*, meaning careful, painstaking, and meticulous.[77] One with this attribute works tirelessly, attempts to always do a respectable job, and completes the task at hand.

You will need *conscientiousness* to successfully navigate the path out of reactivity to a responsive marriage.

Next is *follow-through*. This involves endurance toward achieving long-term goals. Malcolm Gladwell, author of the 2008 book *Outliers*,[78] found that one of the greatest predictors of success is practice with purpose. Apparently, twenty hours per week for ten years, or about 10,000 hours, is the magic number of *follow-through* needed to be a contender.

You will need *follow-through* to keep going on the path out of reactivity to a responsive marriage.

Another essential attribute is *resilience*. A resilient material possesses the power or ability to return to its original form or position after being bent, compressed, or stretched. This is the quality of elasticity, best illustrated by a rubber band. For people, it is the ability to adjust to or recover readily from illness, adversity, or major life changes. This is the quality of buoyancy, staying afloat when the waves are undulating all around you.[79]

You will need *resilience* to stay on the path out of reactivity to a responsive marriage.

Finally, the last characteristic enumerated by the author of the Forbes article on grit is a focus on *excellence vs perfection*. I will let the Forbes author describe this for you:

> *In general, gritty people don't seek perfection, but instead strive for excellence. It may seem that these two have only subtle semantic distinctions; but, in fact, they are quite at odds. Perfection is excellence's somewhat pernicious cousin. It is pedantic, binary, unforgiving and inflexible. Certainly, there are times when "perfection" is necessary to establish standards, like in performance athletics such as diving and gymnastics. But in general, perfection is someone else's perception of an ideal, and pursuing it is like chasing a[n]hallucination. Anxiety, low self-esteem, obsessive*

compulsive disorder, substance abuse, and clinical depression are only a few of the conditions ascribed to "perfectionism." To be clear, those are ominous barriers to success.

Excellence is an attitude, not an endgame. The word excellence is derived from the Greek word Arête which is bound with the notion of fulfillment of purpose or function and is closely associated with virtue. It is far more forgiving, allowing and embracing failure and vulnerability on the ongoing quest for improvement. It allows for disappointment and prioritizes progress over perfection. Like excellence, grit is an attitude about, to paraphrase Tennyson...seeking, striving, finding, and never yielding.

Excellence, not perfection, will be the measuring stick used when we stand before the Lord one day. We know, of course, that forgiveness of sins, reconciliation to God, and entrance into Heaven is unconditional. These elements are based entirely on what Jesus did for us on the cross and not on what we can offer with any ounce of human effort. This is the beauty of grace—unmerited favor.

But Jesus also told several parables to describe the inner workings of the kingdom of Heaven that have implications for us relative to this concept of excellence or "doing our best with what we have." In Matthew 25, Jesus tells the story of three servants each given a different amount of "talents," a denomination of money in that day, by their master before he left on a journey.[80]

Each of the servants deals with the talents differently. The two with the fewest invest them and double the money for the master. The one with the most buries the money in the ground so as not to lose it. In the end, the investors are rewarded, and the hoarder is punished.

We cringe at the implications here. Do you mean, Almighty God desires His children to take risks as they walk with Him rather than take the safe route or do nothing? Apparently so! Could it be that the pursuit of perfection paralyzed the hoarder servant? In his effort to *get it right* and not risk disappointing his master, he opted for inactivity. In business, we call this "the paralysis of analysis." We spend so much time analyzing the problem and considering all the "what if" scenarios, we fail to act when it is necessary, and the consequences can be disastrous. The other two servants, whom the master called "faithful," exhibited attitudes of excellence, opting to act, to risk, in order to "do it well," rather than just "get it right."

The words spoken by the master to his two investing servants upon his return are particularly poignant. "Well done, good and faithful servant," he says. Imagine with me for a moment standing before Jesus someday, face to face, with those grace-filled, tender, and loving eyes focused intently on yours. A smile expands His cheeks as he settles his nail-scarred hands on your shoulders, tilts His head slightly causing an endearing look to emerge across His face, and says to you in a warm and gentle tone, "Well done, good and faithful servant." These are the words I long to hear from my Savior. I hope you yearn for that affirmation as well. Wouldn't it warm your heart for the lover of your soul to say to you, "You loved well my servant?"

You will need to focus on excellence, not perfection, to love well while traveling the path to a responsive marriage. You will need to take risks and try repeatedly. After all, isn't it one of the riskiest chances you take when you stand with your soon to be spouse before God and human witnesses, repeat your vows, and hand them your heart? "What if they mishandle my heart, bruise it, or carelessly drop it on the floor?" "Will they love me, cherish me, and honor me until death separates us or will they escape when the going gets tough?" These are the haunting questions that define the risk of loving. "Will they?" and "What if they don't?"

As flawed individuals, there is no guarantee that another individual will not mishandle our heart at times or hurt it deeply.

We will never be perfect or get it right all the time. But to keep going, to continue to risk, this is the underlying message of this parable of the servants. The story is about acting, investing, and growing rather than sitting idle to protect and guard yourself from possible failure. It is tenacity, perseverance, and resilience that pleases the Master and prompts the words, "Well done." Commit today to pursue excellence in your marriage and stop hoping for perfection or the Hollywood depiction of *love*. Your marriage will stand the test of time, not because your passion or romance is exemplary and enviable, but because you stick with it and keep trying.

Additional Resources for Marriage Improvement

To help you have an excellent, responsive marriage, the Welch Family Therapy Institute provides numerous tools and resources to support you. We call this our Marriage Support Continuum of Services which is layered and progressive to be comprehensive and targeted, depending upon the condition of the marriage, and includes the following:

- **TIER 1: Fundamental Concepts**
  - *The Responsive Marriage Book* (you are completing this now)
  - *The Responsive Relationship Handbook*: a comprehensive handbook containing tools and skill building resources to improve relationships within more than seventy different psychological areas.

- **TIER 2: Individual Exploration**
  - *Self-Awareness Video Package:* Five videos with over two hours of engaging content for individuals desiring to deepen their self-awareness and learn practical methods for self-regulation. Includes the *Responsive Relationship Handbook.*

- *Marriage Readiness Video Package:* Six videos with nearly three hours of engaging content designed for engaged couples or those married less than two years. Includes the *Responsive Relationship Handbook.*
- *Marriage Refresh Video Package:* Ten videos with over four hours of engaging content designed for married couples with a relatively healthy relationship experiencing intermittent irritations and frustrations. Includes the *Responsive Relationship Handbook.*

- **TIER 3: Group Processing**
  - Advisory services and assistance for churches and individuals to start and sustain interactive small groups of couples willing to be transparent and open about their struggles and triumphs in a safe, confidential, and trust-filled environment with the Holy Spirit present. We call these groups *Two Become One Groups* and they use the *Responsive Relationship Video Series,* the *Responsive Relationship Handbook,* and the Welch Responsive Temperament Assessment (WRTA) as curriculum.
  - *Marriage Revitalization Video Package:* Twenty videos with over eight hours of engaging content designed for married couples experiencing enduring irritations and frustrations often causing emotional distance and withdrawal. Includes the *Responsive Relationship Handbook* and discussion starter questions for groups and couples.
  - *Marriage Restructuring Video Package:* Thirty videos with over twelve hours of engaging content designed for: 1) married couples desiring to renew, restore, or renovate their relationship; and/or, 2) pastors or lay persons providing spiritual guidance and/or relationship skills counseling/coaching to couples. Includes the *Responsive Relationship Handbook* and discussion starter questions for groups and couples.

- ○ *Welch Responsive Temperament Assessment (WRTA):* 200+ question scientifically based psychological assessment to provide individuals and couples a detailed profile of their natural temperament within a set of four, and range of responsiveness vs reactivity within nine dimensions of expression. Individuals receive a profile of their self-assessment, and couples also receive a combined profile of their self-assessment and their companion's assessment of them for comparison purposes. For more information on this resource, see details at the end of the Epilogue.

- **TIER 4: Focused Intervention**
  - ○ *Counseling Advisory Services*: Just-in-time guidance on how to effectively coach/counsel individuals or couples with challenging relationship dysfunction from an experienced licensed marriage and family therapist and ordained pastor through remote video interaction(s).
  - ○ *Counseling/Coaching Maps:* Tabular depictions of specific symptoms or conditions seen in marriages with correlated tools, techniques, and resources to help address the condition and improve outcomes for couples.
  - ○ *Targeted Conditions Video Packages:* Sets of one to nine videos from the *Responsive Relationship Video Series* designed to address the specific conditions listed in Counseling/Coaching Maps.
  - ○ *Use of the Welch Responsive Temperament Assessment in a counseling setting*

- **TIER 5: Advanced Intervention**
  - ○ *Professional Counseling Offered Through the Center For Enriching Relationships (available only in certain States)*

Dr. Welch is a licensed marriage and family therapist in California (LMFT #50129), a licensed clinical marriage and family therapist in Kansas (LCMFT #090), and a certified sex therapist with the American Board of Christian Sex Therapists (CST #0204). He holds an M.S. degree in Family Therapy from Friends University (1998); a Ph.D. in Education from the University of Kansas (1994); an M.Div. in Pastoral Ministry/Theology from Nazarene Theological Seminary (1986); an M.A. in Religion from Point Loma Nazarene University (1980); and a B.A. in Religion from Point Loma Nazarene University with a minor in Psychology (1978).

- o *Use of the Welch Responsive Temperament Assessment in a counseling setting*

For more information on these resources, visit:

www.welchtherapyinstitute.com and
www.enrichingrelationships.org.

For more information on booking Dr. Welch for speaking services, contact Karl Christensen, Director of Planning and Client Coordination with the Welch Family Therapy Institute, at kchristensen@welchtherapyinstitute.com

For more information on the WRTA, visit https://www.welchtherapyinstitute.com/wrta. After you purchase the WRTA and begin the process of taking it, you will be asked to enter a facilitator code. Enter *RMBook2023* when prompted.

ENDNOTES

Chapter 1

[1] Mark 10:9

Chapter 2

[2] Detroit, Fox 2. "I-94 Erosion in Roseville Threatening Collapse of the Highway; Officials Order Emergency Stabilization." FOX 2 Detroit, August 9, 2022. https://www.fox2detroit.com/news/i-94-erosion-in-roseville-threatening-collapse-of-the-highway-officials-order-emergency-stabilization.

[3] WebAdmin. "4 Types of Evidence | Daniels, Long & Pinsel, LLC." Daniels, Long & Pinsel, October 15, 2021. https://dlplawyers.com/4-types-of-evidence-you-should-be-aware-of/.

[4] Wikipedia contributors. "Covenant (Biblical)." Wikipedia, April 27, 2023. https://en.wikipedia.org/wiki/Covenant_(biblical).

[5] US Census Bureau. "Census Bureau Releases New Estimates on America's Families and Living Arrangements." Census.gov, November 17, 2022. https://www.census.gov/newsroom/press-releases/2022/americas-families-and-living-arrangements.html#:~:text=Marriage%3A,20.5%2C%20respectively%2C%20in%201947.

[6] "IBISWorld - Industry Market Research, Reports, and Statistics," n.d. https://www.ibisworld.com/us/bed/marriage-rate/29/.

[7] US Census Bureau, "Historical Households Tables." Census.gov, November 10, 2022. https://www.census.gov/data/tables/time-series/demo/families/households.html.

Chapter 3

8   ASIRT. "Road Safety Facts — Association for Safe International Road Travel." Association for Safe International Road Travel, February 24, 2023. https://www.asirt.org/safe-travel/road-safety-facts/.

9   HISTORY. "What Are the Four Waves of Feminism?," March 2, 2022. https://www.history.com/news/feminism-four-waves.

10   Lcsw, Mere Abrams. "68 Terms That Describe Gender Identity and Expression." Healthline, February 9, 2022. https://www.healthline.com/health/different-genders.

11   Warren, Rick, *The Purpose Driven Life: What on Earth Am I Here For?* Zondervan, 2012.

12   Luscombe, Belinda. "Men Want to Remarry; Women Are 'Meh.'" Time, November 14, 2014. https://time.com/3584827/pew-marriage-divorce-remarriage/.

13   Voges, Mona M., Claire-Marie Giabbiconi, Benjamin Schöne, Manuel Waldorf, Andrea S. Hartmann, and Silja Vocks. "Gender Differences in Body Evaluation: Do Men Show More Self-Serving Double Standards Than Women?" Frontiers in Psychology 10 (March 12, 2019). https://doi.org/10.3389/fpsyg.2019.00544.

14   Pietrangelo, Ann. "Left Brain vs. Right Brain: What Does This Mean for Me?" Healthline, May 9, 2022. https://www.healthline.com/health/left-brain-vs-right-brain#takeaway.

15   Northwestern Medicine Staff and Northwestern Medicine. "Battle of the Brain: Men Vs. Women [Infographic]." Northwestern Medicine, July 26, 2018. https://www.nm.org/healthbeat/healthy-tips/battle-of-the-brain-men-vs-women-infographic.

16   Covey, Stephen R., *The 7 Habits of Highly Effective People: Powerful Lessons in Personal Change.* Free Press, 2004.

17   The Gottman Institute. "Love Lab," November 3, 2021. https://www.gottman.com/love-lab/.

18   "Definition of Criticism." In *www.Dictionary.Com*, n.d. https://www.dictionary.com/browse/criticism.

19   Lisitsa, Ellie, "The Four Horsemen: Criticism, Contempt, Defensiveness, and Stonewalling." *The Gottman Institute*, November 3, 2022. https://www.gottman.com/blog/the-four-horsemen-recognizing-criticism-contempt-defensiveness-and-stonewalling/.

20   "Definition of Contempt." In *www.Dictionary.Com*, n.d. https://www.dictionary.com/browse/contempt.

21 Lisitsa, Ellie, "The Four Horsemen: Criticism, Contempt, Defensiveness, and Stonewalling." The Gottman Institute, November 3, 2022. https://www.gottman.com/blog/the-four-horsemen-recognizing-criticism-contempt-defensiveness-and-stonewalling/.

22 "Definition of Defensive." In *www.Dictionary.Com*, n.d. https://www.dictionary.com/browse/defensiveness.

23 Lisitsa, Ellie, "The Four Horsemen: Criticism, Contempt, Defensiveness, and Stonewalling." *The Gottman Institute*, November 3, 2022. https://www.gottman.com/blog/the-four-horsemen-recognizing-criticism-contempt-defensiveness-and-stonewalling/.

24 "Definition of Stonewalling." In *www.Dictionary.Com*, n.d. https://www.dictionary.com/browse/stonewalling.

25 Wooden, John. *They Call Me Coach*. McGraw-Hill Education, 2004.

26 1 John 1:9 and James 5:16

Chapter 4

27 DiDonato, Theresa E., PhD. "Are Couples That Live Together Before Marriage More Likely to Divorce?" *Psychology Today*, August 6, 2021. https://www.psychologytoday.com/us/blog/meet-catch-and-keep/202101/is-living-together-marriage-associated-divorce?amp.

28 "St. Augustine of Hippo : Confessions," n.d. https://www.vatican.va/spirit/documents/spirit_20020821_agostino_en.html.

29 Matthew 26:53

30 "No One Understands Like Jesus," composed by John W. Peterson, 1952.

31 Rowold, Katharina. "What Do Babies Need to Thrive? Changing Interpretations of 'Hospitalism' in an International Context, 1900–1945." *Social History of Medicine 32*, no. 4 (November 1, 2019): 799–818. https://doi.org/10.1093/shm/hkx114.

32 Johnson, Sue. *Hold Me Tight: Seven Conversations for a Lifetime of Love*. Little, Brown Spark, 2008.

Chapter 5

33 Mayo Clinic. "Post-Traumatic Stress Disorder (PTSD) - Symptoms and Causes - Mayo Clinic," December 13, 2022. https://www.mayoclinic.org/diseases-conditions/post-traumatic-stress-disorder/symptoms-causes/syc-20355967.

34   Cherry, Kendra. "Biography of Psychologist John Bowlby." *Verywell Mind*, March 29, 2020. https://www.verywellmind.com/john-bowlby-biography-1907-1990-2795514#:~:text=Bowlby%20defined%20attachment%20as%20a,attachment%20bond%20with%20a%20caregiver.

35   Mcleod, Saul, PhD. "Mary Ainsworth | Strange Situation - Simply Psychology." *Simply Psychology*, May 18, 2023. https://www.simplypsychology.org/mary-ainsworth.html.

36   Thompson, Curt. *Anatomy of the Soul: Surprising Connections Between Neuroscience and Spiritual Practices That Can Transform Your Life and Relationships*. Tyndale House Publishers, Inc., 2010.

37   Thompson, Curt. *Anatomy of the Soul: Surprising Connections Between Neuroscience and Spiritual Practices That Can Transform Your Life and Relationships*. Tyndale House Publishers, Inc., 2010.

38   Eldredge, John. *Wild at Heart: Discovering the Secret of a Man's Soul*. Thomas Nelson Publishers, 2006.

39   Eldredge, John, and Stasi Eldredge. *Captivating Expanded Edition: Unveiling the Mystery of a Woman's Soul*. Thomas Nelson, 2021.

40   Eldredge, John. *Fathered by God – Learning What Your Dad Could Never Teach You*, Thomas Nelson; April 2009.

41   Eldredge, John. *Wild at Heart: Discovering the Secret of a Man's Soul*. Thomas Nelson Publishers, 2006.

42   Eldredge, John, and Stasi Eldredge. *Captivating Expanded Edition: Unveiling the Mystery of a Woman's Soul*. Thomas Nelson, 2021.

Chapter 6

43   ———. "Human Multitasking." *Wikipedia*, April 27, 2023. https://en.wikipedia.org/wiki/Human_multitasking.

44   ———. "MS-DOS." *Wikipedia*, May 6, 2023. https://en.wikipedia.org/wiki/MS-DOS.

45   ———. "Microsoft Windows." *Wikipedia*, May 15, 2023. https://en.wikipedia.org/wiki/Microsoft_Windows.

46   Clear, James. "The Myth of Multitasking: Why Fewer Priorities Leads to Better Work." James Clear, February 4, 2020. https://jamesclear.com/multitasking-myth.

47   ———. "Human Multitasking." *Wikipedia*, April 27, 2023. https://en.wikipedia.org/wiki/Human_multitasking.

48 ———. "Human Multitasking." *Wikipedia*, April 27, 2023. https:// en.wikipedia.org/wiki/Human_multitasking.

49 ———. "Human Multitasking." *Wikipedia*, April 27, 2023. https:// en.wikipedia.org/wiki/Human_multitasking.

50 ———. "Vantage Point (Film)." *Wikipedia*, March 28, 2023. https:// en.wikipedia.org/wiki/Vantage_Point_(film).

51 Gilbert, Beth. "Do You Have a Codependent Personality?" EverydayHealth.com, July 16, 2020. https://www.everydayhealth.com/ emotional-health/do-you-have-a-codependent-personality.aspx.

52 GoodTherapy Editor Team. "What Does Codependency Look Like?" November 21, 2019. https://www.goodtherapy.org/learn-about-therapy/ issues/codependency.

53 MasterClass. "A Guide to the 5 Levels of Maslow's Hierarchy of Needs - 2023 - MasterClass," November 8, 2020. https://www.masterclass.com/ articles/a-guide-to-the-5-levels-of-maslows-hierarchy-of-needs.

54 Tejada, A. Heatley; Dunbar, R. I. M.; Montero, M. *Physical Contact and Loneliness: Being Touched Reduces Perceptions of Loneliness*, Adaptive Human Behavior and Physiology, Nature Publishing Group, May 26, 2020.

55 Dunning, John B. Jr (Editor). *CRC Handbook of Avian Body Masses*; CRC Press; 2009.

56 "A Quote by Walter Hagen," n.d. https://www.goodreads.com/ quotes/3244447-you-re-only-here-for-a-short-visit-don-t-hurry-don-t.

57 McKeown, Greg. *Essentialism: The Disciplined Pursuit of Less* Currency, 2014.

58 Covey, Stephen R., A. Roger Merrill, and Rebecca R. Merrill. *First Things First: To Live, to Love, to Learn, to Leave a Legacy*, Free Press, 1994.

59 Swenson, Richard A. *Margin: How to Create the Emotional, Physical, Financial & Time Reserves You Need*. NavPress Publishing Group, 1992.

60 Lebowitz, Kim Rachelle, Sooyeon Suh, Philip T. Diaz, and Charles F. Emery. "Effects of Humor and Laughter on Psychological Functioning, Quality of Life, Health Status, and Pulmonary Functioning among Patients with Chronic Obstructive Pulmonary Disease: A Preliminary Investigation." *Heart and Lung* 40, no. 4 (July 1, 2011): 310–19. https:// doi.org/10.1016/j.hrtlng.2010.07.010.

Chapter 8

[61] DeAngelis, Tori. "Anxiety among Kids Is on the Rise. Wider Access to CBT May Provide Needed Solutions." *https://www.Apa.Org*, n.d. https://www.apa.org/monitor/2022/10/child-anxiety-treatment.

[62] Prinstein, Mitchell J. "US Youth Are in a Mental Health Crisis—We Must Invest in Their Care." *https://www.Apa.Org*, February 7, 2022. https://www.apa.org/news/press/op-eds/youth-mental-health-crisis.

[63] "Facts & Statistics | Anxiety and Depression Association of America, ADAA," n.d. https://adaa.org/understanding-anxiety/facts-statistics.

Chapter 9

[64] "Definition of Trust." In *www.Dictionary.Com*, n.d. https://www.dictionary.com/browse/trust.

[65] Covey, Stephen R., and Rebecca R. Merrill. *The SPEED of Trust: The One Thing That Changes Everything*. Simon and Schuster, 2006.

[66] Niallmck. "Psychological Flexibility: The Superpower of Mental Health and Wellbeing." *The Weekend University*, November 25, 2021. https://theweekenduniversity.com/psychological-flexibility/.

[67] Penner, Clifford L. and Joyce J., *Restoring the Pleasure*, Thomas Nelson, 2016, 100.

[68] Weir, Kirsten. "Healing the Wounds of Pregnancy Loss." *https://www.Apa.Org*, n.d. https://www.apa.org/monitor/2018/05/pregnancy-loss.

Chapter 10

[69] "Footprints in the Sand Poem - I Carried You," n.d. https://poem4today.com/footprints-poem.html.

[70] National Fatherhood Initiative®, a 501c3 Non-Profit. "Father Absence Statistics." National Fatherhood Initiative, n.d. https://www.fatherhood.org/father-absence-statistic.

[71] Eldredge, John. *Wild at Heart: Discovering the Secret of a Man's Soul*. Thomas Nelson Publishers, 2006, 51–54.

[72] Lewis, Robert. *The Quest for Authentic Manhood (Member Book)*. Lifeway Church Resources, 2005.

[73] Joshua 4:1–24

Epilogue

[74] "Definition of Grit." In *www.Dictionary.Com*, n.d. https://www.dictionary.com/browse/grit.

[75] Perlis, Margaret M. "5 Characteristics Of Grit -- How Many Do You Have?" *Forbes*, October 29, 2013. https://www.forbes.com/sites/margaretperlis/2013/10/29/5-characteristics-of-grit-what-it-is-why-you-need-it-and-do-you-have-it/?sh=1e7c73454f7b.

[76] McCarthy, Erin. "Theodore Roosevelt's 'The Man in the Arena.'" *Mental Floss*, March 9, 2023. https://www.mentalfloss.com/article/63389/roosevelts-man-arena.

[77] "Definition of Conscientious." In *www.Dictionary.Com*, n.d. https://www.dictionary.com/browse/conscientious.

[78] Gladwell, Malcolm, *Outliers: The Story of Success*, Little, Brown and Company, 2008.

[79] "Definition of Resilience." In *Www.Dictionary.Com*, n.d. https://www.dictionary.com/browse/resilience.

[80] Matthew 25:14–30

Made in the USA
Las Vegas, NV
08 February 2024